T0305414

Darwinism and Evolutionary Economics

Photographic portrait of Charles darwin in old age, autographed by Darwin, in John Maynard Keynes's papers, King's College, Cambridge (Courtesy of King's College, Cambridge).

Darwinism and Evolutionary Economics

Edited by

John Laurent

Lecturer in the History of Science and Technology
Griffith University
Brisbane, Australia

and

John Nightingale

Senior Lecturer in Economics
University of New England
Armidale, Australia

With a Preface by Richard R. Nelson

Edward Elgar
Cheltenham, UK • Northampton, MA, US

Published by
Edward Elgar Publishing Limited
Glensanda House
Montpellier Parade
Cheltenham
Glos GL50 1UA
UK

Edward Elgar Publishing, Inc.
136 West Street
Suite 202
Northampton
Massachusetts 01060
USA

A catalogue record for this book
is available from the British Library

ISBN 1 84064 2092

Printed and bound in Great Britain by MPG Books Ltd, Bodmin, Cornwall

Contents

List of Tables and Figures

Tables

Figures

List of Contributors

William Coleman, School of Economics, University of Tasmania, GPO Box 252-85, Hobart, 7001, Australia.

Peter Groenewegen, Department of Economics, University of Sydney, Sydney, 2006, Australia.

Geoffrey M. Hodgson, Department of Economics, Social Sciences and Tourism, Business School, University of Hertfordshire, Hertford Campus, Mangrove Road, Hertford, Herts SG11 8QF, UK

Thorbjørn Knudsen, Department of Marketing, University of Southern Denmark, Odense, Campusvej 55, DK-5230 Odense M, Denmark.

John Laurent, School of Science, Griffith University, Nathan, 4111, Australia.

Richard R. Nelson, School of International and Public Affairs, Columbia University, New York, NY.

John Nightingale, School of Economics, University of New England, Armidale, 2351, Australia.

Jack J. Vromen, Erasmus Institute for Philosophy and Economics, Erasmus University Rotterdam, P.O. Box 1738, 3000 DR Rotterdam,The Netherlands.

John S. Wilkins, Department of the History and Philosophy of Science, The University of Melbourne. Corresponding address: PO Box 542, Somerville 3912 Australia.

Preface

Richard R. Nelson

Economic systems are complex structures, and their workings and their performance tend to change over time, in many countries progressively. Economics grew up as a discipline dedicated to describing and explaining how economies worked and developed, and achieving a firm enough grasp of the relevant phenomena and mechanisms so that economists could make a useful contribution to the major debates about economic policy. These features of the economic ontology – complexity, change and continuing policy debate – were of central interest to the early classical economists. Adam Smith's path-breaking analysis of *The Wealth of Nations* is concerned with all of these.

The brute facts of complexity and change mean that simple theoretical arguments will not explain economic systems very well, unless the subject matter is somehow simplified. For economists who hanker after the elegance of physics, this can be frustrating. There clearly is great attraction in a strategy that would simplify the ontology to be explained, and then devise theories to explain that simplified ontology. The Walrasian characterisation of the economy in terms of a vector of input and output quantities, and prices, is a striking example of one proposal to simplify the ontology, a proposal that modern economics has largely embraced. The explanation of a Walrasian configuration as the equilibrium outcome of the decisions made by profit and utility-maximising actors is a theoretical structure tuned to that simplified ontology.

Scientific disciplines, of course, have the right within themselves to define and prune down the empirical subject matter they address, and to set their own standards for what makes for an acceptable theory. Many of the natural sciences have done this fruitfully. Modern neoclassical economic theory has done this too, along the lines I characterised above.

But the tradition of seeing the subject matter of economics as complex and changing remains alive, if diminished, in a scholarly line that runs from Smith to Marx, to Marshall, to Schumpeter, to many contemporary economists. For these economists, a simple characterisation of the economy in terms of Walrasian variables, and in particular a repression or simplification of the patterns of economic change, misses much of the interesting phenomena to be explained. From this perspective, the task of theory is to come to grips with at least the broad characteristics of these complex and changing phenomena, rather than with a drastically stripped-down ontology. Only if understanding is of the actual economic processes at work, as contrasted with a simple model of these, will economic analysis be able to make a useful contribution to ongoing policy discussions. While making a useful contribution to economic policy-making is not the sole end of economic analysis, it is an important end, and further, provides a powerful test regarding whether or not the theory actually works. While clearly now a minority position among economists, this tradition lingers on among economic historians, among a good portion of the economists trying to advance a new institutional economics, and among a group of economists trying to develop evolutionary economic theory.

This book is about evolutionary economics and its relationships with Darwin, and Darwinian, theory. As the editors and many of the authors recognise, indeed highlight, the range of contemporary economic writing that has adopted the term 'evolutionary' is quite wide. There is, first of all, the kind of evolutionary economic theorising I have introduced above, a body of theorising that rejects the modern neoclassical strategy of stripping down drastically the economic phenomena regarded as appropriate subject matter of economic analysis, and in particular that attempts to bring the processes of economic development back to the centre of the picture where they were with many of the great classical economists, and more recently with Schumpeter and his contemporary followers. I will focus my subsequent remarks on this strand of evolutionary economics because this is where I am. However, as the authors of this book recognise, there are at least two other strands that I believe are quite different in orientation from the one I have been discussing.

One is evolutionary game theory, which to a considerable extent has been motivated by recognition that certain economic contexts modelled as games might have multiple equilibria. In the absence of assumptions implying global rationality, which equilibrium will be reached will be determined by behaviour out of equilibrium. The dynamics of out of equilibrium behaviour have been modelled by evolutionary game theorists as 'evolutionary', or at least given that name. The other is a collection of models that involves non-linear dynamics, and the fascinating set of phenomena that non-linear dynamic processes can generate and the issues they raise. While there is some overlap, I believe that only a few of the writers in these camps have been strongly motivated by a desire to significantly enrich the empirical ontology of economics in the same way that the first group of evolutionary theorists is trying to do; rather, their key motivation is the interesting analytic issues posed by relatively simple models. And the interesting questions about the relationships between these bodies of evolutionary economic theory and

Darwinism, or evolutionary theory in biology more generally, are I believe quite different.

For the most part the evolutionary economic theorists in the first group, which is my focus here, are not particularly motivated by biological ideas, nor are they inclined to simply lift evolutionary ideas from biology and apply them to the domain of their own inquiry. Technological advance, the dynamics of industry structure and competition, and institutional change, have been the three principal topics addressed by this group of economists. Their colleagues located in business schools have worked from the concepts of evolutionary economics, and added to those concepts, by building a theory in which the capabilities of a firm to lead in or take on board new technology or identify the right way to manage or market new technology is the key to firm success. These subjects comprise complex dynamic phenomena in their own right, and as I have stressed, for most members of this group the task is defined in terms of understanding these phenomena. Theories lifted from another discipline, and addressing very different subject matter, are unlikely to be satisfactory in this endeavour, and this group of evolutionary economists generally knows that. Indeed, I would stress the inclinations of this group of evolutionary economists to actually do, or at least to keep their analysis close to, empirical research.

Inductivism as an epistemological strategy is not in good repute. However, it is clear that many successful fields of natural science have been advanced by researchers whose philosophy has been pretty inductive, and that theory building in many successful fields has been strongly oriented towards the empirical phenomena the scientists were trying to understand. As noted, much (certainly not all) of modern evolutionary economics has been developed by economists who had and have a central interest in technological advance as the key driving force behind economic growth, a fact or perception highlighted by neoclassical as well as evolutionary economists. Their interpretation of the available empirical evidence about technological advance led them to highlight the competition among different alternatives that seem always to be present in fields where technological advance is rapid, the central importance of ex-post selection in determining the winners and losers in this competition, and the disequilibrium nature of the processes involved. This led them to a very different kind of theory than that which dominates standard economics. And the resemblance of at least certain aspects of that theory to Darwin's theory is obvious.

But my argument is that they were not led to that theory by thinking about Darwin, but rather by thinking about how to explain the phenomena that were observed. Schumpeter's theory is very much an evolutionary theory, in the sense I am describing, and many of the contemporary evolutionary economists I have been discussing were profoundly influenced by

Schumpeter. But Schumpeter himself strongly resisted the idea that his theory was Darwinian.

But if Schumpeter could deny and ignore the connection, this generation of evolutionary economists cannot. They cannot avoid having had their conceptualisations as economic theorists influenced by their understandings of Darwin and evolutionary biology, even if Schumpeter and not Darwin was their direct theoretical inspiration. And they cannot avoid reflecting on the intellectual similarities and differences, and the connections more generally, particularly in an era when some scholars have proposed a 'Universal Darwinism'.

If my own feelings are any indication, most contemporary economists who embrace an 'evolutionary' theory of economic change, and who propose that satisfactory explanation for prevailing economic phenomena generally must involve in an essential way examination of how the current configuration 'evolved', certainly are interested in exploring the relationships between the economic evolutionary theory they espouse, biological evolutionary theory and Universal Darwinism, but also sceptical regarding efforts to establish common principles. They are interested because it is useful and friendly to get to know one's relatives, and those who claim they are one's relatives, and to sort out which of the latter are also the former. One certainly can learn a lot about oneself by studying one's true relatives. But they also are sceptical because they know they surely are different from any of one's relatives in certain essential ways, and thus resistant to the notion that even well-founded conceptions regarding relatives (for example the misconceptions of Lamarck regarding the processes of biological evolution) can easily carry over to evolutionary economics.

However, the purpose of a preface is not to summarise the book that follows, but to whet the reader's appetite. This is a fascinating and provocative book, and those delving into it will have good reading.

1. Darwinism and Evolutionary Economics

John Laurent and John Nightingale

Darwinism is now becoming an orthodoxy of modern thought, a framework within which a wide range of knowledge communities conduct their discourse. The initial idea for this volume emerged from a meeting of, on the one hand, an interest in the development of ideas in science, technology and economics, and on the other, a concern about the various dead ends into which economists have driven themselves over the past couple of centuries. John Laurent has a background in biological sciences and, more recently, in the study of science in society. He saw the growth of evolutionary ideas amongst economists as if economists were alerted to a need, and as a result, were rushing off in all directions with seemingly little concern to ensure consistency with existing knowledge, or even internal consistency. John Nightingale is an economist who came to evolutionary ideas from reading economics, only much later dipping into the more highly developed biological applications of those ideas. He, too, became concerned at the way ideas were being appropriated and manipulated to suit short-term fixes for problems of economic theory (see Nightingale, 2000).

The explicit, if loose, use of a biological analogy in economics dates from well before Alfred Marshall (see Groenewegen, this volume). But Marshall's use of it marked an ending, rather than a beginning, of the analogy in the mainstream of professional economic discourse during the next half century.[1] Alchian (1950) caused a flurry of interest and controversy. Downie (1958) and Penrose (1959) both theorised evolutionary processes, without invoking biology or even evolution. It was not until Nelson and Winter (1982) that interest revived, and then, not in Darwinism as such, but a loosely defined construction asserted to have Lamarckian tendencies. Not until evolutionary game theory was brought together with neo-Schumpeterian writings by Jack Vromen (1995) was a need to resolve the issues surrounding Darwinism in a social context even hinted at by economists.

The work of the 'hard-line' Universal Darwinists, such as Richard Dawkins (1989) and Henry Plotkin (1994), and the spread of evolutionary epistemology beyond philosophy departments with such works as Callebaut (1993), provided another stimulus to a more rigorous approach to the use of evolutionary theory in economics.

1

In the light of these influences, we found ourselves saying much the same things: how have economists used evolutionary ideas, and can we find any sound basis for those ideas? The authors of the various chapters in this book contribute to understanding the interaction of economists and evolutionary thought in two ways. The first is the study of how earlier economists related their ideas to evolutionary thought. The second is how evolutionary thought can validly be used within the foundations of economics. For this reason we have two parts to this book. Part I examines the influence of evolutionary ideas on economics (and in one case the reverse); Part II consists of chapters presenting various understandings of the proper use of evolutionary theory by economics.

Early Darwinism and Its Lamarckian Heritage

The idea of evolution in nature is an ancient one, going back at least to the first-century A.D. Roman poet Lucretius.[2] In the following century the Roman emperor and Stoic philosopher Marcus Aurelius wrote that 'what keeps the whole world in being is Change: not merely change of basic elements, but also change of the larger formations they compose'. Marcus Aurelius is also interesting for his understanding of *human* nature: we 'share with the beasts of field and forest ... the instinct for gregariousness', and with our 'ascent in the ranks of creation' we experience 'fellow feeling, even when there is no proximity' – a view endorsed by Charles Darwin.[3] St. Augustine, writing in the early fifth century, argued similarly.[4] But specific theories as to *how* evolution might operate in nature had to await Jean Baptiste de Lamarck in the eighteenth century (Lamarck's contemporary, Erasmus Darwin – Charles's grandfather – merely reiterated the *idea* of evolution, updating Lucretius).

Lamarck, as Geoffrey Hodgson and Thorbjørn Knudsen explain in this volume, was an influential botanist and zoologist in his time and afterwards (Louis Figuier's 1872 *The Ocean World* has numerous illustrations of marine organisms described and named by him). Most biologists today would reject Lamarck's evolutionary mechanism involving 'new needs which establish a necessity for some part' which 'really bring about the existence of that part, as a result of efforts' and which is 'preserved by reproduction' (cited Wilkins, this volume). However, there remain a small number of specialists who find his theories attractive. Among these are Ted Steele and his colleagues at the University of Wollongong and John Curtin School of Medical Research at the Australian National University. They have worked out what they call a 'Lamarckian' model to account for what they claim is the inheritance, through the male line, of *acquired* immune responses in laboratory mice.

Steele et al.'s model is not, as yet, well supported empirically, but there are in any case other phenomena not easily explained in conventional Darwinian terms. One of these, as John Wilkins notes, is an increased mutation rate in bacteria in the absence of the usual food source or presence of toxic substances (e.g. antibiotics). As geneticist Barry Hill has observed: 'I can document [purposeful mutations] any day, every day, in the laboratory' (quoted Wesson, 1993, p. 234).

Is this 'Lamarckism' in operation at the biological level, and what has it got to do with economics? These are important questions since, first, evolutionary economists seem apt to posit 'Lamarckian' mechanisms to explain apparent evolutionary phenomena where they find them (see Nelson and Winter, 1982 and Metcalfe, 1993, 1998), and second, we need to know whether Darwinian explanations are sufficient in such situations, and if not, whether anything that *can* be called Lamarckism can be held to apply to the same.

Lamarck (1744–1829) himself was not always consistent in his suggestions as to how acquired changes in organisms came about and were inherited. Sometimes it was through 'efforts' to satisfy some 'need', sometimes it was the direct effect of environment ('the influence of climate, the variations of atmospheric temperature and surrounding environment, the diversity of locations').[5] If things are unclear at the biological level, what of that fuzzy zone where principles of sociocultural evolution are said to operate – the domain of economics? Do Lamarck's theories apply here? Things are complicated, unfortunately, by *Darwin's* recourse to Lamarckian explanations at times, especially when he was discussing the sociocultural sphere.

Darwin had been exposed to Lamarck's ideas when a medical student at Edinburgh in 1825-7, where his tutor in zoology, Robert Grant, whom Darwin accompanied on excursions in search of marine animals, was an enthusiast for Lamarck.[6] This apparently rubbed off on Darwin to some extent. Notwithstanding his later (sometime around 1838) devising of an entirely new theory of evolution – natural selection – Darwin could still, in 1871, in *The Descent of Man*, write a section on 'Effects of the increased Use and Disuse of Parts' (loss of organs through the latter was another element in Lamarck's scheme). Here he describes dexterity in seal-catching among Eskimos, for example, as an instance of the inheritance of 'mental aptitude quite as much as bodily structure' (Darwin, n.d., p. 419).[7] Elsewhere in *The Descent of Man* Darwin wrote of the survival value of 'social and moral qualities' in tribal life. 'In the first place, as the reasoning powers and foresight of the members become improved, each man would soon learn that if he aided his fellow men, he would commonly receive aid in return. From this low motive he might acquire the habit of aiding his fellows; and ...

[h]abits ... *followed during many generations probably tend to be inherited*'
(ibid., p. 499).

We can't be sure, but it is just possible that Darwin had in mind here some
such lines from Lamarck as these quoted by Robert Richards (1992, p. 50):
'[T]he varieties of habits, movements, actions, the means of living, and the
ways of self-preservation, defence, and propagation ... as a result of these
diverse influences, the faculties become extended and strengthen themselves
through use, and they become diversified through new habits which have
been practiced for a long time'. Darwin had as yet no mechanism to explain
the transmission of discrete units of heredity (this awaited the rediscovery of
Mendel's work in 1900), so his difficulty is understandable. However, there
was more to Darwin's conception of sociocultural evolution than a reiteration
of Lamarck and his other writing on the subject has stood the test of time
very well.

The deleted words before 'habits' in the above quote from *The Descent of
Man* read: 'the habit of performing benevolent actions certainly strengthens
the feeling of sympathy which gives the first impulse to benevolent actions'.
Is Darwin referring to the same processes here? Are sympathy and the habit
of aiding one's fellows acquired by the same means? Further reading in *The
Descent of Man* – summarised in the first of Laurent's chapters – shows that
clearly they are not. 'Sympathy', for Darwin, by the time he wrote *The
Descent of Man*, is a biological *proclivity*, naturally selected for over æons of
time (and inherited by humans from pre-human socially-living species) for its
utility in competition between groups (and possibly between species).[8]
'Habits', on the other hand, are *learned* behaviours, made possible, in part, by
the underlying 'impulse' of sympathy. Nevertheless, Darwin still believed in
1871, apparently – with Lamarck – that learned habits etc. could somehow be
biologically inherited. That we now believe this position is untenable is due
to August Weismann's discovery, a few years after Darwin's death, of the
barrier named after him (though Steele et al. dispute this – see Knudsen's
chapter) between the hereditary material in the nucleus of the germ cells and
all other bodily (somatic) cells. Weismann's Barrier became doctrine with
the elucidation of the structure of DNA[9] in 1953 and in the extraordinary
achievements of recombinant DNA technology from the late 1970s onwards.

Darwin's uncertain distinction between inherited tendencies and learned
behaviours is, of course, the basis of the nature–nurture debate of today. That
this debate can be so vociferous is a reflection of our awareness of the
complexity of evolutionary processes at the sociocultural level. One possible
pointer to a way out of the debate is the so-called Baldwin Effect,
independently proposed in 1896 by James Mark Baldwin (1896a, 1896b) and
C. Lloyd Morgan (1896). The Baldwin Effect is discussed in detail by both
Hodgson and Wilkins, below, but perhaps a little more can be said about it

here. In both of Darwin's 'Lamarckian' examples from *The Descent of Man* above, learned behaviours are an important element. But learning presupposes a central nervous system and brain of some sort (depending on the complexity of the task), a product of biological evolution. In other words, and in what we would now call 'Darwinian' terms (neo-Darwinian would be better), learning *capacity*, through the accumulation of chance variations of genetic material resulting in neural developments, will be *selected for* over generations. This is essentially the Baldwin Effect, and can be seen as remaining true in Darwin's examples, even if Darwin himself may not have fully appreciated the implications of what he was saying.

Another example that can be so *interpreted* from *The Descent of Man* can be adduced. In Alfred Russel Wallace's (see William Coleman's chapter) copy of the second edition of the *Descent* sent to him by Darwin,[10] – beside what would appear to be another instance of Darwin's 'Lamarckism' and which reads '... some intelligent actions, after being performed during several generations, become converted into instincts and are inherited, as when birds on oceanic islands learn to avoid man' – Wallace has pencilled in: 'imitation & selection'. With this brief comment Wallace provides a perfectly acceptable 'Darwinian' account of the phenomenon described. What Wallace is surely saying is that a biologically evolved capacity for learning by imitation – a product of normal natural selection processes (which Wallace knew about, having independently formulated the theory) – will in turn be acted upon by natural selection to the effect that those birds most adept at learning to avoid man will be those most likely to survive and pass on their heredity to offspring.

Darwinism and Political Economy

Turning to economists' uses of Darwinian theory, and the extent to which ideology may or may not have entered into this process, the Baldwin Effect is surely an illuminating principle. It enables us to move beyond what we can now recognise as the limitations of Lamarckian theory, including in the social sphere, and which – we would argue – have bedevilled much of the evolutionary economics of recent years. Lamarck no doubt had important things to say – not least being the undeniable pervasiveness of evolutionary processes in nature, including in the human sphere (Darwin acknowledges Lamarck's view that humanity 'is the co-descendant with other species of some ancient, lower, and extinct form').[11] But investigations over the 140 years since publication of *The Origin of Species* have shown us that it is *Darwinian* evolution, modified as particular circumstances may require (as with Steele's mice and Hill's bacteria), that is the best model we have yet for understanding not only the natural world but ourselves and our institutions also.

This does not necessarily mean, however, that there will be universal agreement as to how Darwin's ideas apply to the latter. Friedrich Hayek and John Maynard Keynes, for example, were both deeply interested in Darwin's theories, but had very different understandings of the workings of the economy. While Hayek stressed the self-organising power of the natural adjustment of the needs of evolving individuals to each other (as discussed in Hodgson's chapter), Keynes preferred to focus on phenomena at the group level (which by extension could mean whole nations, locked in 'the competitive struggle for markets' – see Laurent's second chapter). But each in his own way can be seen as emphasising different *facets* of Darwin's writing, rather than having arrived at diametrically opposed interpretations (even if their followers may prefer to see things differently). It may be true, as Hodgson argues, that Hayek could conceive of cultural evolution proceeding in some kind of 'Lamarckian' fashion, given the complexities involved at this level (and Darwin's own difficulties on this question, as already noted), but that Hayek was fully cognisant of the issues involved is clear, for instance, in his understanding of the Baldwin Effect, which he summarised with admirable clarity in a 1971 review of the geneticist C.D. Darlington's *The Evolution of Man and Society* (which takes a strongly hereditarian line): 'Once an innate capacity for learning by imitation is acquired', Hayek writes, 'the transmission of abilities takes a new form – vastly superior to genetic transmission precisely because it includes the transmission of acquired characters which genetic transmission does not' (Hayek, 1990, p. 291).

Here we have, then, 'Lamarckian' inheritance of acquired characteristics but through Darwinian selection processes, as Wallace had recognised. Another economist, Thorstein Veblen, too, clearly saw the importance for the relevance of evolutionary theory to economics of Darwin's distinction between learned behaviours and underlying capacities and propensities. Just as the latter have presumably been the subject of natural selection, so also may be their cultural expressions (including in business culture). In 1914 (see References) Veblen wrote: 'It is a distinctive mark of mankind that the working out of the distinctive proclivities of the race is guided by an intelligence not approached by the other animals. But ... it is only by the prompting of instinct that reflection and deliberation come to be ... employed'. Veblen, as Hodgson shows, retained Darwin's differentiation between instincts (as with 'sympathy'), and 'habits', which are learned. As Veblen is often regarded as the first major institutionalist, it is tempting to associate Veblen's interest in sympathy (or as Darwin sometimes calls it, 'fellow-feeling') with his preoccupation with the group dynamics of institutions, and to see in this some useful perspectives on the egoism versus altruism debate – individual versus group selection – as is taken up in Vromen's chapter.

Darwinism *or* Lamarckism, or Darwinism *and* Lamarckism?

One of the clearest features of evolutionary ideas has been the distinction between Darwinian and Lamarckian processes, and the lack of any other possible processes. These appear to be exhaustive of possibilities and, at the most fundamental level, mutually exclusive.

In the life sciences, where evolutionary thought is most highly developed, genetics has provided the basis for the mechanisms of evolutionary processes to be made explicit. Alternatives or complements to genetics, such as self-organisation and far-from-equilibrium thermodynamics (Kauffman, 1993) have been investigated as a means whereby Darwinian selection is activated. Some popular authors have attempted to make self-organisation an alternative to Darwinism (Wesson, 1993). However, it seems clear that this is nothing more than another possible mechanism through which Darwinian processes operate, in the same way as Mendelian genetics[12] (Maynard Smith, 1998). In the social and cultural sciences and humanities, where more controversy has raged about the role and applicability of evolutionary theory, debate about the precise nature of evolutionary processes has been secondary. Because there is less known about the mechanisms of social and cultural evolution, the roles of various theories, including memetics (see Blackmore, 1999) and self-organisation or far-from-equilibrium thermodynamics (which have their enthusiasts amongst economists, see Foster, 1999) is more difficult to judge. However, it must be said that the various ideas are almost always seen as being within either the Darwinian framework (as, explicitly, memetics) or Lamarckian.

It would appear, then, from the lack of competitors, that the available niches for occupation are full: evolution is either a Lamarckian or a Darwinian process. The philosophical analysis of the question seems to indicate the lack of any such space, on grounds of logic. Two accessible treatments suggest why this is the case. Henry Plotkin (1994) begins the argument by defining the two processes as mutually exclusive and exhaustive. Geoffrey Hodgson (1993), on the other hand, traces the use of 'evolution' in economics through a labyrinth of meanings, all of which ultimately come down to either something which is not evolution in the sense of population dynamics over time, or something which he defines as phylogenetic, and itself either Darwinian or Lamarckian (Hodgson, 1993, Chapter 3). This phylogenetic category includes all current evolutionary economics. This is seen even more clearly when Hodgson's argument is juxtaposed with that of Vromen (1995).

Plotkin's argument is that evolutionary processes can only be the result of either selection and sorting of some kind, or instruction and direction. Lamarck hit upon the latter notion, in his belief that organisms are wonderfully well adapted because they respond to their environment by developing characteristics best suited to that environment: change depends on environment, is called forth by environment. In order for Lamarck's process to operate there has to be a means for organisms to choose to develop characteristics, thus the inheritance of acquired characters is central to his process. Darwin, on the other hand, saw organisms changing, mutating, for reasons independent of their environment. Their success in surviving and propagating is a chance relationship between them and their environment. In order that characters emerge independently of environment,[13] a Darwinian process has to forbid inheritance of characteristics adopted by an organism for its survival. Dependence of changes on environment (Lamarckian instructionism) and independence of changes from environment (Darwinian selectionism) are thus two states of nature which are both mutually exclusive, in that the one process cannot be both dependent and independent; and exhaustive, in that a process has to be one or the other.

Once this is understood, it is easy to see that no other fundamental process is possible. It is also clear that self-organisation and far-from-equilibrium thermodynamics are merely another level on which emergent changes are constrained or directed, in the same way that orthodox theories of genetics constrain and direct emergent changes. In neither theory is the environment the cause of the change; in both cases the theory is about how a change emerges on which selection forces operate. Natural selection remains the meta-theory of evolution.

Our interest is, of course, with social evolution. On the above argument it must be the case that evolution must fall into one or the other camp. If it were clear that social evolution was undoubtedly Darwinian, the arrow of causation from within the social organism to interaction with its environment, there would be no difficulty in articulating social and cultural systems with the biological systems on which the former are founded. It is only if social evolution is clearly Lamarckian that problems arise in delineating boundaries at which Lamarckian processes can be allowed. Here is the nub of the problems attacked in this book by Hodgson, Knudsen and Wilkins, as well as by Vromen in a slightly different context – that of the problem of agency for Darwinian processes. How can we resolve the problem of an evolutionary explanation of social processes, where learning, choice, uncertainty, complexity and novelty are all important phenomena?

Hodgson and Knudsen both seek to retain a Lamarckian theory of economic evolution, but not independent of the underlying Darwinian biological (or even deep social) processes. The motive for so doing is a strong one. It is much easier to present a Lamarckian process, with some semblance of rational choice directed toward satisfying an objective subject to constraints, than it is to present the same phenomena as the outcomes of blindly generated actions. This approach allows seamless adoption of the many economic theories of evolution that emerged in the second half of the 20th century. Nelson and Winter (1982) and Metcalfe (1993, 1998) are only three of the best known theorists to use instructionist logic for their models. The task taken up by Hodgson and Knudsen is to reconcile this with the limitations of instructionism. Both choose to use the device of nesting the Lamarckian process within an underlying Darwinian selectionism. Their arguments are by no means identical. Each suggests an ingenious method for ensuring the logical and scientifically appropriate co-existence of the two processes.

Wilkins and Vromen both take the other view. Wilkins explicitly argues the irrelevance of instructionism, beginning with the biological. He attacks the argument of Steele for an instructionist basis for any biological phenomena, which may have given an excuse for social science to use the Steele argument. In this, the reader will find a direct confrontation with Knudsen's chapter, and thus an opportunity to directly weigh the alternatives. Vromen completes the argument by exploring the seeming contradiction between agency, or volition, and selectionism. This argument is indeed a difficult and subtle one, as befits a question long avoided by most social science, and certainly economics.

Evolutionary Processes and Agency

It is worth our while to introduce this argument, again by reference to the seeming conflict between instruction and selection. Human volition, or agency, apparently directs social evolution. If this is obvious, then is it not obvious that social evolution has to be Lamarckian by nature, that the environment causes changes by directly calling them forth? Unfortunately it is not so obvious once the problem of boundaries between biological and social is acknowledged. Plotkin's *Nature of Knowledge* (1994) attacked this problem by examining the boundary between brain activity (a biological phenomenon, however it may work) and human action. His argument is that brain function (about which our knowledge is very sketchy) at some level has to be selectionist, rather than instructionist, if creativity and novelty is to be explained. Learning may consist of apparent instruction, but it is never wholly instruction; novel insights emerge and these cannot be the product of instruction: 'while selection can mimic instruction, the reverse is never true' (Plotkin, 1994, p. 172). The argument of parsimony completes his choice of selectionist or Darwinian process as against Lamarckian instructionist as the theory up for test in future scientific work on brain function.

But this does not necessarily bind higher levels in the field of social organisation. Is he not simply suggesting that the boundary between phenomena consistent with the biological is at least that of the brain. What about interactions between people, and groups of people such as we are concerned with in economics? Surely the importance of choice, or agency, precludes a selectionist account? But if selection is excluded, how are novelty and error to be treated? Given also that social activity at any level of organisation, from the individual to the corporation or government, is undertaken with radical uncertainty and complexity (as per Simon's 1981 chess example), can instructionist process explain choice?

What seems clear is that the initially 'obvious' Lamarckian instructionism for social activities involving conscious choice creates problems as well as solving them. Is there a way through this which can allow evolutionary analysis to resolve them? What emerges after digesting arguments both for instructionism and selectionism in economic evolution is the conclusion that evolutionary theory is a valid research programme. Whether the scientific community takes up one or the other way of reconciling choice with novelty, it is the case that reconciliation is clearly possible. It cannot be argued that evolutionary economics is any threat to the idea that rational action is part of the human experience. The question becomes one of whether evolutionary theories explain economic phenomena better than alternative theories, in other words, whether evolutionary economics is worth exploring. The answer to that must await theoretical and empirical development of mature evolutionary theory.

Acknowledgements

The editors wish to thank our authors for their support for, and commitment to, this project, not only in writing their papers but in dealing with editorial demands for revisions, not to mention our intransigence and occasional wrongheadedness. We also wish to acknowledge the support and help of our publishing and editorial staff at Edward Elgar Publishing.

In addition John Laurent wishes to thank David Burch, Margaret Campbell, Jacky Cox, Roslyn Cox, Adrian Desmond, Gina Douglas, Athol Fitzgibbons, Sally Hames, Chris Harrington, Peter Healy, Geoffrey Hodgson, Wayne Hudson, Richard Keynes, Mike Kirk and staff at King's College,

Cambridge, Ian Lowe, Roy MacLeod, John Marsden, Phillip McDonald, Jim Moore, Robin and Laurie Neill, Sue Newton, Doug Ogilvie, Peter Pegg, George and Yvonne Simmons, Robert Skidelsky, Andrew and Jill Bowie and David and Isabella Thorpe for all their help in various ways.

John Nightingale would like to add his thanks to all of the above, and add Don Lamberton, Stan Metcalfe, Dick Nelson, Kurt Dopfer and Malcolm Treadgold; Lyn Nyland for dealing with the List of References and Ian Kerr for cleaning up diagrams for conversion into PDF for the publishers.

Notes

1. Copeland (1931) may be an exception. Hobson (1929, and 1936 on Veblen) shows that the idea survived, albeit beyond the mainstream.
2. Titus Lucretius, *On The Nature of Things*, translated and introduced by R.E. Latham, Harmondsworth: Penguin, 1957.
3. Marcus Aurelius, *Meditations*, translated and with an Introduction by Maxwell Staniforth, London: Penguin, 1964; Ch. 2 this volume, note 7.
4. St. Augustine, *The City of God*, a new translation by Henry Bettenson with an Introduction by David Knowles, Harmondsworth: Penguin, 1981, Books XII, XIX.
5. Quoted in Richards (1987), p. 50.
6. See Desmond and Moore (1991), Ch. 3.
7. See also William Platt Bell, *Are the Effects of Use and Disuse Inherited? An Examination of the View Held by Spencer and Darwin*, London: Macmillan, 1890.
8. This argument is cogently put in Niles Eldredge (1986).
9. Of which 'genes' – a term coined in 1909 by the Dutch botanist Wilhelm Johannsen for Mendel's units of heredity – are composed.
10. Now housed in the library of the Linnean Society in London.
11. Darwin (n.d.), p. 390.
12. Plotkin (1994, p. 38) refers to self-organisation as 'handwaving'. This may be too severe, in particular where it includes far-from-equilibrium thermodynamics.
13. The environment selects from amongst independently emerging mutations. Change is thus dependent on environment, but at the first remove.

PART I

2. Darwin, Economics and Contemporary Economists

John Laurent

In an interesting paper a couple of years ago, University of New South Wales economist Geoff Fishburn (1995) argued that Alfred Marshall's predecessor in the Cambridge Chair of Political Economy, Henry Fawcett, was not only an early supporter of Charles Darwin following publication of *The Origin of Species*, but also that Fawcett was helpful to Darwin in reassuring the latter of the soundness of his scientific methodology.[1]

This small episode points to the close, if not always comfortable, association that economics and Darwinian theory have had since the very formation of Darwin's theory. Indeed, this association can be seen well before that date, if one takes into account the intellectual climate in which Darwin developed his ideas (Schweber, 1980; Desmond and Moore, 1991). Paradoxically, very few economists now seem to know anything about Darwin or his writings. Evolution, on the other hand, is a term much bandied about by economists; indeed there is a whole branch of present day economics calling itself 'evolutionary economics', and there is a journal with that name. At least two books with the title *Evolutionary Economics* have been published (Boulding, 1981; Witt, 1993), and several other economics texts with 'evolution' or related words in their titles are currently in print (e.g. Reijnders, 1997; Magnusson and Ottosson, 1997; Hodgson, 1998c). One seeks with difficulty, however, for economics titles with the words 'Darwin' or 'Darwinism' in them, notwithstanding the common use of 'Darwinian' or similar words in everyday economic discourse (a computer search of the 'Worldcat' database revealed just eight, one of them being my own Griffith University working paper on *Keynes and Darwin*). One does, though, happen across pleasant surprises from time to time. Another volume from Geoff Hodgson (1995) – one of the contributors to the present volume – has helpful discussions on the significance of Darwin's theories for economics, as has his earlier book, *Economics and Evolution* (Hodgson, 1993). In a 1997 issue of the *Journal of Evolutionary Economics* (Vol. 7, pp. 97–145) there is an exchange between Hodgson and Matthias Kelm over an attempt by Kelm to provide a 'Darwinian interpretation' to Joseph Schumpeter's economics.[2] And insofar as Schumpeter does not restrict himself to the basic Darwinian principle of selection from pre-existing variety, one prominent writer in 'evolutionary economics', anyway – John Foster (1997) – is at least aware of the tendency of proponents of this school to 'not choose the neo-Darwinian theory of natural selection as their biological analogy' but to 'favour a Lamar[c]kian analogy'. A volume I picked up in a secondhand bookshop in Brisbane recently, published in 1966 by the somewhat obscure Gulf Publishing Co. of Houston, Texas, has the title *Corporate Darwinism*. It contains a generally fair treatment of Darwin's conception of human nature, citing both *The Origin of Species* and *The Descent of Man* as well as important works about Darwin and Darwinism such as Richard Hofstadter's (1955) *Social Darwinism in American Thought*. Juxtaposed with these references are others to important works in economics, such as Robert Heilbroner's *The Making of Economic Society*.

The argument of this obscure volume (Blake, Avis and Mouton, 1966, p. 112) is that '[s]ome students of human behaviour [have] looked at Darwin's theories [and] said, "If we apply the Darwinian concepts to individuals it should account for the differences in human conduct", [but] their results were disappointing'; and: 'The great problem as to why this research was not successful stems from the fact that these concepts were applied to small parts rather than the whole ... [I]t is quite possible that the social organisms to which these ideas apply best are organised entities of people – such as the corporation – rather than individuals considered independently and in isolation from one another'.

There are, I would argue, both truth and the potential for misunderstanding in these sentences. Blake et al. highlight the incompleteness of individualistic interpretations of Darwin, as have a number of other writers. I can mention the Fabian socialist Sidney Webb (1896, 1916), the scientist and co-discoverer of natural selection, Alfred Russel Wallace (1870, 1913b) and the South African general and politician, Jan Christiaan Smuts (1926).[3] At the same time, Blake et al.'s use of the phrase 'social organisms' to describe 'organised entities of people' is unfortunate. Darwin himself, so far as I am aware, never referred to the 'social organism' in print. The closest he seems to have come to using the term – and it is clearly meant only as a figure of speech – is to talk of animals 'living in a *body*'; or, perhaps, when discussing the sting apparatus in bees (which cannot be withdrawn after use, inevitably resulting in the death of the bee from the tearing out of its viscera), to speak of the bee's stinging ability as being 'useful to the *social community*' (the hive), thus 'fulfil[ling] all the requirements of natural selection, though it may cause the death of some few members' (Darwin, n.d., pp. 50, 476).[4]

So Blake et al.'s description of Darwin's 'organised entities of people' as 'social organisms' is not quite right. But it contains an essential truth, and that truth is that Darwin's view of human evolution – as this chapter will try to show – is preponderantly in terms of 'man' (the term Darwin mostly uses) as a social being.

Notwithstanding occasional references by economists to *The Origin of Species* (e.g., Hirshleifer, 1977; Cottrell and Lawler, 1991; Khalil, 1993), the fact of the matter is that there is no discussion of humans in that book except in one paragraph on the second last page. This reads in part: 'In the future I see open fields for far more important researches. ... Much light will be thrown on the origin of man and his history' (Darwin, n.d., p. 373). Where *The Origin of Species* is cited, frequently this is in contexts completely unconnected with Darwin's writing. Cottrell and Lawler (1991), for example, quote Darwin on 'sports' in plants at the head of an article (then do not mention him again) about 'natural rate mutations' in interest rates, whereas the term 'mutation' does not appear anywhere in Darwin (nor does Darwin say anything about interest rates).[5]

Such instances emphasise a fundamental problem with 'evolutionary economics'. That is, besides frequently demonstrating a lack of familiarity with, and understanding of, what Darwin actually wrote (and of modern biology) it is founded almost entirely on analogy. Of course, there is nothing necessarily wrong with this principle. Analogy can be an important aid to thought – and indeed there is a sense in which perhaps most thought depends upon it at base. But analogy has its limitations, and the appropriateness of the analogy that is being drawn is always an important question. For example, Bishop Butler's *Analogy of Religion* may have impressed eighteenth century readers, but we are less convinced today by assertions made in one domain of thought based on alleged similarities with phenomena in the other domains which excited Butler.[6] Similarly, I would argue, one should view with scepticism claims made in one field of thought (economics) based on supposed similarities with another (biology), unless a direct connection can be demonstrated between the two. But I claim such a connection can be made between economics and biology, and that is by way of what Darwin said about human nature and biology. My first task in this chapter is to see what Darwin says about these subjects in *The Descent of Man*. As very few economists, so far as I have been able to discover, ever read this book, it is important – given the frequent invoking of Darwin's name in economics – to look at what Darwin actually wrote about the human condition in it. The contents of *Descent of Man* will be contrasted with the very different 'evolution' of Herbert Spencer's *First Principles*. This is the basis for a study of Alfred Marshall's and Karl Marx's biological analogy which, it will be seen, owes little to Darwin, notwithstanding the occasional invocation of Darwin's name. I will then look at the writing of two early Australian economists who can lay some claim to basing their ideas more firmly in Darwin's theories. A concluding section will return to the subject of the often misleading notions of 'evolutionary' economists who claim a Darwinian pedigree for their arguments.

Darwin's *Descent of Man* versus Spencer

The most relevant chapter of *The Descent of Man* for economics is undoubtedly the fourth (of the second [1874] edition), on 'The Moral Sense'. In this chapter, people like J.S. Mill, Adam Smith (*Theory of Moral Sentiments*) and *Economist* editor Walter Bagehot (*Physics and Politics*) are liberally cited (Malthus is not cited in this chapter, but is in Chapter 2). It is clear that Darwin's reading in their, and other economists', works had a profound bearing on his thinking. The results of this thinking are encapsulated in a sentence in the penultimate paragraph of 'The Moral Sense' which contains the phrase: 'the social instincts – the prime principle of man's moral constitution,'[7] and are more fully elaborated in the following passage, under the sub-heading *Man a social animal*:

> The social animals which stand at the bottom of the scale [of nature] are guided almost exclusively, and those which stand higher in the scale are largely guided, by special instincts in the aid which they give to the members of the same community; [and] are likewise in part impelled by mutual love and sympathy, assisted apparently by some amount of reason. Although man ... has no special instincts to tell him how to aid his fellow-men, he still has the impulse, and with his improved intellectual faculties would naturally be much guided in this respect by reason and experience. (Darwin, n.d., p. 481)

For Darwin, the origin of the 'moral sense' in humans is in those 'social instincts' which enable certain species to act collectively (as in Blake et al.'s 'organised entities of people'). These instincts consist partly in feelings of 'sympathy' – a term which Darwin borrows from Adam Smith's *Moral Sentiments*[8] – between members of animal and human 'communities'. A few pages earlier in 'The Moral Sense' Darwin provides some examples of collective and 'co-operative' behaviour in various species gleaned from the reports of naturalists and travel writers:

> Social animals perform many ... services for each other. The most common mutual service ... is to warn one another of danger by means of the united senses of all. ... [M]onkeys search each other for external parasites ... wolves and some other beasts of prey hunt in packs, and aid one another in attacking their victims. Pelicans fish in concert. The Hamadryas baboons turn over stones to find insects, etc., and when they come to a large one, as many as can stand round turn it over and share the booty. Some animals mutually defend each other. Bull bisons in N. America, when there is danger, drive the cows and calves into the middle of the herd, whilst they defend the outside. (Darwin, n.d. pp. 473–4)[9]

Such behaviour, Darwin believed, is observable today because it has been naturally selected for in terms of the benefits it confers on the species concerned. For example, those gatherings of baboons and bison which, through chance variation of hereditary material (the nature of which remained a mystery for Darwin – the word 'mutation' was not coined until 1901, and 'gene' in 1909)[10] happen to possess these survival-enhancing propensities, will be at an advantage over those groups which do not. Consequently, their hereditary material will tend to spread throughout the population generally at the expense of that possessed by the latter. Adopting Smith's 'sympathy' concept, Darwin summarises his argument this way: 'In however complex a manner this feeling may have originated, as it is one of high importance to all those animals which aid and defend one another, it will have been increased through natural selection; for those communities which included the greatest number of the most sympathetic members would flourish best and rear the greatest number of offspring' (Darwin, n.d., pp. 473–4).

This, for Darwin, is how man, the pre-eminently social animal, inherited his social propensities from primate ancestors: 'Judging from … the majority of the Quadrumana [primates]', Darwin writes (p. 480), 'it is probable that the early ape-like progenitors of man were likewise social'.[11] But with man, the other element that he refers to in the quote above – reason – is also able to come into play; and this faculty, coupled with instinctive impulses for sociability, enables the possibility of co-operation beyond the confines of the immediate social community – indeed, on a global scale. Making allowances for Darwin's Victorian approbation of 'civilisation', the following passage from towards the end of 'The Moral Sense' presents a marked contrast to the kinds of imperialist and racist 'Social Darwinism' (see Hofstadter, 1955) that many people assume stem from Darwin himself:

> As man advances in civilisation, and small tribes are united into larger communities, the simplest reason would tell each individual that he ought to extend his social instincts and sympathies to all the members of the same nation, though personally unknown to him. This point being once reached, there is only an artificial boundary to prevent his sympathies extending to the men of all nations and races. (Darwin, n.d., pp. 491–2)

To those unfamiliar with Darwin's actual writing, this passage may come as a surprise. Darwinism, for most people, undoubtedly tends to be associated with cut-throat competition and the 'survival of the fittest', and it of course provides a perfect rationale for ultra-conservative 'New Right' and similar ideologies (see, e.g., Davidson, 1987). As it happens, 'survival of the fittest' is not Darwin's phrase, but Herbert Spencer's (though Darwin adopted it in the 6th edition of *The Origin of Species*). Spencer, however, is probably better known as the originator (at least in an evolutionary sense)[12] of the 'social organism' concept, a favourite idea in 'evolutionary economics' but having very little to do with Darwin. Spencer's concept is most fully argued in his book *First Principles*, which has chapters on 'The Law of Evolution', 'The Interpretation of Evolution' and 'Evolution and Dissolution'. The 'social organism' idea – or sometimes 'super organism' – is an extension of Spencer's conception of the organism at the biological level of evolution to a collection of biological entities (e.g., people). In 'The Law of Evolution', to illustrate, Spencer first describes how, in his view, all matter passes 'from a relatively indefinite, incoherent homogeneity to a relatively definite, coherent heterogeneity', and then goes on to say, regarding biological evolution:

> [T]he evolution of an organism is primarily the formation of an aggregate, by the continued incorporation of matter previously spread through a wider space. ... Secondary integrations ... accompany [these] primary integrations [and are] displayed not within the limits of an individual only but by the union of many individuals. ... Among the Coelenterata [for example] integration produces half-fused colonies [such as] the Hydrozoa, in which many individuals form an aggregate in such a way as to have a common system of nutrition.

Spencer then proceeds to argue, regarding human social evolution, 'The phenomena set down in the foregoing paragraph introduces us to others of a higher order', by which he means:

> [I]n the *social organism* [my emphasis] integrative changes are abundantly exemplified ... . A civilised society is made unlike a savage tribe by the establishment of regulative classes – governmental, administrative, military, ecclesiastical, legal, etc., which ... are held together as a general class by a certain community of privileges, of blood, of education, of intercourse ... . The integrations seen throughout the operative or industrial organisation, later in origin, [are] consequent on the growths of adjacent parts performing like functions, as, for instance, the junction of Manchester with its calico-weaving suburbs. (Spencer, 1900, pp. 289–90)

Spencer's references to 'civilised society' versus a 'savage tribe' are in keeping with the Social Darwinism that has been associated with his name (see, e.g., Hofstadter, 1955, pp. 170–200), but it is Spencer's organic analogy with which we are concerned here. As just seen, Spencer does not hesitate to use this kind of language in a specifically economic context, where he is describing the 'integrations of industrial organisation'. Further instances in *First Principles* can be cited. One example is the following passage, where Spencer is elaborating upon his understanding of the progression from the 'homogeneous to the heterogeneous' in the differentiation of society into 'distinct classes and orders' (biological taxonomic terms) of workers. 'Political economists', he writes, have long since described the industrial progress which, through increasing division of labour, ends with a civilised community whose members severally perform different actions for one another. ... But there are yet other and higher phrases of this advance from the homogeneous to the heterogeneous in the industrial order of society. Long after considerable progress has been made in the division of labour among the different classes of workers, there is relatively little division ... . Among the widely separated parts of the community ... the nation continues comparatively homogeneous in the respect that in each district the same occupations are pursued. But when roads and other means of transit become numerous and good, the different districts begin to assume different functions, and to become mutually dependent. The calico-manufacturer locates himself in this county, the woollen-manufacturer in that [etc.]. (Spencer, 1900, pp. 317–18)

Such arguments would no doubt be appealing to 'evolutionary' economists interested in organic models of industrialisation (see, e.g., Mokyr, 1990) but again have nothing whatever to do with Darwin's writing. Just how Spencer's evolutionism became influential in economics is an intriguing question, a complete answer to which it is probably impossible to give; nevertheless, suggestions as to at least parts of the answer can be made, and one of these is via Alfred Marshall.[13]

Spencerian Analogy in Marshall and Marx

There is, I take it, little argument among economists about the importance of biological analogy for Marshall (see, e.g., Thomas, 1991; Nightingale, 1993; Groenewegen, 1995). What has received less attention, however, is the role of Spencer, rather than Darwin, in this process, and how Marshall's economics, as a consequence, has little resemblance to anything Darwin wrote. Marshall's debt to Spencer will be dealt with in more detail in Peter Groenewegen's contribution to the present volume. For the present, it is easily demonstrated that Spencer was more important for Marshall than Darwin. To begin with, the final (8th) edition of *Principles of Economics* has nearly twice as many (5) references to Spencer as to Darwin (3). (An earlier edition – the 4th – has 7 entries for Spencer in the index and 3 for Darwin.) Moreover, in the first of the latter, Marshall's usage of Darwin displays a clearly Spencerian rather than Darwinian mode of thinking. Marshall cites an argument by Darwin – to the effect that the parts of an organism most obviously adapted to its habitat are not usually those which throw most light on its origin – to make a case that 'in like manner those properties of an economic institution which play the most important part in fitting it for the work which it has to do now are for that very reason likely to be in good measure of recent growth' (Marshall, 1920, p. 42). As with Spencer, Marshall's words are pure analogy. They do not follow logically from

Darwin's argument, nor is there any obvious physical connection between the phenomenon described by Darwin and the situation to which Marshall refers.

In the second of Marshall's references to Darwin (the third is simply a note about Darwin's capacity for mental work), the conflation of that writer's theories with Spencer is even more pronounced. '[E]conomists', Marshall writes, have

> owed much to the many profound analogies which have been discovered between social and especially industrial organisation on the one side, and the physical organisation of the higher animals on the other. ... [M]any of [these] illustrate a fundamental unity of action between the laws of nature in the physical and in the moral world. This central unity is set forth in the general rule ... that the development of the organism, whether social or physical, involves an increasing subdivision of functions between its separate parts on the one hand, and on the other a more intimate connection between them. ... This increased subdivision of functions, or 'differentiation', as it is called, manifests itself with regard to industry in such forms as the division of labour, and the development of specialised skill, knowledge and machinery: while 'integration', that is, a growing intimacy and firmness of the connections between the separate parts of the industrial organism, shows itself in such forms as the increase of security of commercial credit, and of the means and habits of communication by sea and road, by railway and telegraph, by post and printing-press. (Marshall, 1920, pp. 240–1)

The debt to Spencer is obvious, even while it is Darwin's name that is invoked in this discussion.[14] Furthermore, there are plenty of other places in *Principles of Economics* where Marshall clearly has Spencer in mind, even if Spencer's name is not mentioned. Thus, at one point (p. 39), Marshall says that 'In the late Middle Ages a rough beginning was made of the study of the industrial organism', and that 'Each successive generation has seen further growths of that organism'.[15]

While questions may remain as to how Spencer's purely analogical (and metaphorical) mode of reasoning came to so strongly influence economics at the expense of Darwin's ideas, there can be little doubt that Marshall is partly responsible. Another likely source – at least for some economists – is Marx. Notwithstanding Marx's apparent admiration for Darwin,[16] there is little evidence that he understood Darwin's theories, or that he absorbed any of the author's key ideas. At least such would appear to have been the case from a perusal of *Capital*. Darwin is cited in Vol.1 only of this work, and that is in two footnotes, both of which are concerned with comparisons between human and 'nature's' technology. The longer of the two reads, in part, as follows:

> Darwin has interested us in the history of Nature's Technology, i.e., in the formation of the organs of plants and animals, which organs serve as instruments of production for sustaining life. Does not the history of the productive organs of man, of organs that are the material basis of all social

organisation, deserve equal attention? ... Technology discloses man's mode of
dealing with Nature, the process of production by which he sustains his life,
and thereby also lays bare the mode of formation of his social relations, and of
the mental conceptions that flow from them. (Marx, 1906, p. 406)

Again, the entirely analogical style of argument is apparent. Marx is
hardly pointing to any direct link between Darwin's writing (see footnote 14)
and human nature or history. To be fair, Vol.1 of *Capital* was first published
in 1867, so Marx could not have read *The Descent of Man* (first published
1871). In an essay apparently originally intended to be an Introduction to *A
Contribution to the Critique of Political Economy* – which was published in
1859, the same year as *The Origin of Species* – Marx touches on the theme of
man as a social animal (a phrase first used by Aristotle). The manner in
which he does so is very similar to Darwin, and in a specifically economic
context:

> The further back we trace the course of history, the more does the individual,
> and accordingly also the producing individual, appear to be dependent on and
> to belong to a larger whole ... . Man is a *Zoon politikon* in the most literal
> sense: he is not only a social animal, but an animal that can be individualised
> only within society. Production by a solitary individual outside society ... is
> just as preposterous as the development of speech without individuals who live
> *together* and talk to one another. (Marx, 1977, p. 189)[17]

But there is no evidence that Marx ever followed up these insightful remarks,
and for the most part economists have not felt led to pursue the matter[18] or to
peruse the work which most obviously supports Marx here – Darwin's *The
Descent of Man*.

Early Darwinism in Economics: W.E. Hearn and R.F. Irvine

There have, however, been economists, both 'Right' and 'Left', who have
shown a preparedness to take into account Darwin's arguments concerning
the importance of human sociability. Two who can be cited in this
connection, William Edward Hearn and Robert Francis Irvine, are
particularly interesting from the present author's point of view in that both
did most of their significant work in Australia.

Hearn, Melbourne University's first Professor of History and Political
Economy (1855–78), is probably best known for his book *Plutology*, which
was published in Melbourne in 1863.[19] This work drew praise from W.S.
Jevons, no less, as well as Marshall, as is explained by Joseph Schumpeter in
his *History of Economic Analysis* (see also Groenewegen, 1995, pp. 71, 485).
Schumpeter (1954, p. 826) says that while the book failed to impress him

personally, he did note that 'in part it does read curiously Jevonian', with its stress on the demand side. What is of most interest to us, however, is Hearn's frequent reference to both Darwin and Spencer (he is possibly the first economist to cite both writers in a book), and also the fact that Hearn was able to keep the evolutionary conceptions of each separate. Here, for example, is Hearn's accurate summary of Spencer's metaphorical conception of 'The Industrial Evolution of Society' (Hearn's chapter heading):

> The same phenomena which ... characterise the evolution of an individual may be observed in the evolution of society. In both cases the evolution consists in, or at least is invariably attended by, an increase of bulk, a greater complexity of structure, and a consequent interdependence of parts. The social germ, like the individual germ, has a simple and uniform origin. It too attracts, assimilates, and organises other like bodies; and thereby grows in bulk. It too presents, with every increase in bulk, an increase in complexity; and continually substitutes for a single indefinite and homogeneous structure a series of well-defined and mutually dependant organs. Each of these organs performs its special function; each function acquires its appropriate organ. Each organ is related both to the whole organism, and to every other organ; and depends for its efficiency upon their co-operation. Society therefore, like the individual organism, tends to become more complex, and its parts consequently become more closely interdependent. (Hearn, 1863, p. 384)

That Hearn is not asking his reader to take him literally here, and is merely using Spencer's language as an aid to thought, is clear from references to Darwin's *Origin of Species* and discussions about them a few pages further on. Each species, Hearn notes, 'serves as the food of that above it', and '[E]ven between individuals of the same species ... the feebler are as it were pushed aside and trampled down by the stronger'. Further, it is true that to these 'laws of vegetal and animal life ... man presents no exception'. But Hearn also argues that there are enormous differences between humans and other species, in that humans, in contrast to other species, can artificially increase their food supply. Humans, as well, can mitigate 'the severity of those climatic influences which so powerfully reduce the numbers of other animals', and most importantly, 'While in the lower organisms the excess of their numbers dies, such an excess in the human species ... is never born'. Man 'seldom *will*', according to Hearn, 'do all that he *can* do'. He has indeed the 'power which all other animals possess of annually producing offspring', but he 'does not act, as they act, under the impulse of blind instinct' (Hearn, 1863, pp. 388–90).

There are significant differences, for Hearn, between what happens in human societies and in aggregations of other species: with humans, a role for reason, or agency, is brought into play, as Darwin was to argue in *Descent of Man*. Yet the most interesting feature of Hearn's book is found in the opening paragraphs of the chapter entitled 'Of the Assistance Rendered to

Industry by Government'. This chapter immediately follows the one already examined, 'The Industrial Evolution of Society'. Hearn has been described by his biographer, John La Nauze (1972), as a 'mild conservative, cautious about state intervention in economic affairs but not implacably opposed to it'. Hearn's phraseology in this chapter is remarkably reminiscent of Marx (as quoted above) and Darwin, though neither Marx's essay[20] nor *The Descent of Man* had as yet been published. Hearn sets out by noting that 'Man is not merely a gregarious, but a political animal ... His tendency towards association is an attribute, not so much of his physical, as of his moral constitution'. He elaborates as follows:

> In the lower animals the impulse to aggregation is always the same. Their experience teaches them no improvement in its use. If their combination be excessive, its pressure does not induce their dispersion. But man's sociality continually increases with every advance that he makes in civilisation. ... With every extension of society the reconciliation of these conditions becomes more complete. It appears partially in the family; but it involves for its completion further and other relations. (Hearn, 1863, pp. 406–7)

We might hesitate today to talk confidently about 'advances' in 'civilisation', but it is remarkable how close Hearn is here to *The Descent of Man*, as in the earlier quoted lines from the latter book where Darwin also refers to 'advances in civilisation'. This similarity is further borne out in a comparison with some more lines from Darwin's chapter on 'The Moral Sense' in *The Descent of Man*:

> The feeling of pleasure from society is probably an extension of the parental or filial affections ... and this extension may be attributed in part to habit, but chiefly to natural selection. ... [T]he social instincts, which no doubt were acquired by man as by the lower animals for the good of the community, will from the first have given to him some wish to aid his fellows ... and have compelled him to regard their approbation and disapprobation ... . As man gradually advanced in intellectual power, and was enabled to trace the more remote consequences of his actions ... his sympathies became more tender and widely diffused, extending to men of all races. (Darwin, n.d., pp. 478, 493–4)[21]

Hearn's interest in a 'Darwinian' view of human society, and the relevance of such a view for economics, had an indirect but significant influence on the next Australian economist I wish to discuss, Robert Francis Irvine. Irvine was born in the Shetland Islands and educated in New Zealand. He moved to Sydney in the 1890s and eventually, after several years as a headmaster and as an examiner in the New South Wales Public Service Board, was appointed lecturer in economics at Sydney University. He became the university's first Professor of Economics in 1912. In 1902 Irvine had published, with O.T.J. Alpers, a former fellow student at Canterbury University College,

Christchurch, New Zealand, *The Progress of New Zealand in the Century* (Irvine and Alpers, 1902). This was a general economic and social history of the country, in which Irvine (who wrote the chapters concerned) has much interesting material on both natural history and on the lifestyle of the Maoris.

This material reveals, first, a considerable knowledge of Darwinian theory on the part of the author. For example, Irvine discusses the displacing of the native rat by the introduced European species – a topic of obvious interest from a Darwinian point of view and in fact discussed by both Darwin (1890) and A.R. Wallace (1879) (Campbell and Laurent, 1987). Irvine would also seem to have had in mind Darwin's understanding of the survival value of human solidarity in his account of the Maoris. As Darwin had written in *The Descent of Man*, 'Every one will admit that man is a social being [who] would inherit a tendency to be faithful to his comrades, and obedient to the leader of his tribe' and to be 'willing to defend, in concert with others, his fellow-men; and would be ready to aid them in any way which did not too greatly interfere with his own welfare' (Darwin, n.d., pp. 480–1). Irvine's description of Maori life in *The Progress of New Zealand in the Century* perfectly fits this image of at least one side of human nature.[22] 'The Maori tribe', Irvine explains,

> was a commune organised for peace or war. Its communal character escaped the notice of the early settlers, who were extremely puzzled to understand the nature of Maori customs and especially their land laws ... . There was no individual ownership in the English sense. When an individual cleared a patch of forest and cultivated it, it was recognised as his property; but he had no right to sell without the permission of the tribe ...
> The Maoris had no desire to accumulate wealth or property. A large catch of fish was valued merely because it permitted a lavish hospitality. So in other matters it was deemed a disgrace to possess riches except for the purpose of squandering it. The father did not accumulate for the spending of the son: his weapons of war, whatever belongings he set most store by, were interred with his bones. Under these circumstances and in a country where food was obtainable at a moderate expenditure of labour, there were no glaring inequalities of social condition. None were rich and none were absolutely destitute. Even the lazy man whose 'throat was deep' could get himself fed, and the feeble or unfortunate were able to share in the results of the fishing or snaring. (Irvine and Alpers, 1902, pp. 22–3)

As explained by his biographer, Bruce McFarlane (1966), Irvine, as an economist, was deeply interested in radical and left-wing politics, probably from about the 1890s onwards, and this shows in his writing. The idyllic picture of 'primitive communism' among the Maoris given by Irvine can be seen to partly reflect similar accounts of other 'primitive' peoples in Engels, Annie Besant (a founder of the Fabian Society) and other writers.[23] But as we have also just seen, Irvine's picture accords with Darwin's, who certainly can't be accused of being a communist. He is also in accord with A.R.

Wallace,[24] who wrote, in *Contributions to the Theory of Natural Selection* (Wallace, 1870), for example: 'Capacity for acting in concert for protection, and for the acquisition of food and shelter; sympathy, which leads all in turn to assist each other ... are all qualities, that from their earliest appearance must have been for the benefit of each community, and would, therefore, have become the subjects of "natural selection"'. Whether Irvine directly read Darwin is difficult to say, as he doesn't cite his name in any of his writings that I've been able to consult.   But he was certainly aware of Darwin's arguments concerning the importance of co-operation in human societal evolution as outlined in at least one secondary source.   This was Alexander Sutherland's *The Origin and Growth of the Moral Instinct* (Sutherland, 1898), to which Irvine refers in his *The Place of the Social Sciences in a Modern University*, published by Sydney University in 1914.

Sutherland, a fellow Scot who migrated to the antipodes at a young age, was a student of Hearn at Melbourne University (and in fact was the writer of Hearn's obituary in the Melbourne *Argus*, in 1888).   It would seem very possible that Sutherland acquired his interest in Darwin from Hearn.   In any event, Sutherland's later consuming interest in Darwin's theory concerning the origin of morality in human instinctive propensities for mutual help is evident throughout his closely argued 2-volume treatise.[25]   As with Darwin, Sutherland founds his understanding of the moral sense on 'sympathy', a term which he, too, adapts from Adam Smith's usage of the word and which he, like Darwin and Hearn, sees as arising from parental instincts.   Sutherland argues his case this way:

> [T]he ... roots of sympathy which the parental and conjugal relations have already established, are always there, prepared to spread out into a general social sympathy, whenever and wherever an advantage is likely to arise therefrom ... . Thus the emergent type in the end is that wherein parental and conjugal sympathies widen out, as possibilities arise, into social sympathies; for, where the individual favoured of fortune is impelled ... to lend a helping hand to other individuals under less happy circumstances, the average chances of the race are thereby improved. (Sutherland, 1898, Vol. 1, p. 292)

The similarities between Sutherland's generalised account of human co-operativeness, and Irvine's specific description of Maori tribal life, are unmistakable.   One is easily drawn to the conclusion that this is not coincidental and that Irvine was profoundly influenced by Sutherland, if not directly by Darwin (apart from whatever bearing similar ideas in Marx and Engels had on his thinking).   The extent of this influence may be judged by the fact that the above-quoted paragraphs from *The Progress of New Zealand in the Century* are reprinted verbatim in a chapter titled 'The Way We Have Come' in Irvine's last book, *The Midas Delusion*, published in 1933.[26]   Using this description of Maori life in 'The Way We Have Come' as an illustration,

Irvine argues that in 'primitive' societies 'the group was paramount' and that 'all within the group were regarded as comrades'. While all without were viewed as enemies or strangers, '[h]ospitality to strangers was also a common feature', according to Irvine.[27] The clan might consist of a number of families, and 'The original social binding force appears to have been the instinctive love of mothers for their offspring' (Irvine, 1933, pp. 29–30).

Irvine rejects 'The Immutable Laws', including 'The Invisible Hand' (two more chapter titles in *The Midas Delusion*) commonly invoked in the economic orthodoxy of his time, preferring, rather, the view of human nature presented by people like the demand-side economist J.A. Hobson. It was 'probably true', Irvine agrees (quoting Hobson), that 'no greater injury has ever been inflicted on the mind of man, in the name of science, than the prepotence assigned to the competitive and combative aspects of individual life', and that such a philosophy had 'stifled the growth of intellectual and moral sympathy between the human centres of the industrial system, and impaired the sense of human solidarity which ... is the mainspring of efficient economic organisation' (Irvine, 1933, p. 49).

So Irvine's leanings are clear: they are towards a more co-operative rather than competitive vision of human nature, and an economic system built on this principle. In this, Irvine can be seen to be interested in 'organic' models of community and society, something after the manner of Herbert Spencer, or Hobson, whose suggestively titled *Physiology of Industry* (with A.F. Mummery) and *Evolution of Modern Capitalism*, as well as *Economics of Unemployment*, are cited by Irvine as books that had been influential in his thinking (pp. 4 and *passim*). In *The Physiology of Industry*, for example, Hobson and Mummery (1888, p. 158) argue that abnormal demands on an economy, such as wars, can be seen to have had the effect of 'providing a full use for all the superfluous capital which tended to *congest the industrial body* [my emphasis] in stimulating to the utmost the productive powers of the community'. In earlier writings, such as a report of a commission of enquiry into working-class housing to which he had been appointed by N.S.W. Premier W.A. Holman, Irvine uses expressions suggesting an organic model. One example is 'like other things, the city must grow and take on new functions'.[28] But Irvine's organicism, like Hearn's, was a more nuanced conception than either Spencer's or Hobson's. It took into account to a greater extent than either of these writers the actual motives and characteristics of human beings as understood in Darwinian terms. Irvine's position can best be demonstrated from an examination of his *The Place of the Social Sciences in a Modern University*, the text of an address to the Melbourne University Association in May 1914.

That Irvine, firstly, is interested in organic models is clear enough from the following sentences in this booklet:

> There have been many attempts to express the nature of the unity we call society. Most of them have been based on imperfect analogies. Thus it has been figured as a mechanism or as an organism of a particular kind; but these analogies, though sometimes helpful, have often proved misleading. The most we can say is that society, though not an organism, is nevertheless organically connected, held together by pervasive psychical forces.

'But', Irvine continues, 'however we conceive this unity, the centre of interest must always and everywhere be men ... red-blooded men and women, driving through as best they could their judgements, ideals, passions and interests'. If we forget this, Irvine insists, 'we spend our days in a make-believe world of abstractions' (Irvine, 1914, pp. 19–20). Irvine's reference to 'psychical forces', those bonds between human beings based on verbal and non-verbal communication (the concrete expression of underlying social proclivities) represents an important advance beyond Spencer's largely mystical conception of social cohesiveness. Society 'evolves through the interaction of individuals and groups of individuals', Irvine argues, something commonly overlooked by 'economists [who] have too frequently succeeded in putting abstractions in place of living men' (pp. 12, 15).[29] And in a direct reference to Spencer, Irvine explains that '[t]hough he [Spencer] did so much to popularise the idea of evolution, the total effect of his interpretation of society is a denial that any conscious social force can hasten or alter anything' – the 'orbit of civilisation is apparently independent of the human will and outside human control'. In the new 'social science' envisaged by Irvine, rather, data derived 'from Biology and Psychology on the one hand, and from the special social sciences on the other' will provide concrete 'evidence as to the process of human association and evolution as a whole' (pp. 16, 19).

Conclusion

R.F. Irvine's waxing eloquent about human evolution as a whole may go beyond Darwin's concerns (and indeed can be seen as actually closer to Spencer's abstractions), but he is at least attempting to bring a more Darwinian emphasis on the character of human beings to bear on economic questions. In this, I would suggest, Irvine is taking a more valid approach than, say, Joel Mokyr (1990, pp. 6–7, 104–5). Mokyr thinks that 'macroinventions' in economic history – those 'inventions in which a radical new idea, without any clear precedent, emerges more or less *ab nihilo*' – can be regarded as the equivalent of the biologist Richard Goldschmidt's 'macromutations', which 'create new species altogether' (Allen, 1979, pp.

66, 198–200). For Mokyr, in other words, 'macroinventions' bring into existence new 'species' in his version of 'economic evolution' – a mode of thinking of the same order as Marx's 'productive organs of man'. This, I would suggest, is analogy run wild. There is no obvious direct comparison between biological species (for Darwin, living beings which can interbreed) and human inventions. Some evolutionary economists prefer the firm as the unit of selection, following Alchian (1950) and Downie (1958), others, organisational routines (Nelson and Winter, 1982; Kelm, 1997; Hofer and Polt, 1998). Still other evolutionary economists move further away from Darwin when they substitute mathematical notation for 'mutations' (are these supposed to include changes in human agents?), as in Bergin and Lipman (1996). Kenneth Boulding (1992) is engaging in more pure abstraction with his notion of 'noogenetic' mutations (changes in technology – human knowledge of techniques): 'In both social and biological systems … we see evolution as the process of the filling of empty niches in ecosystems, either by biogenetic or noogenetic mutation … . The automobile is now as much a species in the world ecosystem as is the horse'. (p. 173)

These kinds of speculations, fuelled by a growing disenchantment with equilibrium models in economics, and an attempt to more adequately take into account the historical dimension (see, e.g., Setterfield, 1997), all have in common a tendency to employ inappropriate analogy. This is why it is so important for economists interested in recovering a 'Darwinian' approach to their subject to look at what Darwin actually wrote about the human condition. This chapter has endeavoured to provide something of the tenor of Darwin's views, as mainly contained in *The Descent of Man*. It has contrasted these with the evolutionary theories of Herbert Spencer and others which, while now almost universally rejected by biologists, nevertheless continue to hold some sway – even if unconsciously – amongst 'evolutionary' economists largely unfamiliar with Darwin's writing. One result of the tendency in economics to engage in Spencerian-like abstraction and inappropriate analogy is that the discipline has not infrequently become almost totally divorced from the realities of human life. As Heilbroner and Milberg (1996, p. 6) have expressed it, the problem with much economic analysis in recent years has been a seeming widespread belief that such analysis 'can exist as some kind of socially disembodied study'. In an Australian context, Michael Pusey (1991, p. 10) has said much the same sort of thing. His argument is that the depredations of 'economic rationalism' in Australia have been allowed to take place in an intellectual environment in which projections of reality have given 'primacy to "the economy", second place to the political order, and third place to the social order'. Part of what this present volume seeks to do is to contribute something towards a reversing of this order of priorities, in which, the editors believe, a rediscovery and application of Darwin's ideas concerning human nature and society can play some part.

Notes

1. Strangely though, Geoff Fishburn does not quote one of the most famous of Darwin's statements about scientific method. This was in a letter to Fawcett dated 19 Sept. 1861. It reads: 'How odd it is that anyone should not see that all observation must be for or against some view if it is to be of any service' (quoted in Clark, 1984, p. 140).
2. Hodgson shows that while Schumpeter may be described as an 'evolutionary' economist, there is nevertheless 'no legitimate basis for describing his approach as Darwinian'.
3. Webb's 1896 pamphlet, originally published in the *Economic Journal* (June 1891), can admittedly be taken as a program for the 'struggle for existence' between nations, as in Thomas Henry Huxley's (1888) rather infamous *Nineteenth Century* paper along these lines (which indeed Webb cites, p. 17). But at least, at this level, the pamphlet's collective understanding (i.e. within nations) of struggle is in line with Darwin, as is *Towards Social Democracy?* (Webb, 1916), which similarly argues that socialism is in accord with 'the lessons which Political Economy has learnt from biology and from Darwinism as a fundamental necessity of national existence' (p. 29). A more sophisticated understanding of Darwin can be found in another Fabian socialist (at least for a time), and labour organiser, Tom Mann. Mann had a deep interest in Darwinism and evolution. He argued not only that 'the law of mutual interdependence was just as true as the struggle for existence', but also that 'Time was when a tribesman would hate and fight the members of every tribe but his own ... . But a better knowledge tells us the residents of one village are the same as those of another country', and 'we know that men in other countries are like ourselves'. (See 'Tom Mann on Wages War', *The Socialist* [Melbourne], 10 June 1921; and Laurent, 1994). In later years Mann was recommending books like Julian Huxley's *What Dare I Think?* (Mann to Mrs Mann, 25 October 1931, Modern Records Centre, University of Warwick), which decries simplistic models of human nature which 'attempt to follow the methods of the bees and ants' and avers, on the contrary, 'since mutual understanding ... constitute[s] the basis of human progress, it is extremely important that any machine-like or ant-like specialisation should be avoided' (Huxley, 1933 [first published 1931], p.144). For more on Mann see Laurent (1988), and for a good general discussion of collectivist models of evolution, see Ogilvie (1990), pp. 7–13.
4. Even in his private notebooks (1837–42) Darwin gets no closer to speaking of the 'social organism' than to allude to the 'social animal' (specifically referring to dogs, cattle and deer), and to 'insects which become *in imago* state social' (see Gruber, 1974, pp. 349–51).
5. The quote reads 'I have given in another work a long list of "sporting plants", as they are called by gardeners; – that is, of plants which have suddenly produced a single bud with a new and sometimes widely different character from that of other buds on the same plant'; after which the authors cite the source as 'Charles Darwin ([1859] 1958, 33–34)'. As the other work referred to by Darwin, *The Variation of Animals and Plants under Domestication*, was not published until 1868, Cottrell and Lawlor cannot be citing the 1859 edition of the *Origin of Species* as they say, but a later edition (probably the final edition, the 6th, of 1872). For a recent discussion of the use of the 'mutation' idea in economic

modelling, see Bergin and Lipman (1996). The authors present a generally sceptical view of the usefulness of the transference of the notion from biology to economics, and conclude that 'in the absence of a concrete model of what mutations are (in evolutionary economics) and why they arise', any number of scenarios can be envisaged.

6.   Typical of Butler's 'arguments' is this one for the 'Future Life': 'From our being born into the present world in the helpless imperfect state of infancy, and having arrived from thence to mature age, we find it to be a general law of nature in our own species, that the same creatures, the same individuals, should exist in degrees of life and perception, with capacities of action, of enjoyment and suffering, in one period of their being, greatly different from those appointed them in another period of it. And in other creatures the same law holds. For the difference of their capacities and states of life at their birth (to go no higher) and in maturity; the change of worms into flies, and the vast enlargement of their locomotive powers by such change: and birds and insects bursting the shell, their habitation, and by this means entering into a new world, furnished with new accommodations for them, and finding a new sphere of action assigned them; these are instances of this general law of nature. Thus all the various and wonderful transformations of animals are to be taken into consideration here. But the states of life in which we ourselves existed formerly in the womb and in infancy, are almost as different from our present in mature age, as it is possible to conceive any two states or degrees of life can be. Therefore, that we are to exist hereafter in a state as different (suppose) from our present, as this is from our former, is but according to the *analogy of nature* [my emphasis]; according to a natural order or appointment of the very same kind, with what we have already experienced'. (Butler, 1824, pp. 16–17)

7.   Interestingly, Darwin here cites *The Thoughts of the Emperor M. Aurelius Antoninus* (English translation, 2nd ed., 1869).

8.   See Smith (1853), the first chapter ('Of Sympathy') of which begins: 'How selfish soever man may be supposed, there are evidently some principals in his nature which interest him in the fortunes of others, and render their happiness necessary to him, though he derives nothing from it, except the pleasure of seeing it. Of this kind is pity or compassion, the emotion which we feel for the misery of others, when neither we see it, or are made to conceive it in a very lively manner. That we often derive sorrow from the sorrow of others is a matter of fact too obvious to require any instance to prove it; for this sentiment, like all the other original passions of human nature, is by no means confined to the virtuous and human ... . The greatest ruffian, the most hardened violator of the laws of society, is not altogether without it'. See also Fitzgibbons (1995); and there is an excellent discussion of Smith's 'sympathy' concept in a specifically Darwinian context in Prince Kropotkin's *Anarchist Morality* (London: 'Freedom Pamphlets No. 6', n.d. [c.1886]).

9.   Warning signals can even operate across species, as has long been known to naturalists. McKie (1967), writing of his friend Jim Hislop's observations in the Malayan jungle, for example, notes (p. 128): 'Jim has no doubt that monkeys have special calls for their own kind which other living things recognise. His presence has been signalled by them often and he has followed the progress of tigers, without being able to see them, by listening to the trail of monkey calls through the jungle. He thinks that jungle monkeys have a limited vocabulary of warning calls, alarm calls, social chatter ... . A warning call undoubtedly alerts a monkey colony, but an alarm call – a distinctly different sound – sends them fleeing'. I myself have seen various species of birds scattering at the sound of a particular call from the Australian 'Noisy Miner' bird (*Manorina melanocephala*) when a hawk approached, as was shown to me by my brother, Robert Laurent, on his property near Cabarlah, Queensland; and studies by Evans et al. (e.g., 1993a, 1993b) have confirmed the reality of such phenomena. I am

also indebted to Jim Davis for further help on this subject. Watkins (1998) has recently drawn attention to the challenge that such 'symbiosis' in nature poses for simplistic 'Darwinian' notions in economic theory.

10. The term 'mutation' was first used in a biological sense in the title of the Dutch plant breeder Hugo de Vries's *Die Mutationstheorie* (Leipzig: von Veit & Co., 1901–3); and 'gene' was coined by the Danish botanist Wilhelm Johannsen to describe Mendel's 'factors'. See Allen (1979), and Clark (1984).

11. Elsewhere in *The Descent of Man* Darwin writes (perceptively: his suggestion was confirmed with the discovery of Australopithecus – see, e.g., Chilvers, 1929, pp. 320, 382): 'It is ... probable that Africa was formerly inhabited by extinct apes closely allied to the gorilla and chimpanzee; and as these two ape species are now man's nearest allies, it is somewhat more probable that our early progenitors lived on the African continent than elsewhere' (Darwin, n.d. p. 520).

12. As a metaphor of society the idea goes back at least to St. Paul (1 Cor.12), and later Shakespeare (Coriolanus Act 1, Scene 1). Schabas (1994) thinks the term 'social organism' might actually have originated with Auguste Comte rather than Spencer.

13. Another author who may have had some influence in this connection is the not widely known (and rarely cited) *Financial News* editor, Ellis Powell (1868–1920). The author's foreword in his *The Evolution of the Money Market* (London: *Financial News*, 1915) suggested that 'the ever-increasing stability and potency of modern finance were attributable to something in the nature of organic development operating by means of Natural Selection, and therefore completely in accordance with the main postulate of the Darwinian theory' (pp. vii–viii). However, he has only one reference to Darwin (interestingly, to the same passage about 'sporting plants' cited by Cottrell and Lawler) but nine to Spencer (including a quote from Spencer's *The Study of Sociology* on the title page). Significantly, there is no entry under 'Darwin' in Powell's index, only 'Darwinism (see Organism)'.(I am indebted to David Edmunds for drawing my attention to this volume.)

14. Just before this quote Marshall has: 'Before Adam Smith's book [i.e., *Wealth of Nations*, on 'increased efficiency which labour derives from organisation'] had yet found many readers, biologists were already beginning to make great advances towards understanding the real nature of the differences in organisation which separate the higher from the lower animals; and before two more generations had elapsed, Malthus' historical account of man's struggle for existence started Darwin on that enquiry as to the effects of the struggle for existence in the animal and vegetable world' (Marshall, 1920, p. 240). It is true, also, that at one point in *The Origin of Species* Darwin (n.d., p. 86) makes a passing allusion to Smith's Division of Labour: 'The advantage of diversification of structure in the inhabitants of the same region is, in fact, the same as that of the physiological division of labour in the organs of the same individual body `... . No physiologist doubts that a stomach adapted to digest vegetable matter alone, or flesh alone, draws most nutriment from these substances. So in the general economy of any land, the more widely and perfectly the animals and plants are diversified for different habits of life, so will a greater number of individuals be capable of there supporting themselves. A set of animals, with the organisation but little diversified, could hardly compete with a set more perfectly diversified in structure'. In turning the analogy back onto human society, however, Marshall clearly has Spencer's usage in mind.

15. Among Marshall's books in the Marshall Library, Cambridge, are copies of 13 works by Spencer, a number of which are heavily annotated by Marshall. His copies of *The Origin of Species* and *The Descent of Man*, now housed by Cambridge University Library, have no annotations in them (Laurent [in press]; P. Groenewegen to John Nightingale, 10 November 1998).

16. There is a copy of a letter from Darwin to Marx in Darwin's house in Downe, Kent, in which Darwin thanks Marx for sending him a copy of *Capital*, adding: 'I believe we both earnestly desire the extension of knowledge, and that this in the long run is … all to the happiness of mankind'. The letter is dated 1 October 1873. For more on Marx and Darwin, see Urina (1977), Taylor (1989) and Trent-Band (1991) (I am grateful to Adrian Desmond for this last reference).

17. The essay was found amongst Marx's belongings after his death, and was first published (in German) in 1903.

18. In one apparent exception, Rudolf Hilferding, in *Boehm-Bawerk's Criticism of Marx* (Glasgow: Socialist Labour Press, c. 1914) argues for the inadequacy of a view which 'starts from the individual relationship between a thing and a human being instead of starting from the social relationship of human beings one with another' (p. 11).

19. This was reprinted in London the following year – see Treloar and Pullen (1998). For an excellent overview of Hearn's evolutionary thinking, see Arndt (1981), footnote 4. Arndt notes that Hearn not only appears to have been the first economist to take up Spencer's notion of the 'evolution of the simple into the complex', but also to marry Darwin's 'struggle for existence' with the laissez-faire principle. I am grateful to Professor Arndt for his kindness in sending me a copy of his paper, which was reprinted in his *Fifty Years of Development Studies*.

20. See note 17.

21. Interestingly, in a lecture to the Melbourne Mechanics' Institute in 1856, Hearn referred to 'those sciences which have for their object man, whether as an individual, or as a member of society'. These include logic, i.e., those 'rules to which every mind, consciously or unconsciously, conforms'. In an age of widely assumed European superiority, this is a remarkable acknowledgement of the commonality of the human species, with its universal capacities (Hearn, 1856). I am grateful to Philip Candy for this reference.

22. Susan Rose-Ackerman (1996) has persuasively argued (against the socio-biological explanations of E.O. Wilson and others) that 'evolutionary models, *not* [my emphasis] based on kinship, demonstrate how altruistic traits such as heroism, trust … can have survival value' (pp. 711–2).

23. See F. Engels (1977); and A. Besant (1887, pp. 78–9). In *The Midas Delusion* Irvine acknowledges an intellectual debt to John Ruskin, especially that author's *Unto This Last*, which is 'almost as revolutionary as Karl Marx', and in which Ruskin argues for the co-operative spirit being one of the 'laws of life' (see Laurent, 1991).

24. See Coleman, this volume, for Wallace's political views.

25. For a useful discussion on Sutherland, see Wallace Nelson, 'An Australian Philosopher', in *Foster Fraser's Fallacies and Other Australian Essays*, Sydney: Gordon & Gotch, 1910, pp. 131–6. Sutherland's earlier (with George Sutherland) *The History of Australia from 1606 to 1888* (Melbourne: George Robertson and Co., 1891) has interesting material on the Australian aborigines.

26. This book contains, it has been argued (e.g., McFarlane, 1966), anticipations of much that Keynes was to say three years later in *The General Theory*.

27. In *Social Environment and Moral Progress*, A.R. Wallace (1913b) similarly argues that 'Affection, sympathy, compassion form as essential a part of human nature as do the higher intellectual faculties. [These qualities] are fully manifested not merely between members of the same family, but throughout the whole tribe, and also in most cases to every stranger who is not a known or imagined enemy' (pp. 100–1). Wallace, unlike Darwin, took his interest in collectivist models of human nature to what he regarded as their logical conclusion and became a socialist in later life (see Coleman, below). He was president of the Land Nationalisation Society from 1881, and in this capacity worked closely with Keir Hardie's Independent Labour Party from its foundation

(Wallace to Hardie, 31 March 1894, London School of Economics archives). See also Wallace (1913a) and Gaffney (1997).

28. Irvine (1913), p. 259.   It should be said, though, that while retaining Spencer's broad model, Hobson allows a greater role for human agency (in a vision of public intervention which prefigures Keynes somewhat, as indeed Keynes himself acknowledges – see chapter on Keynes and Darwinism, below).   The following lines from Hobson (1895, pp. 402, 417–18) give something of the tenor of his broader position: 'The progressive adjustment of structure to the environment in the unconscious or low-conscious world is necessarily slow.   But where the conscious will of man, either as an individual or as a society, can be utilised for an adjusting force, the pace of progress may be indefinitely quickened ... .   So soon as the idea of a social industrial organism is grasped, the question of State interference in, or State assumption of, an industry becomes a question of social expediency.   ... The indictment against social control over industry is an indictment against a natural order of events, on the ground that nature has taken a wrong road of advancement.   It is only possible to regard the legislative action by which public control over industry is established as "unnatural" or "artificial" by excluding from "Nature" those social forces which find expression in Acts of Parliament, an eminently unscientific mode of reasoning'.   Irvine also mentions (p. 4) that he had benefited from a reading of J.B. Crozier's *The Wheel of Wealth* (1906) – a 'fine piece of literature as well as a vigorous polemic'.   However, from a Darwinian perspective, it is not clear what Irvine could have gained from this book.   Discussion of 'evolution' as such is limited to the Introduction (it contains 3 of the 4 references to Darwin listed in the Index), and this is mainly in terms of an attempt to encompass natural selection within a generalised, Spencerian understanding of the term.   Crozier cites Hobson extensively but, again, within a Spencerian context: of Hobson's notion of 'The Physiology of Industry', for example, Crozier agrees that, at first sight anyway, this 'symbol of a biological organism ... gives a greater appearance of *life*, perhaps, to a science which is essentially a human one' (p. 509).   In the final analysis Crozier's own preference – notwithstanding his book's subtitle – is for a mechanical model employing the 'wheel of wealth'.

29. One is reminded of a remark by Keynes in *The General Theory*: 'Too large a proportion of recent 'mathematical' economics are mere concoctions, as imprecise as the initial assumptions they rest on, which allow the author to lose sight of the complexities and interdependencies of the real world in a maze of pretentious and unhelpful symbols' (Keynes, 1936, p. 298).

3. The Strange 'Laissez Faire' of Alfred Russel Wallace: The Connection between Natural Selection and Political Economy Reconsidered

William Coleman

Alfred Russel Wallace (1823–1913) is remembered as the naturalist who devised the principle of natural selection independently of Darwin. But Wallace spread his intellectual energies well beyond the subject of biology. He was the author of a profusion of speculations, on matters stretching from vaccination and astronomy to spiritualism and phrenology.

Wallace also had a strongly expressed suite of economic ideas. These ideas are of slight value in themselves. They lack both originality and depth; they made little or no contribution to the development of economic thought. But Wallace's economic ideas are relevant to the drawn-out debate over the connection between political economy and Darwinism.

Many commentators have contended that there is a close connection between political economy and Darwinism. This supposed connection has two distinct characterisations, and they are worth distinguishing. The first maintains that the connection is merely one of 'transference': Darwinism transferred ideas from economics to biology (e.g. Cowles, 1936, p. 341). The second maintains that Darwinism amounted to a 'transcription' or 'projection' of political economy on to biology (e.g. Schweber, 1980, p. 277).[1]

The first characterisation is more modest, and the second more radical. Whereas the first assumes that biology was prior in the minds of natural selectionists, and the transference amounted to no more than the opportune exploitation of ideas in another field (political economy), the second believes that political economy was prior in the minds of natural selectionists, and that biology was deliberately (if unconsciously) wrought in the image of political economy. Whereas the first allows the possibility that natural selection had a disinterested and scientific genesis, the second suggests that natural selection was ideological in its origins. In the second characterisation, the natural selectionists made nature in the image of political economy because political economy was apologetic for the establishment, and the conformity of nature to political economy would further the effectiveness of that apologetic.[2]

The advocates of both characterisations of the connection typically draw strongly on (i) the explicit expression of debt to Malthus by Darwin, and

(ii) the fact that both natural selection and political economy stress the benefits of competition.

Both versions of the connection hypothesis have critics. These critics point to the uneconomic character of that part of Malthus's thought which Darwin drew upon, and to Darwin's relative lack of interest in, and knowledge of, political economy (Gordon 1989).

This chapter argues that the case of Alfred Russel Wallace is strong evidence against there being an ideological connection between natural selection and political economy. The argument is simple. Wallace was a keen advocate of natural selection. Yet he was also the ardent adversary of several of the most important claims of political economy. Further, he was a champion of the interests of that section of the population that political economy, and even natural selection, was supposedly antagonistic to: the working class. If natural selection was a matter of projection of an apologetic political economy on to biology, how was it that Wallace devised the principle?

The fact of Wallace's natural selectionism is celebrated, and the characteristics of his political economy are well known to those interested in his life (Clements, 1983). Yet the plain significance of the conjunction of both these features of his thought for the debate over economics and natural selection has not been pressed. It is the purpose of this paper to do so

The first section of the chapter briefly rehearses Wallace's Darwinian credentials. The second section outlines Wallace's deprecatory views of orthodox political economy. The third section considers the suggestion that Wallace, despite these views, was nevertheless an 'individualist'. The fourth section casts some doubt on the other evidence in favour of a natural selection/political economy connection. The fifth section touches on the sociology of knowledge issues raised by the case of Alfred Russel Wallace.

Wallace and Natural Selection

From the age of 35, and until his death at the age of 90, Wallace was a firm advocate of natural selection. He had devised the thesis independently of Darwin, and did not falter in its advocacy.[3]

There were some differences between Darwin and Wallace over evolution (Hartman, 1990; Kottler, 1985; Wallace, 1905, v.2, pp. 6–22). They differed over the possibility of inheritance of acquired characteristics (Darwin believed in it, Wallace did not). They differed over the reality of sexual selection, as distinct from ecological selection (Darwin believed in it, Wallace did not). They differed over whether natural selection explained the origin of man (Darwin believed so, Wallace did not). But these disagreements were disagreements between allies. Wallace has been described as 'second to none in

his defence of Darwin's view' (Durant, 1979). 'The original concept of natural
selection as the sole agency for explaining modifications in the organic world,
except for those in man, boasted no more staunch defender than Alfred Wallace'
(Turner, 1974, p. 94).

Wallace on Political Economy

Wallace's advocacy of natural selection coexisted with a strongly held suite of
views on economics. However, he cannot be described as an 'economist'.
There is no positive evidence that he read any economic writing before he
formulated the principle of natural selection in 1858, with the exception of
Malthus's *Principles of Population*. But by at least the latter stage of his life
he was certainly acquainted with the theses of political economy. He quoted
the economic works of Smith (Wallace, 1900, v.2, p. 202: the first line of
The Wealth of Nations), Ricardo (Wallace, 1895, p. 128),[4] Mill (Wallace,
1913a, p. 71: 'Of International Trade', *Principles of Political Economy*),
Senior (Wallace, 1900, v.2, p. 289: *Essays on Ireland*), Jevons (Wallace,
1900, v.2, p. 145: *Money and the Mechanics of Exchange*), Cairnes
(Wallace, 1898, p. 356: *Leading Principles of Political Economy*) and
Fawcett.[5] Darwin, by contrast, never refers to, or quotes from, the economic
writings of any of these authors.[6]

   Wallace rejected much of what he read.[7] Specifically:

1. Wallace opposed free trade. To Wallace, 'free trade' was a system of 'free
    imports'. 'Our boasted freedom of trade ... consists in our being at a great
    disadvantage in half the markets of the world' (Wallace, 1900, v.2, p.
    181). He favoured imposing tariffs in accordance with the tariffs that
    foreign countries imposed on the home country. He also maintained that
    free trade imposed external costs, in the form of environmental
    degradation, and that this recommended the restriction of free trade
    (Wallace, 1900, v.2, p. 177).[8]
2. He favoured the introduction of minimum wages. He recommended 'a
    very high minimum wage for really necessary or useful work' (Wallace,
    1913a, p. 30).
3. He proposed the creation of an inconvertible note issue (Wallace, 1900,
    v.2, p. 147).
4. He was hostile to interest and profit income. Wallace believed lending at
    interest should be illegal, except for personal loans of a fixed duration.
    Not even such personal loans would be enforceable by law; the loans
    would be made at the risk of the lender (Wallace, 1905, p. 246).

5. He championed the nationalisation of land. In Wallace's view private property in land was 'barbarism' masquerading as 'civilisation' (Wallace, 1905, p. 235). In 1870 he joined the Land Tenure Reform Association, and later organised the Land Nationalisation Society (Wallace, 1892; Gaffney, 1997; Gould, 1988). He scorned the Free Trade in Land movement which sought to abolish entails and to make conveyancing cheap and expeditious: Wallace believed the elimination of such market imperfections would only lead to a further concentration of land ownership (Wallace, 1900, v.2, p. 255).
6. He advocated the prohibition of the export of coal and iron, and the extensive regulation of any other industry that was producing a product 'essential to comfort' and in 'practically limited quantity' (Wallace, 1900, v.2, p. 140).
7. He proposed the management by state authority of all industries 'essential to public welfare'.
8. He entertained doubts over Say's Law, leaning, instead, toward a pre-Keynesian under-consumptionist view. In Wallace's opinion 'every pound paid extra in wages is a pound more expended in food, clothing, furniture, houses, and other necessaries of life. It will, therefore, benefit the makers and growers and retailers of those commodities by the increase of their trade (Wallace, 1913a, p. 36)'.
9. He believed 'capital' was 'the tyrant and enemy of labour' (Wallace, 1905, p. 247).
10. He urged the provision of bread free to anyone who was 'in want' of it (Wallace, 1913a, p. 25).

The incongruity of these 10 propositions with orthodox political economy need not be laboured.

Accordingly, Wallace did not hold orthodox political economy in any great esteem. In a public lecture in 1886 on 'Social Economy and Political Economy' he described the 'old political economy' (i.e., laissez faire economic theory) as 'effete and useless' (Wallace, 1905, v.2, p. 129). At greater length he complained,

> For more than half a century both our Government and our mercantile classes have acknowledged the importance of political economy, or the science of the rod of wealth; and they have made it their guide in trade, in manufacture, in foreign commerce, and in legislation. ... Yet after fifty years ... of following what was professed to be an infallible guide, we find ourselves in the present day (1886) in the terrible quagmire of commercial depression. ... In all our great cities we have stagnation of business, poverty and even starvation. Certainly, according to the doctrines of the political economy which we have followed, none of these things ought to have happened (Wallace, 1900, v.2, p. 188).

With more choler he declared,

> Everywhere, to-day, it [political economy] is being denounced by thinking
> men as a false science – as a delusion and a snare – as an *ignis fatis* [i.e.
> delusive light], leading men away from the paths of happiness and true well-
> being, and guiding them towards the quagmires of unhealthy competition,
> poverty and discontent. ... Surely a science like this – so narrow in its
> scope, so powerless for good, so utterly divorced from all considerations of
> morality, of justice, even of broad and enlightened expediency – should be
> treated as a blind and impotent guide, which, if any longer followed, will lead
> us on to social and political ruin (Wallace, 1895, pp. 126–8).

It may be noticed that Wallace's grievance in the last quotation is not that
economics is actually at fault. Its defect lies in its unconcern with, and
unhelpfulness to, the working class. Here we arrive at a key to Wallace's
economic views: his urgent concern to find a remedy for the plight of the
working class. He believed this plight was desperate. He went so far as to
claim (in 1898) that the proportion of Britons in poverty was larger than at
any time in her history (Wallace, 1898, p. 342). He felt that 'the condition
of the workers as a whole is absolutely unbearable, is a disgrace to
civilisation, and fully justifies the most extreme demands of the workers'
(Wallace, 1913a, p. 12).

His own political economy was always, therefore, governed by a concern to
increase the wealth of (British) workers. For example, he opposed the
unhindered export of coal and iron from Britain largely on the ground that it
would raise the price of these products for British workers (Wallace, 1900, v.2,
p. 143). In a similar vein he opposed public funding for science, while
supporting public funding for 'popular' museums, on the grounds that workers
would patronise popular museums but would not participate in scientific
research (Turner, 1974, p. 86).

In the light of this class sympathy it is not surprising that Wallace treats
Marx favourably in comparison to the 'old' political economists. Marx is
described as a 'social reformer'. One of the principles of the Land
Nationalisation Society is judged by Wallace to resemble the 'main thesis' of
Marx.[9]

Wallace joined Marx in faulting political economy for being apologetic for
dominant class interests. He complained that political economy (along with
clergy) 'enforced' the belief that it was 'natural and inevitable that there should
be rich and poor' (Wallace, 1913a, p. 5).

This all leads to the question: how can natural selection be a projection of
an apologetic political economy if one of the discoverers of natural selection
championed the interest of labour, spurned political economy and chastised its
doctrines as apologetic for capital?[10]

Wallace the Individualist?

A critic may charge that the previous section has exaggerated the distance between political economy and Wallace. Were not the precepts of economic policy in English political economy in 1860 some distance from the laissez faire of Ricardo or James Mill? And did not Wallace identify himself at some stages in his life an 'individualist'?

It is true that some of Wallace's ideas on land would have found nurture in the thought of Mill and Cairns: it was Mill who invited Wallace to join Mill's Land Tenure Reform Association.[11] It is also true that Wallace admired some aspects of Herbert Spencer, and in 1884 recommended that Britain adopt what he described as the 'true system of laissez faire'. (Laissez faire, he complained, was 'abused as if it had failed, when really it has never been tried'). Further, Wallace was capable of suddenly stating, in the midst of a polemic against political economy ('blind', 'impotent', 'altogether insufficient'), that political economy was 'mainly true' (Wallace, 1895, p. 126). Finally, in autobiographical writings Wallace represented himself as an individualist in youth, who only became a 'socialist' in his late 60s.[12] In the light of such apparent incongruities one recent critic has described him as 'libertarian', as well as socialist (Wallace, 1991, p. 164).[13] Nevertheless, one may doubt whether these remarks amount to evidence that Wallace had to any significant degree assimilated economic liberalism.

Consider Wallace on Herbert Spencer, the supposed missionary of laissez faire and individualism. What specific views of Herbert Spencer impressed him? It was Spencer's *Social Statics* (1851) that sent him into an enthusiasm shortly after its publication (Wallace, 1900, v.2, p. 333). What so excited him there? Spencer's blunt condemnation of private property in land.[14] Wallace was also impressed by Spencer's depiction of progress as consisting of the extending victory of social man over anti-social man.[15] Is this the mindset of an individualist?

Further, it has to be understood that Wallace's use of the terms 'individualist' and 'laissez faire' was eccentric.

Consider Wallace on 'individualism'. In 1900, after his own self-described conversion to socialism, Wallace published a paper entitled, 'True Individualism – The Essential Preliminary of a Real Social Advance' (Wallace, 1900, v.2, p. 510). This paper is largely devoted to arguing that society must implement 'a strict regulation of the transmission or inheritance of wealth'. This sentiment is closer to the *Communist Manifesto* than individualism as it is commonly understood.[16]

Or consider his expression, 'true laissez faire'. Wallace explains that his 'true' system of laissez faire included land nationalisation, and the state management of all industries essential to the public welfare. Is this laissez faire? We can agree with Wallace that his 'true' laissez faire had (at that date) never been tried.

What should we make of Wallace's references to individualism and laissez faire?

First, Wallace was a man of many thoughts, to the extent that he was an 'intricate', and sometimes even flatly inconsistent, author.[17] He could, for example, deny 'general over-production' (Wallace, 1900, v.2, p. 190) as a cause of slumps on one page, and literally on the next page advance an under-consumption explanation of slumps. With such an inconsistent author, surely the best procedure is to find the position which gives the 'best fit' to the author's varied remarks. A position of interventionist egalitarianism will give a far better fit than a laissez faire one.

The second appropriate inference from Wallace's individualist remarks is that there was undeniably an 'individualist' accent to Wallace's program of interventionist egalitarianism. Wallace was not a collectivist. His socialism was never an attraction to a great and organising state. 'Socialism' was to Wallace 'the use by everyone of his faculties for the common good, and the voluntary organisation of labour for the equal benefit of all' (Wallace, 1905, v.2, p. 274). The use of the word 'voluntary' in his definition of socialism is surely significant. Under Wallace's socialism industry would be run by enterprises composed of capital-owning workers. Land nationalisation would not amount to a system of state farms or agricultural collectives. Rather, the state would be the sole owner of land, and would rent out its land to a throng of individual tenants.[18]

Nevertheless, Wallace's individualist accent was still far removed from the individualism of ordinary political economy. If Mill and Cairnes favoured restrictions on property rights in land in particular situations (especially Ireland), they never advocated the nationalisation of land. Wallace allowed his land nationalisation to be 'strongly opposed by all the recognised authorities in political economy' (Wallace, 1905, p. 249). Further, and above all, Wallace's 'individualism', whatever it was, cannot be described as apologetic for the wealthy.

What Is Left of the Natural Selection–Political Economy Connection?

If Wallace is evidence against a connection between political economy and natural selection, is there not some evidence for it? This evidence in favour includes, and above all other, the fact that the two discoverers of natural selection both refer to Malthus as a critical catalyst of their thoughts (Darwin [1884] 1974; Wallace, 1916, p. 113).[19] But what did Darwin and Wallace use in Malthus? There are many possible things. To political economists, there is a thesis of a long-run equilibrium level of per capita consumption that is invariant to transfers from rich to poor. But this is not what Malthus meant to Darwin and Wallace. What they used of Malthus was the suggestion that not all who were born could survive to reproduce.[20] This proposition is entirely unnecessary for political economy's Malthusian thesis concerning per capita consumption; that thesis can be secured by allowing everyone born to live, but having fertility rates vary. And the presumption of political economists is that the Malthusian mechanism would operate through fertility rates (see Gordon, 1989, p. 443).[21] In this connection it is worth noting that Malthus is not treated by Wallace as a political economist: Wallace described Malthus's work as 'philosophical biology'(Wallace, 1905, v.1, p. 232).

There are two other themes of political economy that might have lent themselves to natural selection:

1. *Competition for wealth as productive of wealth*: This was at the heart of classical political economy, and its congruence with natural selection is plain. Wallace, however, believed that the 'struggle for wealth' had 'deplorable results' (Wallace, 1898, p. 367). Hostile references to 'unhealthy competition' in the human world are plentiful in Wallace.
2. *The existence of design without a designer (the invisible hand)*: This notion is present in Smith, Hume, Mandeville and other Enlightenment authors with respect to economic and social worlds. This notion would suggest the possibility of design in the natural world without a designer. Hume explored design without a designer in the natural world in his *Dialogues Concerning Natural Religion*. There he also took up the question that, if there is design without a designer, how does this design occur? He edges close to the notion of the selection of fit forms and the elimination of the unfit: 'It is in vain, therefore, to insist upon the uses of the parts in animals or vegetables, and their curious adjustment to each other. I would fain know how an animal could subsist, unless its parts were so adjusted?' (Hume [1779] 1935, p. 227). One can only speculate as to whether notions of design without a designer may have at least allowed the very question of the origin of design in the natural world to be put in Wallace's youthful agnostic mind.[22]

There is a third possible influence from social thought. It is plausible to suppose that the dissolution of the 18th century's complacent presumption of social equilibrium, and the eruption of the 19th century's preoccupation with social fractures, was congenial to the genesis of natural selection. A static and placid picture of society is less congruous with the drama of the survival of the fittest than the theory of social turbulence. But this transformation in social thought only slightly touches political economy. Ricardo's economic theory does have the seeds of social clash *in nuce*; but almost the same could be said of Smith. And it was not the political economists who cultivated these seeds, it was their adversaries: the St. Simonians, Comte and Marx. These thinkers were apt to fault political economy for missing the social clash, and for rejoicing in a non-existent harmony.

The Case of Alfred Wallace and the Sociology of Knowledge

The previous sections have used the case of Alfred Russel Wallace to scrutinise the proposition that natural selection was a projection onto nature of a political economy apologetic for a dominant class interest. This proposition is just one manifestation of a general and familiar vision of science. This vision is summarised by Gross and Levitt (1994, p. 46): 'Science is not a body of knowledge: it is rather, a parable, an allegory, that inscribes a set of social norms and encodes, however subtly, a mythic structure justifying the dominance of one class, one race, one gender over another'. This vision further maintains that the 'scientific aristocracy' which practises science is 'organically connected to the ruling elite. ... [I]ts prestige, authority and epistemological monopoly are guaranteed by the power of the state and the social formations it principally serves' (Gross and Levitt, 1994, p. 63).

Alfred Wallace's scientific achievement, we have argued, makes for a jarring disconfirmation of this theory. Rather than seeking to inscribe norms justifying the dominance of one class, one race, one gender, Wallace sought to overturn such conventional dominance: of the wealthy, of the white race and (we may add here) of men.[23] And, rather than being 'organically connected' to science's ruling elite, few could be less connected than Wallace to the elite and its social formations.[24] 'Wallace was different from most of his scientific contemporaries because his life had been different from theirs. Those typical English institutions of the family, the church, the public service, the military or the university did little or nothing to mould his character' (Turner, 1974, pp. 69–70; Moore, 1997). His biographers are unable to point to distinguished family connections to commerce, or to plump investments of his own. His education finished at 14. His brothers were apprenticed to building trades, he to a land surveyor.

The teenage Alfred Wallace, without any scientific education or encouragement, spent his evenings at an Owenite 'Hall of Science'. The meagre material rewards of a career in science were augmented by the prospect of the sale of insects collected from the Amazon and, later in life, by a government grant. His mind was animated by the new idea of evolution. Perplexed by its mechanism, he seeks the intellectual company of the like-minded. One is Darwin who, like himself (as Wallace notes), was a beetle collector, a traveller and a reader of Malthus. He produces an idea which threatens to eliminate the remaining rational authority from Christianity, its teachings and temporal instruments.[25] It threatens more: Marx writes to Engels with the news that natural selection has shown that the proletarian critique of capitalism has a basis in nature (Marx, 1941, p. 126). Wallace's idea succeeds with biologists and the public, and that success is born of an intellectually honest attempt to remove perplexity. But the logical faculty is not the only source of reward in his mind; that faculty yields without struggle to wish fulfilment in the face of spiritualism and pseudo-astronomy.

The vision of science of which A.R. Wallace is most suggestive is best entered by considering the individual rather than society: not because the individual is exogenous to society, but because the individual is the plainest proximate cause of scientific activity. That activity begins with an individual which is both like and unlike other individuals. This individual is like others in that their beliefs are chosen as instruments to best obtain rewards they value. Their beliefs are, therefore, self-serving, or 'ideological' in broad terms. But what makes the individual unlike others is that their rewards are to a considerable degree immaterial, and include, critically, the satisfaction of a logical faculty: a soothing of a sensitivity to problems and errors, the tickling of a sensibility to order and clarity, a relief of an itch understood. The reward to this faculty does not preclude other rewards, material or immaterial. Neither does it preclude the existence of a countervailing reward to believing things contrary to good reason. This individual (i.e. the scientist), therefore, is neither a priest of power, nor a robot angel, calmly, rationally and disinterestedly pursuing truth. They are neither noble or ignoble, they are merely human.[26]

Being human, they are not solitaries, and will associate with their own kind in order to obtain esteem, and to secure intellectual exchange. In brief, they form a scientific community, and that is critical to the prosperity of science.

The relations of this scientific community to society at large are ambiguous. Trivially, there will be a relationship of dependence. The larger society will provide material rewards (or perhaps penalties). Further, that larger society's ideology may impart biases to members of that community. These biases may be so strong that the only science is bad science, i.e. unsuccessful science.[27] It is in this field of bad science that ideology hunters will find their richest quarry.

But even though science is dependent on larger society, successful science is also autonomous within that society. It is capable of disturbing that society. Its attachment to the logical faculty allows it to reach conclusions hostile to traditional teachings (regarding, for example, race, gender, species, class). Science is not a projection of society, it is a subculture. And like the more familiar subcultures it will have ambivalent relations to the larger society in which it exists.

Conclusion

This chapter has scrutinised the economic positions of one of the two co-discoverers of natural selection: Alfred Russel Wallace. It has shown that Wallace rejected many of the key tenets of the orthodox political economy of his contemporaries: free trade, the gold standard, competition, the market determination of wages and interest rates, the demerits of state property, and the merits of private property. It has been argued that this rejection of political economy has been motivated by his concern to improve the welfare of the British working class. The paper concludes that the case of A.R. Wallace makes for a pungent falsification of the popular thesis that natural selection was a projection onto biology of orthodox political economy. A more likely location of the metaphysical roots (in a non-pejorative sense) of Wallace's thought is the Owenism of his youth. There one will find socialism and religious scepticism. In that scepticism lies latent a question which Christianity did not need to answer: how can design come to an undesigned world?

Notes

1. Darwinism was an extension of laissez faire economic theory from society to biology' (Young, 1985, p 3). 'What Darwin did was take early-nineteenth *political* economy and expand it to include all of the *natural* economy' (Lewontin, quoted in Mogie, 1996, p. 2086).
2. 'It is beyond doubt that their [Darwin's and Lyell's] theories were central to others reconciling and apologetic doctrines' (Young, 1985, p. 199). Darwin's theory 'made Nature an ally of the middle-classes' (Moore, quoted in Mogie, 1996, p. 2086). 'Darwin was not averse to making social and economic applications of his theory. He clearly linked economic success with selective fitness and thought his theory supported individualist economic competition' (Weikart, 1995, p. 611).
3. Indeed, partisans of Wallace have argued that Darwin appropriated the idea from Wallace (see Bernstein, 1984, p. 235). However almost all historians of this episode would classify natural selection as a genuine doubleton.
4. Wallace quotes Ricardo as writing, 'There is no gain to society at large from a rise in rent; it is advantageous to the landlords alone, and their interests are thus permanently in opposition to those of all other classes'.
5. Wallace also read Henry George's *Progress and Poverty*.
6. There are only two economic works for which there is positive evidence that they were read by Darwin: McCulloch's *Principles* and Sismondi's *New Principles* (Gordon, 1989, p. 451). Darwin once declined Wallace's invitation to read Henry George on the ground that political economy was

'destructive' of his mind (Wallace, 1905, v2, p. 14). Darwin does refer to the non-economic works of Smith and Mill.

7.   See Gaffney (1997) and Clements (1983) for commentaries on his economic ideas.

8.   Wallace draws from Smith in an attempt to turn the tables on free-traders. 'It is a maxim of political economy', writes Wallace, 'that the home trade is the best trade for the prosperity of the country' (1913a, p. 36). This supposed maxim is drawn from Smith's reasoning concerning the relative productivity of capital in domestic industry and foreign trade (*Wealth of Nations*, Book II, Chapter 5). Protectionists before Wallace had used Smith's 'maxim' to embarrass free traders (Byles, 1893).

9.   *Prop XIII.* It is out of the pauper and floating masses who have been separated from the land, and have consequently no option between starvation and selling their labour unconditionally, that capital is originally formed, and is, therefore, enabled absolutely to dictate to the very labour that creates it, and to defraud that labour of those surpluses which ought to remain wholly with the latter' (Wallace, 1892, v.2, p. 242).

10. Another who combined an adherence to natural selection with an hostility to political economy was Wallace's companion in the struggle, A.J. Ogilvy (1834–1914). Ogilvy founded the Tasmanian Land Nationalisation Society, and the Democratic League, the forerunner of the Tasmanian Labor Party. He wrote *The Third Factor of Production*, and *A Colonist's Plea for Land Nationalisation*, to which Wallace supplied a foreword. In 1901 his pen yielded *Elements of Darwinism*, and in 1913 *The Ape Man*.

11. Wallace quotes Cairnes approvingly on the unmerited income of the landlord (1892, p. 116).

12. Wallace began to call himself a socialist from 1889 (Durant, 1979, p. 48). In his autobiography Wallace records that his absorption of Owenism in his teenage years did not prevent 'my adopting the individualist views of Herbert Spencer and the political economists' (Durant, 1979, pp. 36 and 74).

13. In sympathy with this position, one critic has identified Wallace with the new puritanism' of the mid 19th century, which sought to achieve social reform by the physical reformation of the individual (Turner, 1974, p. 80).

14. 'Equity, therefore, does not permit property in land ... . On examination all existing titles to such property turn out to be invalid ... . It appears that not even an equal apportionment of the earth amongst its inhabitants could generate a legitimate proprietorship. ... [W]e find ... that the theory of the co-heirship of all men to the soil, is consistent with the highest civilisation'. (Spencer, 1851, p. 125)

15. Wallace had an entirely different judgement from the political economists about the importance of altruism (or what he called 'hospitality'). Hospitality is, in fact, one of the most general of all human virtues, and in some cases almost a religion. It is an inherent art of what constitutes "human nature" '. (1913b, p. 101)

16. Point 3 of the *Communist Manifesto*'s 10 point program: 'Abolition of all right of inheritance'. The first point is: 'Abolition of property in land'.

17. See Durant (1979, p. 51) for Wallace's self-contradictions over eugenicism.

18. Wallace's economic position is reminiscent of the curiously anomalous figure of Thomas Hodgskin ([1827] 1966): simultaneously anti-capitalist and anti-collectivist.

19. Inevitably, perhaps, some critics are unimpressed by this reference (de Beer, in Darwin, 1974). The 'personal response' of the present writer to these facts is that it is absolutely remarkable that both Darwin and Wallace give high credit to Malthus, and it must signify.

20. Notice that whereas Malthus's world picture is one of long-run stationarity, that of Darwin and Wallace is one of long-run movement.

21. Ricardo is not forward in identifying whether it is through death rates or birth rates that the Malthusian mechanism operates. But his objection to the Poor Laws is that they remove the rewards of 'restraint' (Ricardo [1821] 1973, p. 62). Mill explicitly states that in developed societies it is variations in the birth rate (not the death rate) that is the means of the Malthusian mechanism (Mill, [1848] 1974, Book I, Chapter 10, Section 3, p. 156).

22. Later in life Wallace moved from agnosticism to a belief in an 'overarching intelligence' and theism. It is worth noting that Wallace seems to have been attracted to Malthus's theodicy (Wallace, 1905, p. 237).

23. Wallace once described white man as the true savage (Durant, 1979, p. 3).

24. Late in life Wallace was laden with honours. But the situation was the reverse in 1858, when his first paper on natural selection was jointly read with one by Darwin before the Linnean Society (neither paper received much interest at the time). Even in 1864 his application to be secretary of the Royal Geographical Society was rejected. 'He remained outside the professional community of scientists, whether he liked it or not' (Durant, 1979, p. 33).

25. Both radicals and conservatives have believed that Darwinism was subversive. Marx told Lassalle that it dealt the 'death-blow' 'for the first time to "teleology" [i.e., creationism] in the natural sciences' (Marx, 1941, p. 125). A prominent conservative of the 20th century writes thus of the subversive effect of natural selection: 'It was, of course, Darwin's theory of natural selection which first popularised the notion that Man and his environment are involved in an endless automatic process of improvement. Who can measure the consequences of this naïve assumption? What secret subversive organisation, endowed with unlimited funds and resources, could hope to achieve the thousandth part of what it achieved by discrediting the then prevailing morals and values?' (Muggeridge, 1988, p. 62) For more in the same vein, see Carroll (1994).

26. See Leonard (1999) for an extended attempt to analyse the scientist in terms of a model of rational economic man.

27. Society may be such that (successful) science will not exist. Perhaps that is the most normal state of affairs.

4. The Evolutionary Economics of Alfred Marshall: An Overview

Peter Groenewegen

Marshall's saying, 'the Mecca of the economist lies in economic biology', is well known, as is the fact that this gave an evolutionary slant to his economics. This is also captured in the Latin motto which graced the frontispiece of his *Principles* – *natura non facit saltum* – designed to draw attention to the principle of continuity as the underlying 'special character' of the book. Marshall may have derived his fondness for this saying from his youthful studies of the philosophy of Kant or, equally plausible, from the pages of Charles Darwin's *Origin of Species*, a book he likewise studied during this time (see Groenewegen, 1995, pp. 130, 411). The evolutionary thrust of Marshall's work is frequently explicit, especially in his *Principles of Economics*, the work for which he is now mainly remembered, and which spread his economic message of the wide-ranging benefits of progress over its eight editions from 1890 to 1920 and its subsequent frequent reprintings.

This chapter intends to trace the development of Marshall's evolutionary economics. It does so in the following way. Its first substantive section examines Marshall's interest in and acquaintance with evolutionary thought, largely acquired during the second half of the 1860s when he turned away from the study of mathematics to the moral sciences of philosophy and psychology and, eventually, economics. It also looks at the impact thereof on his early economics. Subsequent sections then review the evolutionary content of Marshall's economics in two further distinct stages: first, that in the various editions of the *Principles* and associated work; and second, in the books he described as his later volumes, particularly *Industry and Trade*. A final section offers some conclusions on the nature and growth of this important aspect of the Marshallian tradition.

In short, the emphasis of this chapter is on both the preparation for, and the practice of, Marshall's construction of his evolutionary economics. The former is essential because it enables a demonstration of the wide intellectual currents which shaped the mind of this economist during the 1860s and early 1870s and which included, in rich measure, philosophies of history, evolution and progress.

Evolution and Marshall's Early Economics

Despite Marshall's later claims about the relevance of biological knowledge for the student of economics, his own knowledge of biology was practically non-existent. This is implicitly confessed in one of his youthful, philosophical papers, 'Ye Machine' (Marshall, 1869, pp. 127) and in some remarks, recorded by John Neville Keynes after a dinner party in 1877, in which Marshall lamented the time he had wasted at school in learning classics because this could have been much better spent on the study of 'music, drawing, sculpture, a few modern languages, biology and general culture' (cited in Groenewegen, 1995, pp. 60). Such admissions notwithstanding, Marshall did spend considerable time studying aspects of evolutionary theory during the 1860s, though never in a formal manner.

It should be noted here, as in any case is widely recognised in the history of ideas, that the general notion of evolution was an exceedingly widely held scientific belief among the intellectual community during the 1860s, and that, in addition, a public acceptance of the principle of evolution was equally widespread (Niman, 1991, p. 21 n. 2). This was of course the decade of Marshall's formative intellectual period during which he gradually moved to the study of economics after having taken the final examinations of the Mathematical Tripos (with their emphasis on the physical sciences), from 1865 switching to the moral sciences including the various branches of philosophy, psychology, the theory of knowledge and associated inquiries.

The sources for evolutionary thinking available to Marshall at this time were manifold. By 1867, Marshall claimed he had worked through Darwin's *Origin of Species*; during this period he had also become fascinated with Herbert Spencer's work, especially his *First Principles* (Groenewegen, 1995, pp. 118–26). This not only dealt with certain problems in the theory of knowledge of the type in which Marshall was particularly interested in his formative period as a social scientist, it also presented a theory of evolution as applied to society, in the context of social progress and, something which may have intrigued Marshall even then, aspects of the division of labour and its cumulative effects on industrial organisation. In fact, Spencer's book offered a considerable amount on the importance of industrial organisation, the essentially evolutionary nature of its progress, location and growth, and the importance of that growth and progress for the wider development of society (Spencer, 1900, e.g. pp. 289–93, 312–8, 390–3).

There were other, more derivative, sources on the importance of evolutionary thought of economic, social and political argument. One of these was the economic textbook, *Plutology*, by the Australian academic, W.E. Hearn (1864). This was probably one of the first texts to use Darwin's theories to elucidate economic principles (see e.g. La Nauze, 1949, p. 192

and Laurent, above, pp. 23–5) and which, at an early stage, became a favoured book for Marshall (see Groenewegen 1988, pp. 2–4). Another was the widely read *Physics and Politics* by Walter Bagehot, which likewise brought out important evolutionary relationships in the process by which contemporary societies progressed, and which was among the many books on such subjects the young Marshall studied with considerable interest.[1]

The impact of these evolutionary writers on Marshall's early economics is not all that easy to detect. For example, there is little direct evidence of such influence in the material Whitaker (1975) edited as the *Early Economic Writings of Alfred Marshall*. As Denis O'Brien indicates in his introduction to a reprint of *Economics of Industry* (Marshall and Marshall, 1879), the influence of Hearn's *Plutology* is evident in the book even if Hearn is not cited by name (O'Brien, 1994, p. xvii). Parts of its methodological discussion also reveal shades of Spencer's perspectives (e.g. Marshall and Marshall, 1879, p. 314), as do other parts of the book (e.g. p. 9 on civilisation and the balance of mental and manual labour). Likewise the chapters on industrial organisation, with their treatment of localisation of industry, and on the division of labour, may have used something of Spencer's treatment of the subject[2] given the breadth of their social inferences. An example is the manner in which the link is drawn between division of labour and manual dexterity (Marshall and Marshall, 1879, p. 49, n. 1) and the localisation of industry (pp. 52–3).

The picture which is given from this overview of Marshall's acquaintance with biological, evolutionary thought, is that it was not particularly large in these years. This is despite the fact that during the second half of the 1860s, Marshall had worked quite solidly at Darwin's major works, and even more at the philosophy of Herbert Spencer, including the strong, evolutionary contents of his *First Principles* (Groenewegen, 1995, pp. 118–26). Knowledge gained from such study was probably reinforced by reading popular secondary sources, such as the books by Hearn, Bagehot and others. It is particularly striking that his knowledge is only marginally reflected in Marshall's early economic writings, an inference reinforced by the very few references to such subjects in his surviving correspondence, and in his complaint to John Neville Keynes about his lack of biological knowledge and its absence from the syllabus, given the over-emphasis on classical studies in his early education. The last is also revealed in his discussion with Benjamin Kidd[3] in correspondence in which, in an almost uncharacteristically candid manner, Marshall confessed an inability to grasp some arguments of Weismann, the eminent zoologist and evolutionary theorist (who first proposed the separation of germ and somatic plasm), in his quarrel with Herbert Spencer, even though Marshall had sought the assistance of William

Bateson, a colleague at St John's College, Cambridge, and a pioneer in the study of heredity.

In a reminiscing paper, written in 1896 when he was already well at the top of the economics profession in the United Kingdom, 'The Old Generation of Economists and the New', presented to the members of the Cambridge Economic Club at their inaugural meeting, infatuation with Darwin's 'development of the laws of struggle and survival' was argued by Marshall to have perhaps given 'a greater impetus to the careful and exact study of facts than any other event that has ever occurred' (Marshall, 1997, p. 532). This statement needs to be recalled in the context of the subsequent two sections of this chapter. A letter, almost a decade later, written to the editor of the *Daily Chronicle* in response to the paper's suggestion for a national memorial to Herbert Spencer, called attention to the enormous stimulus Spencer had given to younger Cambridge graduates of the 1860s and early 1870s and averred that, on the Continent, 'no one had exercised greater influence among English writers, with the exception of Darwin' (Whitaker, 1996, III p. 97). Complimentary though this appreciation was, its praise was limited to precisely two ways. Explicitly, the impact was confined to the late 1860s and early 1870s, coinciding with the time of Marshall's own philosophical and methodological investigations. Secondly, and implicitly, Marshall's own philosophical investigations had expressly criticised any applications of evolutionism beyond 'its appropriate, but limited, area, that is, one in which the phenomena studied, are very homogeneous' (Marshall, 1867, 1990, p. 53). In some ways it is therefore not surprising that Marshall used evolutionary doctrine and biological propositions in such a limited way in his early work.

Evolution and the *Principles*

As already indicated, the *Principles of Economics* is Marshall's major repository of biological and evolutionary material. Much of this, however, was confined to a few parts of the book: the preface, and some chapters in Book IV dealing with the organisation of industry (Chapter VIII) and with the correlation of tendencies to increasing and diminishing returns (Chapter XIII). A few references to such matters also occur in the opening three chapters of Book V, which introduce the subject of markets and provide the preliminary exposition of supply and demand. Generally speaking, the setting for this biological and evolutionary content is methodological. This makes it surprising that the explicitly methodological material of the first two books is completely free of biological and evolutionary analogies. It can also be noted by way of introduction that much of this material was included from the first edition of the *Principles*, and was only lightly revised over the seven subsequent editions, and then largely during the preparation of the sixth edition.

The preface makes a number of interesting links between economics and nature, biology and evolution. It does so in the first instance with respect to the problem of time, where nature is said 'to know no absolute partition of time into long periods and short', though such distinctions were claimed to be particularly instructive in economic study, such as, for example, the distinction between rent and interest, or the associated one between fixed and floating capital (Marshall, 1961, pp. vii, viii). In the context of the various meanings of continuity discussed at some length in the preface, biological influences (as represented by Spencer's work) are contrasted with the historical and philosophical influences (represented by Hegel's philosophy and history) and notions of mathematical continuity, represented by Augustin Cournot. The first of these, Marshall indicated, were major influences on the substance of his *Principles* (perhaps a bow in the direction of the importance for him of the contents of Book IV for the argument of the *Principles*), whereas Cournot's mathematical reasoning had influenced much of its form, with special reference to issues of mutual causation. However, in the context of the last, Marshall warned the reader that '[n]ature's action is complex: and nothing is gained, in the long run, by pretending that it is simple and trying to describe it in a series of elementary propositions' (Marshall, 1961, pp. ix–x).

The above comes from the preface to the first edition (reproduced in varying degrees in every subsequent edition) – the problems associated with time to which attention was drawn being more fully appreciated and elaborated in an article in the *Economic Journal* (Marshall, 1898) not long after revising the text of the fourth edition of the *Principles* for publication. This article provided Marshall's famous remark that 'the Mecca of the economist lies in economic biology rather than in economic dynamics' (Marshall, 1961, p. xiv), which implicitly stressed both the desirability and necessity, as well as the difficulties, of satisfactorily incorporating time into economics, largely because 'biological conceptions' are so much 'more complex' than those borrowed from mechanics. This remark likewise allowed a subtle reintroduction of the distinction between form and substance in the contents of the *Principles*: its substance lay in the material devoted to 'the forces that cause movement', the dynamics described as the 'keynote', while the form was largely mechanical, and often statical, because such material was so much easier to handle. The remainder of the final (or eighth) edition's preface then played on instances of the static/dynamic ('or rather, biological') distinction, in which the actual issues for economic study of progress and improvement were to be handled largely, but not exclusively, by statical methods and assumptions because the book, after all, was only a volume of foundations.

Not surprisingly, therefore, those sections of the *Principles* most concerned with progress retained the greatest emphasis on biological analogies. These were particularly drawn from nature's operations in the practical organisation of higher animals, based on survival of the fittest in the universal struggle for existence, seen as particularly pertinent to the understanding of industrial organisation. This is the case, for example, with the introductory chapter to this subject (Book IV, Chapter VIII), which in its opening paragraphs draws attention to the mutual debts of biology and economics, and the immense role of subdivision in the development of organisms, both physical and social. Moreover, this chapter pays particular tribute to the insights of Darwin into natural selection (Marshall, 1961, p. 240) and to Spencer's (Lamarckian) stress on the strengthening of organs and other faculties from being actively used and exercised, and illustrated with interesting biological examples discussed later. Survival and heredity were explicitly linked to progress in population quality, with special emphasis to the important role for families in this survival process, and for that of eugenics in improving quality and racial purity of the population (Marshall, 1961, pp. 242–3, 248–9). This chapter reveals Marshall the Social Darwinist in perspectives which he shared with many of his social scientist contemporaries. Of more relevance to his economics, his observations reveal the stress he laid on the time-intensiveness of progress in both the economic and other worlds, and the urgency of his warning, drawn from nature via its interpreters, that *natura non facit saltum.*

Chapter XIII of Book IV presented Marshall's famous (infamous?) 'tree in the forest' analogy, which influenced crucial aspects of the theory of the firm, initially as developed by him, and subsequently by some of his leading Cambridge followers, including Arthur Pigou and Dennis Robertson. As one of Marshall's most colourful biological analogies, it can be quoted in full :

> But here we may read a lesson from the young trees of the forest as they struggle upwards through the benumbing shade of their older rivals. Many succumb on the way, and a few only survive; those few become stronger with every year, they get a larger share of light and air with every increase of their height, and at last in their turn they tower above their neighbours, and seem as though they would grow on for ever, and for ever become stronger as they grow. But they do not. One tree will last longer in full vigour and attain a greater size than another; but sooner or later age tells on them all. Though the taller ones have a better access to light and air than their rivals, they gradually lose vitality; and one after another they give place to others, which, though of less material strength, have on their side the vigour of youth.
> And as with the growth of trees, so was it with the growth of business as a general rule before the great recent development of vast joint-stock companies,

which often stagnate, but do not readily die. Now that rule is far from universal, but it still holds in many industries and trades.

Nature still presses on the private business by limiting the length of the life of its original founders, and by limiting even more narrowly that part of their lives in which their faculties retain full vigour. And so, after a while, the guidance of the business falls into the hands of people with less energy and less creative genius, if not with less active interest in its prosperity. If it is turned into a joint-stock company, it may retain the advantages of division of labour, of specialised skills and machinery: it may even increase them by a further increase of its capital; and under favourable conditions it may secure a permanent and prominent place in the work of production. But it is likely to have lost so much of its elasticity and progressive force, that the advantages are no longer exclusively on its side in its competition with younger and smaller rivals (Marshall, 1961, pp. 315–16).

In fact, Marshall liked the analogy so much, that it was repeated at the start of Book V (Marshall, 1961, p. 323) and again (Marshall, 1961, p. 367) in the context of substantiating the 'worth' of his notion of the 'representative firm'.

This one major biological flourish from Marshall's pen was designed, once again, to indicate the limitations of statical analysis for economists, particularly in the context of the theory of the firm and, more generally, for the theory of value as a whole. The implications of this methodological stance are particularly plain to see in the discussion of internal and external economies, which continually blends statical with dynamic considerations (much to the annoyance of Stigler, 1941, esp. pp. 71–2). Biology, therefore, served Marshall as a reminder of important truths, essential to a realistic portrayal of economic behaviour, and which could never be attained through the more simple, statical analysis. Such matters related to the importance of change, technological developments, evolution in behaviour and learning by doing, which for Marshall were all parts and essential ingredients in a realistic presentation of the economics of business enterprise.

A specific aspect of the need for such realism in the construction of diagrams illustrative of the theory of the firm can be found in Appendix H (Marshall, 1961, pp. 807–08). There Marshall drew attention to an illegitimate consequence of seeing supply and demand adjustments as perfectly reversible in time. The relevant material can be quoted:

> It must however be admitted that this theory is out of touch with real conditions of life, in so far as it assumes that, if the normal production of a commodity increases and afterwards again diminishes to its old amount, the demand price and the supply price will return to their old positions for that amount.

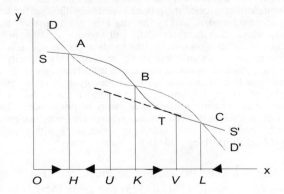

Whether a commodity conforms to the law of diminishing or increasing return, the increase in consumption arising from a fall in price is gradual: and, further habits which have once grown up around the use of a commodity while its price is low, are not quickly abandoned when its price rises again. If therefore after the supply has gradually increased, some of the sources from which it is derived should be closed, or any other cause should occur to make the commodity scarce, many consumers will be reluctant to depart from their wonted ways. For instance, the price of cotton during the American war was higher than it would have been if the previous low price had not brought cotton into common use to meet wants, many of which had been created by the low price. Thus then the list of demand prices which holds for the forward movement of the production of a commodity will seldom hold for the return movement, but will in general require to be raised.[*]

Again, the list of supply prices may have fairly represented the actual fall in the supply price of the thing that takes place when the supply is being increased; but if the demand should fall off, or if for any other reason, the supply should have to be diminished, the supply price would not move back by the course by which it had come, but would take a lower course. The list of supply prices which had held for the forward movement would not hold for the backward movement, but would have to be replaced by a lower schedule. This is true whether the production of the commodity obeys the law of diminishing or increasing return; but it is of special importance in the latter case, because the fact that the production does obey this law, proves that its increase leads to great improvements in organisation.

For, when any casual disturbance has caused a great increase in the production of any commodity, and thereby has led to the introduction of extensive economies, these economies are not readily lost. Developments of mechanical appliances, of division of labour and of the means of transport, and improved organisation of all kinds, when they have been once obtained are not readily abandoned. Capital and labour, when they have once been devoted to any particular industry, may indeed become depreciated in value, if there is a

---

[*] That is, for any backward movement of the amount offered for sale, the left end of the demand curve would probably need to be raised in order to make it represent the new conditions of demand.

falling off in the demand for the wares which they produce: but they cannot quickly be converted to other occupations; and their competition will for a time prevent a diminished demand from causing an increased price of the wares.**

The methodological import of this aspect of Appendix H was grasped particularly vigorously by Joan Robinson who, in her lecture delivered at Oxford by a Cambridge economist, emphasised the one-way nature of time, ever forward, never backward: 'in time, the distance between today and tomorrow is twenty-four hours forward, and the distance between today and yesterday is eternity backwards. There is a lot about this written in verse ...' (Joan Robinson, 1953, p. 12). In this context, Marshall is singled out for some praise: 'The one who understood it thoroughly well was Marshall. This is not a learned lecture. I will only refer you to Appendix H in his *Principles*. Read it over again, and you will see how right I am' (Joan Robinson, 1953, p. 13).

Marshall, as has already been argued, was too wily to be caught by the assumption of reversible time which so often is implicitly assumed in 'mechanical economics'. He was all too well aware from his appreciation of nature that time was irreversible; the past can only be painfully undone, whereas everything in the future is still open. This aspect fills the *Principles of Economics*, guiding its theories of production, distribution and exchange, at many stages of the argument.

Evolution and the Later Works

Biological and evolutionary material is less frequently encountered in Marshall's second major book, *Industry and Trade*. Yet, in a manner quite similar to the *Principles*, evolutionary and biological perspectives guide the method of the work, as is made clear in much of the methodological material included in its opening sections. Section 2 of the opening chapter (Marshall, 1919, 1920, pp. 5–7) thus recalls the gist of the motto of the *Principles* – *natura non facit saltum*. A few pages later, the phrase 'economic evolution' is used to describe the gradual growth in capital intensity of production and

---

** For instance, the shape of the supply curve in fig. 38 [reproduced above, Eds] implies that if the ware in question were produced on the scale OV annually, the economics introduced into its production would be so extensive as to enable it to be sold as a price TV. If these economies were once effected the shape of the curve SS' would probably cease to represent accurately the circumstances of supply. The expenses of production, for instance, of an amount OU would no longer be much greater proportionately than those of an amount OV. Thus in order that the curve might again represent the circumstances of supply it would be necessary to draw it lower down, as the dotted curve in the figure.

its consequences in terms of the 'diminished ... strain thrown on human muscles' (Marshall, 1919, 1920, p. 19). Economic evolution is in fact the term used on other occasions in the book to describe the development theme underlying the industrial economic history which features so strongly in much of its contents.

In this context, and also at a later stage, Marshall draws attention to the relevant findings of biology. For example, when discussing the growth of the 'business point of view' (Marshall, 1919, 1920, p. 163), Marshall reminded his readers that biology had been 'discovering numerous ways in which inheritance and natural selection – supplemented by the imitation of successful actions of parents and other older individuals – have enabled even low grade animals so to adjust their structure and their operations to their environment that they may be able to utilise it for their own benefit with ever increasing ease, efficiency and certainty'.[4] However, in the methodological appendix, Marshall indicates that in the biological sciences, 'the area over which certainty extends is relatively very small', even though in the social sciences, including economics, it is even smaller (Marshall 1919, 1920, p. 673).

Overall, the tone of Marshall's application of biology and evolutionary doctrine to economics seems somewhat more cautious in *Industry and Trade* than in the *Principles*. Yet such analogies were still clearly seen as relevant, as can be illustrated by a rather long set of remarks in which Marshall was critical of socialist doctrines and particularly of the view of human nature espoused therein (notwithstanding some sympathy with these doctrines in earlier writings – see Laurent, below, p. 71). These can be quoted extensively, again because they demonstrate this rather cautious tone, which, with respect to the conclusions, is explicitly seen in the final sentences.

> Darwin's 'law of the survival of the fittest' is often misunderstood; Nature being supposed to secure, through competition, that those shall survive who are fittest to benefit the world. But the law really is that those races are most likely to survive, who are best fitted to thrive in their environment: that is, to turn to their own account those opportunities which the world offers to them. A race of wolves that has well organised plans for hunting in packs is likely to survive and spread; because those plans enable it to catch its prey, not because they confer a benefit on the world.
>
> The common opinion is, however, not as wholly false in substance as it is in form. For almost every increase in power, which any race of men has acquired, can be traced to some social qualities which have enabled that race to overcome the difficulties that lie in the way of obtaining the necessaries and comforts of life; or to overcome its human enemies, or both. Success in war may indeed be partly due to ferocity of character. But, though it could perhaps not have been predicted *à priori,* the social qualities, habits and institutions of a conquering race have in the past generally been of a stronger fibre than those of the conquered. The temper which enables wolves to maintain the discipline of the pack, has in it something that is noble; and the world has in fact gained a good

deal from those qualities which have enabled the dog, a domesticated wolf, to take a high rank among living creatures. But man is not bound to follow the slow steps by which the race of wolves has passed through disciplined ferocity to higher things.

Again, by aid of 'natural selection' certain insects, and flowers from which they gather honey, mutually modify one another, till the insects ensure themselves an abundance of food by the untiring efficiency with which they fertilise the flowers. And in like manner, while it is true that those institutions tend to survive which have the greatest faculty for utilising the environment in developing their own strength; it is also true that, in so far as they in return benefit the environment, they strengthen the foundations of their own strength, and thereby increase their chance of surviving and prospering. On this account then we may admit that the mere existence of broad tendencies towards the dominance of the joint-stock form of administration and towards combinations of semi-monopolistic scope, affords some reason for thinking that these tendencies make for the public good. But it is only a *primâ facie* reason, and not a very strong one. (Marshall 1919, 1920, pp. 175–6)

Given the acknowledgement of the relevance of *natura non facit saltum* in matters relating to industry and trade, it is perhaps interesting to draw attention to a seeming negation of this 'law of nature' in the context of railway technology, with respect to capacity increases by adding to the number of lines. If it is decided, Marshall says, 'to have two lines instead of one, or three or four instead of two ... , the increase in expenses *makes some great jumps*' (Marshall 1919, 1920, p. 458). However, the reader is not explicitly alerted to the fact that this aspect of lumpiness in investment somewhat contradicts the maxim mentioned in the opening pages as 'especially applicable to economic developments'.

Although lip service to the motto of the *Principles* – 'economic evolution is gradual and continuous on each of its numberless routes' – is paid in the preface to Marshall's final volume, *Money, Credit and Commerce* (Marshall, 1923, p. v), that book is otherwise not replete with biological or evolutionary content. The opposite is in fact the case. Apart from a reference to Smith's inadequate allowance for 'natural selection' in his discussion of wage equalisation (Marshall, 1923, p. 5) and a reference (Marshall, 1923, p. 107) to the relevance to economics of the methods of Darwin, as well as those of Bacon and Newton, biology and evolution are absent from the text of this final volume. Perhaps its relevance was less to the world of banking and trade, or, perhaps more pertinent, the manner in which this book was written relied far less on the skill at constant revision of its author (but see Laurent, p. 76 below).

Time, Change and the Biological Analogy

Biology, and evolutionary theory, as was pointed out at the end of the
material on the *Principles* in Section III above, served Marshall as a reminder
of a number of important truths, which clearly constrained, though did not
totally destroy, the value to be attached to more mechanical, statical analysis.
A crucial matter here was the notion of time, a strictly one-way phenomenon
for realistic economics, and one which entered nearly every feature of
economic life since virtually all economic activity, from the most trivial act
of consumption upwards, involved the passage of time. Awareness of this
elementary fact, and a willingness to act on it in his economic analysis, is one
of the great services Marshall rendered to economic analysis. It was one, as
already indicated, which Joan Robinson increasingly appreciated after her
initial wrong turning in her *Economics of Imperfect Competition* of 1933.

Time is not only associated with difficulties. With time also come
opportunities for change, and with change the possibilities for progress and
improvement. Hence evolutionary theory which, for Marshall, imparts to
animals the actualities of change and adaptation over the long course of their
history in the form of modification of some of their organs through use,
emphasised one such avenue for improvement which greatly impressed him.
An example he used in the early editions of the *Principles* included the
Lamarckian story of the long necks of the giraffe. Subsequent editions used
the biologically safer examples of the development of webbed feet in
waterbirds. The relevant passages are as follows, and are quoted in full to
illustrate the pitfalls in the use of such illustrations for persons not adept in
the mysteries of biological science:

> If members of any species of bird begin to adopt aquatic habits, every increase
> in the webs between the toes – whether coming about gradually by the
> operation of natural selection, or suddenly as a sport,– will cause them to find
> their advantage more in aquatic life, and will make their chance of leaving
> offspring depend more on the increase of the web. So that, if $f(t)$ be the
> average area of the web at time t, then the rate of increase of the web increases
> (within certain limits) with every increase in the web, and therefore $f''(t)$ is
> positive. Now we know by Taylor's Theorem that
>
> $$f(t + h) = f(t) + hf'(t) + \frac{h^2}{1.2} f''(t + \theta h);$$
>
> and if h be large, so that h^2 is very large, then $f(t + h)$ will be much greater than
> $f(t)$ even though $f'(t)$ be small and $f''(t)$ is never large. There is more than a
> superficial connection between the advance made by the applications of the
> differential calculus to physics at the end of the eighteenth century and the
> beginning of the nineteenth, and the rise of the theory of evolution. In
> sociology as well as in biology we are learning to watch the accumulated
> effects of forces which, though weak at first, get greater strength from the

growth of their own effects; and the universal form, of which every such fact is a special embodiment, is Taylor's Theorem; or, if the action of more than one cause at a time is to be taken account of, the corresponding expression of a function of several variables. This conclusion will remain valid even if further investigation confirms the suggestion, made by some Mendelians, that gradual changes in the race are originated by large divergences of individuals from the prevailing type. For economics is a study of mankind, of particular nations, of particular social strata; and it is only indirectly concerned with the lives of men of exceptional genius or exceptional wickedness and violence. (Marshall, 1961, I, pp. 843–44)

The giraffe whose long neck enables it to survive by feeding on the shoots of trees when the grass is dried up, may possibly lengthen its neck further by constantly stretching it, and thus further increase its power of surviving; but this effect is not purposely sought. Again, the tendency for all peculiarities of this sort to increase their rate of growth as time goes on, within certain limits, is allowed to work itself out unopposed (unless by sexual selection) in the animal kingdom. The longer, within certain limits, a giraffe's neck is, and the more exclusively he feed on the shoots of trees, the more will his chance of survival depend on the length of his neck; and the greater will be the force which the struggle for survival will exert in tending to accelerate that growth (see Note XI in the Mathematical Appendix). (Marshall, 1961, II, p. 326)

Nature, for Marshall, and hence 'fact' revealed by biological and evolutionary study, had a further important role to play in the aid it gave to the elucidation of sound economic methods. In the first place, the complexity of nature is fully reflected in the complexity of the details in most actions in human life, therefore including economic actions. Hence economics cannot be an easy subject and those resolved to make it easy need to be characterised as fools. This was particularly the case in what Marshall identified with the substance of economics, much of which he presented in the rich material on production and development in Book IV of the *Principles* and from where, as shown previously, most of the important biological material originates.

Unfortunately, the Mecca which defined the relationship, so strikingly necessary for Alfred Marshall, between the economist and economic biology – as identifiable from its appearances in Marshall's writings – remains a somewhat wide and ill-defined entity. The usefulness of that relationship needs continual testing in the practice of the economist in trying to understand economic reality. The extent to which this was caused by Marshall's own lack of biological knowledge, as illustrated here in various ways, is by no means clear.

Notes

1.	Other books of this genre which Marshall appears to have studied and which in any case formed part of his library, together with various titles by Herbert Spencer, were Haycroft (1895) and Kidd (1898).
2.	See Spencer (1900), pp. 289–93, 312–8 and, on homogeneity in evolution, pp. 308–12. Passages such as these may have influenced the nature of Marshall's inductions in the 1870s and the search for specific type of phenomena during these fact-finding tours in Great Britain and Europe. The last are examined in some detail in Groenewegen (1995), Chapter 7, esp. pp. 208–14.
3.	Alfred Marshall to Benjamin Kidd, 6 June 1894 (in Whitaker, 1996, II pp. 114–15) and see Groenewegen (1995, pp. 482–4) which summarises Marshall's correspondence with Bateson (not included in Whittaker). It mentions his Freudian slip therein, revelatory of Marshall's inferiority complex with respect to eminent biologists such as Bateson.
4.	A long footnote warns of the difficulties in this context of distinguishing between inherited characteristics and those acquired from their environment. It can be reproduced in full since it provides a relatively concise example of Marshall's use of this sort of material.

> This remark does not assume that acquired faculties are inherited from parents by children at their birth: it is sufficient for the argument that children automatically imitate the actions of those by whom they are surrounded, and are especially sensitive to suggestions from the examples of mother and father: while acquired skill and faculty in small matters, as well as in large, pass from parents to children by definite instruction. But a protest may be permissible against the pretensions of some exponents of Mendelian doctrine that arithmetical averages of observations of inheritance of mice and vegetables afford conclusive proof that the characters which children bring into the world with them, are incapable of being affected by the past mode of life of their parents. Mendelians do not claim to know what causes originate differences between elementary germs: it seems to be certain that changes in the mental and moral habits of a human being are reflected in his face: and Mendelian arithmetic has little direct bearing on the question whether the nutrition supplied to germs in the body of a person excessively addicted to drink or other sensual indulgences may not result in the birth of a child with less firm character than it would have had, if the parent had lived soberly and chastely. Some Mendelians concede that it does: and the gradual development of trustworthy statistics of inherited mental and moral characters may ultimately lead to further admissions in the same direction. (Marshall, 1919, 1920, pp. 163–4, n. 1)

5. Keynes and Darwinism

John Laurent*

Biological analogy has a significant place in Alfred Marshall's economics, as shown in my earlier chapter. In his use of this kind of language Marshall makes at least some reference to Darwin. This is not a matter of dispute among historians of economic thought (see also Limoges and Menard, 1994; Schabas, 1994). But did Marshall's most famous pupil, John Maynard Keynes, adopt his teacher's methodology in this respect, and if so, did Keynes accept Marshall's usage of biological language? More importantly, to what extent did *Darwinism*, specifically, influence Keynes's thinking?

Keynes's 'Organicism'

Edward McKenna and Dianne Zannoni (1997–8) have referred to what they call an 'ongoing debate' over whether Keynes was a 'methodological individualist' or an 'organicist', and declare that they agree with 'those who believe that Keynes eventually came to adopt an organicist view'. Geoffrey Hodgson (1993), too, notes one or two authors who point to an 'organicist' style of argument in Keynes's *The General Theory of Employment, Interest and Money*. An instance of the latter is Keynes's acknowledged debt to and further development of the arguments of J.A. Hobson's and A.F. Mummery's *The Physiology of Industry* (pp. 364–71), which, as I indicated in my earlier chapter, contains much organic metaphor.

Yet citations from *The Physiology of Industry* apart, closer inspection of *The General Theory* does not, in fact, reveal a great deal of usage of organic language. I have searched Keynes's most famous volume carefully, and the nearest examples that I can find to such idiom are where Keynes speaks of 'the community as a whole', or 'the social structure', or perhaps, in the book's last paragraph, 'the evolution of political society' (Keynes, 1936, pp. 110, 245, 383). It *is* true, however, that Keynes *does* use organic and biological metaphor extensively in earlier writing. In his first book, *Indian Currency and Finance*, for instance, Keynes refers to the 'economic organism' (Keynes, 1913, p. 101), and in *A Revision of the Treaty* nations are 'vast organic units' (Keynes, 1922, p. 10). In *A Tract on Monetary Reform* Keynes (1923, pp. 65, 68) speaks of 'the body politic' and of the state as a 'sovereign body', and in some lecture notes from around 1910 he gives as one model of society 'the hive or community'.[1] This latter motif is also alluded to by Keynes in *The General Theory*, where he cites Bernard Mandeville's *Fable of the Bees* (Keynes, 1936, pp. 359–62). Here it is clear that the story – a celebration of the virtues of conspicuous consumption – is not meant to be taken in any serious scientific sense. Sociobiologists such as E.O. Wilson (1975), whose original research was on ants and bees, and their followers in economics (e.g. Hirshleifer, 1977; Tullock, 1979) seem to have difficulty in appreciating this. Mandeville's message is in the form of an allegory, a rhetorical device, as Keynes himself notes (p. 360).[2]

So Keynes, I would argue, by the time he wrote *The General Theory*, was no 'evolutionary economist' in the sense discussed in Chapter 2, and his 'organicism' was not meant to be taken literally. This does not mean, however, that Keynes was not interested in evolution. On the contrary, it is here suggested, it was *because* of his interest in *Darwinian* evolution that mere organic analogy had ceased to hold much appeal for Keynes by that time, or indeed for some time before this. Before pursuing this argument further, Keynes's interest in Darwin's ideas generally should be looked at.

Keynes's Darwinism

The evidence for Keynes's interest in Darwin is unmistakable. Take for example these lines from Keynes's essay, 'Economic Possibilities for Our Grandchildren', published in *The Nation and Athenaeum* in October 1930:

> [I]f, instead of looking into the future, we look into the past, we find that the economic problem, the struggle for subsistence, always has been hitherto the primary, most pressing problem of the human race – not only of the human race, but of the whole of the biological kingdom from the beginning of life in its most primitive forms.
>
> Thus we have been expressly evolved by nature – with all our impulses and deepest instincts – for the purpose of solving the economic problem. If the economic problem is solved, mankind will be deprived of its traditional purpose (Keynes, 1930b, p. 96).

In *The General Theory*, Keynes shows that he was as fully aware as the most doctrinaire market economist of the reality of this Darwinian 'struggle for existence'. It 'accords with our experience of human nature', Keynes wrote, that the 'struggle for [relative] money wages' is likely to be 'intensified' as the bargaining position of workers improves with fuller employment. At the same time, Keynes defends his case for domestic policies of full employment achieved through the 'socialisation of investment', partly on the grounds that such policies would be more favourable to world peace, since a principle cause of war was 'the pressure of population and the competitive struggle for markets'. International trade under such a system, Keynes insists, would 'cease to be what it is', namely a 'desperate expedient to maintain full employment at home by forcing sales on foreign markets', which merely shifts the problem of unemployment to the neighbour who is 'worsted in the struggle' (Keynes, 1936, pp. 252–3, 381–3).

Keynes's reference to population pressure points to a pivotal element in the Darwinian system: the tendency towards geometric growth in numbers in all species (modified, perhaps, in the case of humans – see Chapter 2 re Hearn) compared with the merely arithmetic growth in the means of subsistence – an element which Darwin obtained from Malthus. As many readers will know, Keynes (1936, pp. 362–4) devotes some space to Malthus in *The General Theory*. In this instance, it was in terms of Malthus's importance as an early demand-side theorist rather than in the context of population: For Malthus, 'the notion of insufficiency of effective demand takes a definite place as a scientific explanation of unemployment'. Keynes also wrote an essay on Malthus for his *Essays in Biography (CW*, X, pp. 71–103), and indeed Robert Skidelsky (1992, p. 416) considers Malthus undoubtedly 'Keynes's favourite economist of all'. But arguably it was Malthus on *population* that most interested Keynes, and this was substantially in terms of the Darwin connection.

In his second book, *The Economic Consequences of the Peace*, Keynes (1919, pp. 8–13) contended, citing Malthus, that population pressure in Germany had been a major factor leading to the outbreak of World War I. In an article in *The Nation and Athenaeum* in October 1923, he replied to some deprecatory remarks about his views made by Sir William Beveridge[3] as follows: 'What is the use or the purpose of all our strivings if they are to be neutralised or defeated by the mere growth of numbers? Malthus's Devil is a terrible devil because he undermines our faith in the real value of our social purposes, just as much now as when Malthus loosed him against the amiable dreams of Godwin [the eighteenth-century Utopian]' (*CW*, XIX pp. 121–2). In an earlier lecture to undergraduates he had argued that it was 'a fallacy to believe that the population of Europe has been profoundly affected by the war', and that 'the birth-rate is increasing and the death-rate diminishing', which was bound to result in 'mighty problems' for the future.[4] Actually, in early May 1914 – three months before the outbreak of World War I – Keynes had warned of the dangers of over-population in a paper read before the Political Philosophy and Science Club in Cambridge (see Cox, 1995, p. 33; Toye, 1997). In some lecture notes for a course on 'Principles of Economics' taught at Cambridge in 1911 Keynes made the specific link with Darwin:

> If Malthusian ideas originally stimulated Darwin's ideas, the latter now lead us to modify the former. There is a marked process of selection at work in favour of the element which we regard as least good.

> In a given country it is the poorest and least intelligent part of the
> population which reproduces itself most rapidly; and it is in the most civilised
> countries that the birthrate is falling off fastest.
> We are faced by a dilemma. The Malthusian Law of Population, when it is
> in operation, maintains the lower classes of the population in a condition of
> perpetual misery. But it is the engine of evolutionary progress, and those
> classes of society, or portions of the world, for which its operation is
> suspended, are liable to be overwhelmed by the rest.[5]

As Keynes says, he is going beyond Malthus here, in that he is looking at
Malthus's writings in the light of Darwin's theory of natural selection. This
is based on the assumption that numbers of any given species will always
tend to outstrip the means of subsistence, so that only those most favourably
adapted will survive and leave offspring: the 'Malthusian Law' (populations
increase geometrically while the means of subsistence only increase
arithmetically). This, as Keynes says, 'is the engine of evolutionary
progress'. The importance, then, of Malthus's and Darwin's ideas for Keynes
is obvious in this lecture. But Keynes's words show that he is actually going
beyond Darwin as well as Malthus in the lecture, in that he is fairly clearly
presenting a case for eugenics, a creation not of Darwin's but of his cousin,
Francis Galton, who coined the term eugenics in 1883.[6] While it has to be
admitted that there are passages in *The Descent of Man* which *could* be cited
in a eugenics context – this is one side of Darwin – Darwin's discussions in
this area are mainly limited to a summary of his cousin's views. An example
is the following passage from Chapter 5 – 'The Development of the
Intellectual and Moral Faculties during Primeval and Civilised Times' – in
The Descent of Man:

> A most important obstacle in civilised countries to an increase in the number of
> men of a superior class has been strongly insisted on by ... Mr Galton, namely,
> the fact that the very poor and reckless, who are often degraded by vice, almost
> invariably marry early, whilst the careful and frugal, who are generally
> otherwise virtuous, marry late in life, so that they may be able to support
> themselves and their children in comfort. Those who marry early produce
> within a given period not only a greater number of generations, but ... they
> produce many more children. The children, moreover, that are born by mothers
> during the prime of life are heavier and larger, and therefore probably more
> vigorous, than those born at other periods. Thus the reckless, degraded and
> often vicious members of society, tend to increase at a quicker rate than the
> provident and generally virtuous members. (Darwin, n.d., p. 505)

Keynes and Eugenics

So there is eugenics of a sort in Darwin, and Keynes was aware of this;
moreover, to judge from his 1911 lecture notes, Keynes was apparently
sympathetic to eugenics's concerns. There is in fact plenty of evidence of

Keynes's continuing interest in eugenics, as is witnessed by his presentation, in February 1946, of the Galton Medal to Sir Alexander Carr-Saunders (an economist who had originally studied zoology) at a meeting of the Eugenics Society.[7] This interest of Keynes's is rarely mentioned by Keynesians, especially those on the Left of the political spectrum, and for understandable reasons. After Nazism, few people, today, would want to argue for eugenics as a social policy. Yet it is remarkable just how pervasive eugenicist views were in the decades before World War II, including among people on the Left. The enthusiasm of H.G. Wells and G.B. Shaw, for example, for eugenics has been well documented (see, e.g., Carey, 1992), and to their names could be added lesser known identities such as the biologist and Communist, J.B.S. Haldane, author of books like *The Inequality of Man* (Haldane, 1932). A paper on 'Economics over Eugenics' by a Dr. H.J. Muller in a journal called *Fact*, in 1939, and whose 'contributing editors' included Wells, Margaret Cole and Labour Party leader George Lansbury, approvingly cites some of Haldane's genetic research in a case made for '[t]he social direction of human evolution [which] can only occur under a socially directed economic system' (Muller, 1939, p. 61). Wells's (1932) *The Work, Wealth and Happiness of Mankind* contains a chapter on eugenics which praises the recently introduced compulsory sterilisation 'of certain types of defectives' in a number of American states.

In his introduction to *The Work, Wealth and Happiness of Mankind*, Wells thanks Keynes for reading part of the manuscript and discussing it with him, and indeed the two had some association in the 1920s and 1930s in the context of population and eugenics. In 1927 Keynes chaired a dinner commemorating the fiftieth anniversary of the Bradlaugh–Besant trial (in which the noted atheist Charles Bradlaugh and his then partner – later Shaw's – Annie Besant, were prosecuted for publishing a pamphlet on contraception) and the subsequent foundation of the Malthusian League. Toasts were proposed by both Keynes and Wells and responded to by special guest, Annie Besant.[8] In September the same year Keynes was on the 'advisory council' for a World Population Conference in Geneva, in which he was associated with Haldane. A printed brochure for this conference among Keynes's papers explains that addresses were to be given on such topics as the 'Results of Differential Birthrate in Germany', and an outline of the conference's concerns reads in part as follows:

> The work of Malthus, scarcely more than a century ago, first made the world think seriously about the problem which the growth of population was preparing for humanity. The rapid growth of wealth consequent upon the industrial revolution caused his forebodings to be largely forgotten, but the last thirty or forty years has once again brought before men's minds the spectre of a world which is rapidly being filled up with people ... .

Meanwhile, another problem of population has obtruded itself upon the world – that of quality. The pioneer in drawing attention to this was Sir Francis Galton. Today, a great volume of scientific work has been devoted to a study of the alarming fertility of some stocks and classes, the alarmingly slow reproduction of others, to the question of the inheritance of mental and physical defects, and, in brief, to discovering whether the quality of the national stock is deteriorating, and if so, what steps could be taken to stem the process.[9]

In his address prior to his presentation of the Galton Medal, Keynes said that the 'peculiar quality' of Galton's mind had always held a 'special fascination' for him, and that he [Keynes] had 'possessed all his [Galton's] books' while still an undergraduate.[10] Keynes's interest in eugenics during his undergraduate years has indeed been noted by one or two authors (e.g. Kevles, 1985). Amongst Keynes's papers from the time are a number of card notices of debates organised by the Social Discussion Society at Cambridge on such topics as 'Heredity and Social Progress' and 'Evolution and the Social Problem'.[11] The first of the latter was held in Keynes's fellow undergraduate 'E. Darwin's rooms, Trinity' in December 1904 – i.e., Erasmus Darwin, son of Charles Darwin's youngest son, Sir Horace Darwin, an engineer and designer of scientific instruments and Mayor of Cambridge in 1896–7. The Keyneses' association with the Darwins in Cambridge was in fact quite close at this time and remained so for many years. J.M. Keynes's mother, Florence, who was herself to be Mayor of Cambridge (in 1932–3), and Horace Darwin were members of the Cambridge University Eugenics Society. From as early as January 1900 Keynes had 'dined with the Horace Darwins'.[12] Keynes also had some contact with two other of Charles Darwin's sons, the astronomer and mathematician Sir George Darwin, from at least 1899, and Leonard, a Major in the Royal Engineers and Liberal M.P. for Lichfield from 1892 to 1895. George had wide interests, including Egyptology (an interest Keynes shared).[13] His daughter, Margaret, married Keynes's brother Geoffrey in 1917. Leonard was perhaps best known as president of the (national) Eugenics Society (from 1911 to 1928) and author of books like *What is Eugenics?* (Darwin, 1928).

Keynes read an *economic* text by Leonard Darwin – *Bimetallism* (L. Darwin, 1897) – in 1906 (and was recommending it to his students a few years later).[14] Another book by Leonard Darwin, *Municipal Trade* (L. Darwin, 1903 – Horace Darwin's copy of which I have), was later commended by Keynes as one of those rare books which are characterised by a 'freedom ... both from socialistic and from anti-socialistic bias'.[15] Leonard Darwin also took a deep interest in his father's theories in general, publishing, for example, a work on *Organic Evolution* (L. Darwin, 1921). In this he defended Charles Darwin's broader views on human nature against Social Darwinist distortions of his theories (i.e., that war was an inevitable

Portrait of John Maynard Keynes by Charles Darwin's grand-daughter,
Gwen Raverat, 1908 (Courtesy of the National Portrait Gallery, London).

result of the 'struggle for existence') during World War I.[16] In April 1909 Leonard Darwin spoke at a public meeting in Cambridge on 'Free Trade', under the auspices of the Cambridge University Free Trade Association, of which Keynes was secretary at the time.[17]

The Influence of the Left

But while a fascination with eugenics (perhaps initiated by a reading of Galton) may have been strengthened through Keynes's contacts with the Darwin family, it is clear that eugenics was not the full extent of Keynes's Darwinian interests. That Keynes's understanding of what Darwin had to say about the human condition went beyond narrow eugenics concerns is evident from Keynes's further notes for his 1911 lectures on 'Principles of Economics':

> The struggle between different races and countries is, at the present time as it has been at other times, confusedly reflected in national prejudices and policy – alien acts, military strength, imperialism, yellow peril, South African, Australian and American feeling against coloured immigration. In these times the primitive instinct for the preservation of one's own race, whatever it may be, now shows itself.
> On the other hand we have policies and sympathies dictated by leaders who have freed themselves from or who are less susceptible to the primitive instinct.
> They feel sympathy with the anxieties of other and very alien races; they are pleased by the existence of varied civilisations and would assist weaker nationalities; they are less convinced than the former that their own race contains within itself all that there is in the world most desirable; they are open to the charge of being cosmopolitan; and they are occupied by the task of improving the moral and material conditions of their own and other races ... .
> *My own sympathies are with the cosmopolitans*, but it is necessary for a cosmopolitan never to forget the struggle for survival of races and classes which the progress of civilisation has done very little to weaken [present author's emphasis].[18]

In the penultimate paragraph of *The Economic Consequences of the Peace* (Keynes, 1919, p. 219), Keynes refers to 'the universal element in the soul of man', and these words, taken together with the above references to 'cosmopolitan' sentiments and to 'sympathy with ... other races', remind one of *another* side of Darwin discussed in my earlier chapter: the Darwin who can talk of an individual's sympathies 'extending to the men of all nations and races'. There is good evidence that Keynes was well aware of this universalist dimension of Darwin's thought as well as the more familiar 'struggle for existence' side, and that this was important for Keynes's own thinking. In his biography of Keynes, Roy Harrod (1951, p. 20) quotes a 1908 letter from Keynes to his friend from Eton days, Bernard Swithinbank, in which Keynes writes: 'Really, the most substantial joys I get are from the perception of logical arguments, and, oh, from reading Darwin's life. How superb it is'. And in Keynes's papers at King's College there is a letter from his brother Geoffrey, from the same year, in which the latter says that he has 'just finished the first Darwin volume and find that your praise was not displaced'.[19] Francis Darwin's (1887) three-volume *Life and Letters* of his father is in the card catalogue for Keynes's library (bequeathed to King's College). Though these volumes are, unfortunately, missing, we know that Keynes read them closely, from the 14 pages of notes transcribed from them among his notes for his Fellowship dissertation from 1905–7.[20]

Darwin's *Life and Letters* contains correspondence to and from Darwin (Vol. 3, pp. 136, 150) in connection with his chapter on 'The Moral Sense' in *The Descent of Man*, including his views on ethical universalism discussed in Chapter 2, above. Also in Keynes's library is a first edition of *The Origin of Species* (and a large, autographed photographic portrait of Darwin – see frontispiece) in which, while it contains virtually nothing about *human* evolution, Keynes could read – under the sub-heading, 'The Struggle for Existence', in Chapter 3: 'I should promise that I use the term Struggle for Existence in a large and metaphorical sense, *including dependence of one being on another*' (Darwin, n.d., p. 52, my emphasis). Again, this aspect of Darwin's thinking will come as a surprise to those who think that his most well-known work is all about unmitigated competition and the survival of the fittest. Co-operation is as much a part of nature as competition, in Darwin's view, and this extended to *human* nature, as we have seen. While ideologically bound individualists of Keynes's day may have been unaware of this side of Darwin's writing, and in any case probably not interested, there is at least circumstantial evidence that this was not the case with Keynes. Apart from the evidence of Keynes having read the relevant sections of Darwin's *Life and Letters*, we know from his records that he also purchased (in 1906) and read L.T. Hobhouse's *Morals in Evolution*.[21] This volume is heavily dependant on Darwin's chapter on 'The Moral Sense' in *The Descent of Man*, as is clear from passages like this one:

> Historically, both the fundamental requirements of a given stage in social evolution have deeply influenced ethical growth. ... Instinct ... is bound in the main to subserve and to hinder the needs of the living animal [and to shape] the moral judgement, for if the standard of conduct were so perversely formed as to favour actions tending to the dissolution of the social bond, it would in the end be self-destructive. (Hobhouse, 1925 [first published 1906], pp. 16–17)

But that Keynes would have been well aware in any case of this 'collective' dimension of Darwin's thought, and that this very likely influenced his 'cosmopolitan' position on inter-racial issues, is fairly confidently established by a consideration of his contacts with the Left – among whom such notions were commonplace – at around the time he read the Francis Darwin and Hobhouse volumes. Robert Skidelsky (1983, pp. 239–241) has drawn attention to the powerful influence of the Fabian Society at Cambridge at this time. He mentions – though he cautions against making too much of it – Keynes's speaking with Sidney Webb in February 1911 in support of a motion that 'The progressive reorganisation of Society along the lines of Collectivist Socialism is both inevitable and desirable'.[22] Just how committed Keynes was to such views, and how long they may have stayed with him, is open to question,[23] but however this may be, Keynes would have been familiar with the collectivist interpretations of evolution of the Webbs (see Chapter 2, Note 3) and others. And these often directly utilised Darwin's own writing: The Fabian socialist and eventual Labour M.P. Harry Snell, for instance, besides describing socialism and co-operation as 'in harmony with the forces of social evolution', could quote Darwin's words, 'I use the term Struggle for Existence in a large and metaphorical sense, including dependence of one being on another' in making a case that 'those who knew how to combine for common ends would better serve the progress of the race' (Snell, 1906, 1936).

It is also not unlikely that Keynes would have imbibed some of this kind of thinking from Marshall. In Chapter 2 I gave some examples of Marshall's use of Spencer's 'social organism' idea in *Principles of Economics*, and earlier in the present chapter I cited some instances of Keynes's employment of the same metaphor in his earlier writings. Marshall's 'small s' socialism has been noted by one or two writers (e.g. Henry, 1995), and when one peruses addresses by Marshall such as that to the 1889 Co-operative Congress, one finds them peppered with phrases like the 'whole body' of co-operators (Marshall, 1889, p. 9). In his *Memoir* of Marshall, Keynes (1924) relates how his mentor had sometimes invited prominent labour leaders like Tom Mann and Ben Tillett to spend weekends with him. Both apparently spoke at meetings of the Social Discussion Society at Cambridge, which Marshall founded. There is no question about the deep interest of both these men – and other trade unionists and co-operators of the time (the 1890s) – in evolutionary and 'organicist' models of society.[24]

But Marshall's evolutionism may actually have extended beyond Spencer's conception (notwithstanding little indication of this in *Principles of Economics*, as seen), and in this he may well have learnt something from Mann and other labour leaders. Mann's interest in evolution has already been looked at (Chapter 2, Note 3), and it was noticed that this could take in a more Darwinian understanding of 'the law of mutual inter-dependence'. Tillett, similarly, in a pamphlet published in 1896, spoke of 'superficial people' who talk as if they had really read Darwin 'but who had not the least

notion of what survival means or what fittest means'. We 'have behind us
the force of the altruistic principle', Tillett continued, in our efforts to
'substitute combination for competition'.[25] Perhaps it was in deference to
Marshall's sympathies that Keynes in later years (1913), as editor of *The
Economic Journal*, asked Dennis Robertson to review Emile Pataud and
Emile Pouget's *Syndicalism and the Co-operative Commonwealth*. This has
a Foreword by Mann and a Preface by Kropotkin, both of whom receive
attention by Robertson.[26]

The Left, then, cannot be discounted as having had some bearing on
Keynes's understanding of Darwin. This is further attested to in Keynes's
own review of H.G. Wells's *The World of William Clissold* in *The Nation
and Athenaeum* in January 1927. *Clissold*, Keynes wrote, was a 'great
achievement', an 'abundant outpouring of an ingenious, truthful and generous
spirit' (*CW*, IX, p. 320); but the feature of the novel that is of particular
interest to us here is its frequent appeal to the evolutionary idea from a
socialistic perspective – a favourite theme of Wells (who was an early
member of the Fabian Society and a Labour candidate in the 1923 General
Election). While Wells's 'organic' view of society may not have been
altogether to Keynes's taste (as in his references to the 'racial brain', p. 397),
passages like the following must surely have caught his attention: 'In the last
million years or so our breed has changed ... to habits more social and co-
operative than those of any other animal. ... The emotions of sexual abandon
and maternal and even paternal love as the ape knew them have ... been
seized upon by nature and broadened and utilised for social ends. There is
now in man a desire to serve. There is a pleasure in and a craving for co-
operation and associated action' (Wells, 1926, pp. 89–90). Similarly, in *The
Work, Wealth and Happiness of Mankind*, Wells (1932, pp. 32, 37),
notwithstanding the book's eugenicist elements, notes the biological fact that
'all mankind now living' are members of the same species *Homo sapiens*,
and that 'Nature is a great friend of co-operation; it is a gross libel upon her
to say she is always "red in tooth and claw"'.

G.E. Moore

So Keynes had had considerable exposure to Darwin's ideas, and the various
interpretations of these by both 'Left' and 'Right', by the time he wrote both
'Economic Possibilities for Our Grandchildren' and *The General Theory*, and
he knew what he was talking about when he referred to the 'struggle for
subsistence'. But an additional and perhaps at first sight unlikely source of
Keynes's knowledge of Darwin's theories was the philosopher G.E. Moore,
whose lecture course on 'Modern Ethics' Keynes took as an undergraduate in

Lent term, 1903. As Keynes explained years later in his oft-quoted 'My Early Beliefs' essay (Keynes, 1938b), Moore was an intuitionist, for whom '[n]othing mattered, except states of mind ... chiefly our own'. Or, as Robert Skidelsky has elaborated, for Moore, the only things 'good in themselves' were 'certain states of consciousness' such as 'the pleasures of human intercourse and the enjoyment of beautiful objects' (Skidelsky, 1997, p. 3). Moore saw himself as in the Kantian idealist tradition, and regarded 'intuition' as a capacity of the human mind for direct knowledge of the 'good' and other qualities. As Keynes jotted down in his lecture notes: '*Intuitionism* is doctrine that certain principles need no proof. That we can tell what is right without investigating consequences'.[27] Or as Moore put it himself in his 1903 textbook, *Principia Ethica*:

> We cannot tell what is possible, by the way of proof, in favour of one judgement that 'This or that is good', or against another judgement 'That this or that is bad', until we have recognised what the nature of such propositions must always be. In fact, it follows from the meaning of good and bad, that such propositions are all of them, in Kant's phrase, 'synthetic': they all must rest in the end upon some proposition which must simply be accepted or rejected, which cannot be logically deduced from any other proposition. This result, which follows from our first investigation, may be otherwise expressed by saying that the fundamental principles of Ethics must be self evident. (Moore, 1903, p. 143)

Evolutionary ('materialist') explanations for the origin of ethical systems (as in Darwin's 'Moral Sense' chapter in *The Descent of Man*), then, were of little interest to Moore, as is reflected in Keynes's further lecture notes from Modern Ethics: 'What is origin of moral sentiments and moral judgements? Wholly irrelevant'; and 'Belongs to genetic psychology mainly'. Further down the page, in an evident summary of the 'naturalistic fallacy' with which Moore's name was later to become prominently associated, Keynes recorded:

> Evolutionists – *all* Hedonistic. ... Evolutionists, even when they hold pleasure to be only good, think this done by increase in life (H. Spencer) or preservation of society (L[eslie] Stephen [Virginia Woolf's father]). ... The Evolutionists confused the ethical judgement with the judgement of fact [by] holding that the q. whether a thing leads to a good result is exactly the same as whether the thing tends towards the preservation of the [race] or the preservation of society. ... Consequently they hold that you can ascertain empirically whether the consequences are good. Hedonists tend to confuse with Psychology. The Evolutionists with Sociology, Biology etc.[28]

Just what Keynes made of all of this is uncertain – he does not mention the naturalistic fallacy in 'My Early Beliefs'. But while it is clear from the latter that he and the other Apostles (the Cambridge society to which Keynes was elected in 1903) were much taken with Moore, this does not have to mean that Keynes accepted all that Moore had to say. In any case, there *was* much that Moore said that made a great deal of sense. In this connection, it is interesting that in his copy of *Principia Ethica* Keynes has his heaviest marginal scoring against the following passage:

> Spencer ... constantly uses 'more evolved' as equivalent to 'higher'. But it is to be noted that this forms no part of Darwin's scientific theory. ... The survival of the fittest does *not* mean, as one might suppose, the survival of what is fittest to fulfil a good purpose – best adapted to a good end: at the last, it means merely the survival of the fittest to survive; and the value of the scientific theory, and it is a theory of great value, just consists in showing what are the causes which produce certain biological effects. Whether these effects are good or bad, it cannot pretend to judge. (Moore, 1903, pp. 47–8)

This is a perfectly fair summation of Darwin's position (cf, e.g., Gould, 1983) and, one feels, acknowledged as such by the young Keynes. Whether in spite of his obvious antipathy to evolutionary ethics Moore actually stimulated Keynes into looking into Darwin more closely cannot be determined, but it is at least interesting that within three years of taking Moore's course Keynes was not only purchasing volumes by Leslie Stephen, and L.T. Hobhouse's *Morals in Evolution* (see above), but also *selling* 'three Herbert Spencers'[29] (which author Keynes was describing by the time he wrote his *Memoir* of Alfred Marshall as 'unreadable'[30]).

The New Liberalism

L.T. Hobhouse, besides being the author of *Morals in Evolution* and other works on evolutionary subjects,[31] is also important, of course, as a major theorist in the reformulation of Liberal philosophy in response to the rise of socialism and the Labour Party in the years before and after World War I, as in his book *Liberalism* (1911). As discussed by Michael Freeden (1978) in a chapter on 'Biology, Evolution and Liberal Collectivism' in *The New Liberalism*, much of this philosophising borrowed from the organic models of society of the Webbs and others, and can be described as 'ethical evolutionism' (Freeden, 1978, p. 85). J.A. Hobson, too, made important contributions to these developments (see his *The Crisis of Liberalism*), and given Keynes's respect for Hobson, as illustrated in his lengthy acknowledgment of his and A.F. Mummery's *The Physiology of Industry* in *The General Theory*, and Keynes's deep commitment to Liberalism (see any biography of Keynes, but especially Skildelsky, 1983, 1992; Moggridge, 1992), it is reasonable to suppose that these ideas had some influence on Keynes's thinking. In any event, it is certain that by the 1920s both Keynes and Hobson were speaking at Liberal Summer Schools at Cambridge and elsewhere, and that Keynes, as Robert Skidelsky (1992, p. 224) expresses it, 'was willing to acknowledge that man, processes of production and consumption were "organic" rather than atomistic'.

While it is also true that a contest was taking place at this time between competing visions of Liberalism, as described in Freeden's (1986) *Liberalism Divided*, and that Keynes was one of those attempting to steer the debate more towards specifically economic questions (Robert Skidelsky, conversation with the author), it is perhaps not insignificant that in the typescript for his address, *Am I a Liberal?* given at Cambridge in the summer of 1925, Keynes has the words 'the liberalism of to-day' crossed out and replaced with 'New Liberalism' – the phrase which, as Freeden (1978, 1986) shows, was adopted by that faction interested in evolutionary models of society.[32]

By this time also, Keynes's evolutionary interests were less Spencerian and more in line with Darwin's conception of 'human nature', as discussed in Chapter 2. 'Man', it will be recalled, for Darwin, was a 'social being', a product of aeons of evolution, and it was on this basis, in Keynes's understanding, that 'organic' human society is founded. That Keynes thought this way is not explicitly stated, but it is everywhere assumed. Human nature, however complex, is a given: it cannot be reshaped to suit social theories or economic policies. Mostly Keynes expressed this in psychological terms. In an article on 'The Stabilisation of the European Exchanges' in the *Manchester Guardian Commercial* of 20 April 1922, for example, Keynes spoke of 'deep … psychological causes which are not easily disturbed', and in the *General Theory* he refers to 'habits' as distinct from 'more permanent psychological propensities' (Keynes, 1936, p. 96). On page 91 of *The General Theory* Keynes writes of 'those psychological characteristics of human nature … which … are unlikely to undergo a material change over a short period of time'. By the 1920s Hobson, too, had abandoned the naive organicism of *The Physiology of Industry*, and was writing of the impossibility of 'sudden transformations, either in human nature or the institutions it imposes' (Hobson, 1922, p. 118). It was probably true, Hobson admitted, that the competitive 'struggle for markets' reflected one side of this human nature; nevertheless, there was a widespread belief 'held in common by individualist free traders and by socialists, that industry and commerce are, or should be, essentially processes of human co-operation' (Hobson, 1922, pp. 132–3).

Keynes's 'Intuition'

Just as Alfred Marshall's 'small s' socialism may have had some influence on Keynes's understanding of Darwin, so too may have Marshall's growing interest in human psychology in the latter part of his life. Margaret Schabas (in Mirowski, 1994) has noted Keynes's recollection of Marshall's wish, in his last years, that he had devoted himself more to psychology, and in Keynes's letters at King's College is one from Marshall from early 1922 thanking Keynes for a copy of *A Revision of the Treaty* (with its compelling portraits of some of the main players in European economic affairs), and adding that he was 'inclined to think that the mixture of good and evil ... is universal in human nature'. In his last book, *Money, Credit and Commerce* (Marshall, 1923, p. 260), Marshall, like Hobson, expresses the opinion that 'economic institutions are the products of human nature and cannot change much faster than human nature changes'[33] – a classic statement of the institutionalist position in economic theory, which is now receiving renewed attention (see, e.g., Hodgson, 1988, 1999a; Bryant and Wells, 1998). But whatever the bearing of Marshall's opinions on Keynes's thinking in this respect, it is clear that Keynes had had a long-standing interest in psychology, and that this interest contained significant Darwinian elements.

In 1905 Keynes read psychology for the Civil Service Examination. His notes from this reading contain points such as 'All science goes to show that psychical activity is uniformly accompanied by physical (nervous) activity'; 'Perception is probably aided from the first by definite inherited tendencies'; and, interestingly, in terms of Keynes's earlier exposure to G.E. Moore's ideas, 'Many of our judgements are arrived at *intuitively* [my emphasis], and apart from a process of reasoning'.[34] Such views must surely have enabled Keynes to see Moore's 'self evident' perceptions of 'the good' etc. in a new light, and must have suggested that, rather than evolution being 'irrelevant' to such matters, as Moore held, Darwin's theories could be seen as highly relevant. That is to say, in Darwinian terms, our 'moral sense' may be regarded as a product of evolution. In any case, Keynes's further notes from his reading confirm an evolutionary emphasis in his psychology studies. The subject matter included 'The mental life of lower animals'. Previous examination questions with Keynes's notes include 'Discuss the nature of instinct in animals', 'Discuss different theories of the origin and evolution of purposive action', and 'Does the principle of biological evolution seem to you to throw any informative light on the main problems of philosophy?'[35]

This term 'intuition' is a crucial one, I would suggest, in appreciating the importance of Darwinism for Keynes's economics. John Davis, in *Keynes's Philosophical Development*, attaches considerable significance to the term, but, I believe, in a misconceived sense. According to Davis, Keynes's philosophical development can be seen to be largely a matter of his eventual rejection of Moore's concept of intuition and its replacement with a 'conventionalist' understanding, whereby the term acquired a 'social dimension', becoming a psychological *skill* dependant upon language conventions, as in the later Wittgenstein (Davis, 1994, p. 70). In support of his case Davis cites sentences from *The General Theory* such as that where Keynes refers to the 'psychological expectation of further yield from capital assets', and describes the successful investor on the stock exchange as one whose energies and skills are concentrated upon 'foreseeing changes in the conventional basis of valuation a short time ahead of the general public' (Keynes, 1936, pp. 154, 247, quoted in Davis, 1994, pp. 122, 126–7).

There is something in Professor Davis's argument, but clearly it is not the whole story concerning Keynes's interest in intuition and psychology generally – specifically, Davis's account leaves out Keynes's *own* reference to a Darwinian dimension.

I mentioned above that Keynes had been using expressions like 'deep psychological causes which are not easily disturbed' from at least 1922, and that this language carried over into *The General Theory*, where Keynes speaks of 'those psychological characteristics of human nature', etc. That such expressions suggest the importance of *evolutionary* concepts for Keynes, and are not merely language conventions, is indicated by Fitzgibbons (1988, p. 87), who says that there were, for Keynes, good 'evolutionary reasons' for our thinking the way we do. The passage in Keynes's writing to which Fitzgibbons is referring (see also Skidelsky, 1992, pp. 72–3; Moggridge, 1992, pp. 365–6) occurs in a review by Keynes of the mathematician Frank Ramsey's posthumous *Foundation of Mathematics and other Logical Essays* (Ramsey, 1931, pp. 160–6), in which Ramsey, in an essay on 'Truth and Probability', criticised Keynes's argument in *A Treatise on Probability* (Keynes, 1921) that there existed a level of objective reality in our probability estimations. Such a claim, Ramsey wrote, confuses probability relations, which are arrived at subjectively – and are of 'merely psychological importance' – with 'necessary' logical relations. In response, Keynes wrote that he agreed with Ramsey that there was an element of subjectivity involved, but that nevertheless 'the basis of our degrees of belief – or the *a priori* probabilities, as they used to be called – *is part of our human outfit, perhaps given to us by natural selection*, [and] analogous to our perceptions and memories, rather than to formal logic' (*CW*, X, pp. 338–9, my emphasis).

Keynes is here stating the evolutionary epistemological argument (cf, e.g., Plotkin, 1994) – that we think as we do about the world around us because there have been strong evolutionary pressures to do so: any radical mismatch between the way we think and the way the world is would be rapidly 'selected out'. H.G. Wells put the case succinctly in his 1917 novel *The Soul of a Bishop*: 'Of course there must be a measure of truth in our illusions, a working measure of truth, or the creature would smash itself up and end itself' (Wells, 1917, p. 102). For Keynes, then, 'those psychological characteristics of human nature' were at least partly the product of evolutionary processes; and his understanding of 'intuition' took into account this Darwinian dimension. Thus in *A Treatise on Probability*,[36] Keynes sometimes uses the phrase 'direct knowledge' for intuition. While this phrase may have derived something from Moore's somewhat mysterious 'self-evident' truth, Keynes clearly has in mind a more mundane understanding. Such is outlined in L.T. Hobhouse's chapter on 'Simple Apprehension' in *The Theory of Knowledge* (Hobhouse, 1896), which is in the Bibliography of the *Treatise* and which Keynes's notes show he read around the same time as he read Hobhouse's *Morals in Evolution*.[37] In 'Simple Apprehension', Hobhouse argues for the primacy of sense data and certain innate capacities of the human brain to organise the same, and this could surely at least partly underlie such statements by Keynes in the *Treatise* as 'About our own existence, our own sense data, some logical ideas, and some logical relations, it is usually agreed that we have direct knowledge' (Keynes, 1921, p. 14).

Other sentences in *A Treatise on Probability*, such as 'Inductive processes have formed, of course, at all times a vital, habitual part of the mind's machinery', and '[I]t is not easy to draw the line between conscious memory, unconscious memory or habit, and pure instinct' – or, perhaps, '[O]ur ordinary methods of procedure in inductive argument [tend to] justify common sense' (Keynes, 1921, pp. 14, 217, 261) support, I would suggest, this interpretation. Statements like these also help to illuminate Keynes's allusions to psychology quoted above from *The General Theory* and elsewhere, as well as further instances in the *Treatise* such as '[J]udgements of probability, upon which we depend for almost all our beliefs in matters of experience, undoubtedly depend on a strong psychological propensity in us to consider objects in a particular light' (p. 52), and also such later expressions as in *The Means to Prosperity* (Keynes, 1933, p. 7) where Keynes asks his readers to consider whether his proposals agree with 'the instinctive promptings of ... commonsense'. In answer to Ramsey, Keynes could have referred to some more lines in the *Treatise*, where he argues: '[T]he fact that we ultimately depend upon an intuition need not lead us to suppose that our conclusions have, therefore, no basis in reason, or that they are as subjective in validity as they are in origin' (p. 70). Our intuitions are, for Keynes, 'subjective' in that they are the product of our own minds, but their reliability has been honed through aeons of evolution.

The End of Laissez Faire

One last piece of Keynes's writing in which he refers to Darwinism should now be looked at. In *The End of Laissez-Faire* (Keynes, 1926), as readers will know, Keynes writes in a couple of places (pp. 14, 31): 'The principle of the Survival of the Fittest could be regarded as a vast generalisation of the Ricardian economics', and 'The parallelism between economic *laissez-faire* and Darwinianism, already briefly noted, is now seen, as Herbert Spencer was foremost to recognise, to be very close indeed'. Such words have been seized upon by sociologists of science (e.g., Francis, 1986) to buttress their case that Darwinism is largely a social construction, a projection onto the natural world of the free-market economic ideologies which predominated in nineteenth century Britain (see also Gould, 1980a). However, against the claim that Keynes's words constitute a *rejection* of Darwinism, two points can be made. Firstly, Keynes's reference in *The Nation and Athenaeum* article cited earlier to the 'economic problem, the struggle for subsistence', which has 'always been' the primary problem not only of the human race but also of the 'whole of the biological kingdom' should leave little doubt as to Keynes's firm commitment to the essential truth of the competitive side of Darwin's theory. But secondly, I would suggest that Keynes's words here are carefully chosen. It will be noticed in the first sentence quoted from *The End of Laissez-Faire* that Keynes says that the principle of the 'survival of the fittest' could be regarded as a generalisation of Ricardian economics. This phrase, as I mentioned in my earlier chapter, is in fact not Darwin's but Herbert Spencer's (though, as I explained, it is true that Darwin eventually adopted it), as Keynes would have known from his reading of Darwin's *Life and Letters*.[38] Also, as can be seen, Keynes explicitly refers to *Spencer's* association with laissez faire economics, not Darwin's, restricting himself to the generalised 'Darwinianism'.

Keynes is fairly obviously here criticising laissez faire Social Darwinism, largely a creation of Herbert Spencer's (and like-minded individuals such as Sumner and Kidd – see Depew and Weber, 1995). That this is so is surely indicated on the next page of *The End of Laissez-Faire*, where Keynes describes the theory he is criticising as one depending on 'a variety of unreal assumptions', and following 'not from the actual facts, but from an incomplete hypothesis introduced for the sake of simplicity' (Keynes, 1926, p. 32). Contrast this with Keynes's assessment of *Darwin's* methodology on page 5 of *A Treatise on Probability* (in his first reference to *any* authority in this work): 'When we agree that Darwin gives valid grounds for our accepting his theory of natural selection, we do not simply mean that we are psychologically inclined to agree with him; it is certain that we also intend to convey our belief that we are acting rationally in regarding his theory as probable. We believe that there is some real objective relation between Darwin's evidence and his conclusions, which is independent of the mere fact of our belief'.

Conclusion

A perusal of Keynes's published writings then, attests to his familiarity with and interest in Darwin's ideas, and this is confirmed from an examination of his unpublished letters, notebooks, etc. But it can also be argued Keynes would have had little interest in the abstractions of 'evolutionary economics' described in Chapter 2, abstractions which have a tendency to treat 'the economy' as an autonomous entity, moving under its own laws seemingly almost independently of the human agents which comprise it. Keynes, like Irvine, was interested in *people*, and in what Darwin had to say about what motivates us to behave as we do in the business of making a living. Keynes's eventual loss of interest in Spencer's and Marshall's organic analogies can be seen to reflect his growing interest in 'human nature' throughout his life.[39] It is true that this took in a fascination with eugenics, which many would now regard as eccentric at best. But at the same time, there is ample evidence of Keynes's awareness of other dimensions of Darwin's thought, as was highlighted, for example, in his enthusiasm for some of H.G. Wells's writing. This allowed him to have a more balanced appreciation of Darwin than was the case with many of his contemporaries on either the 'Right' or 'Left' of the ideological spectrum, who emphasised either the competitive or co-operative ('collective') side of Darwin. Keynes was an economist whose views were often seen as falling somewhere between market and socialist economics.[40] It is thus most fitting that this balance can be seen in the evidence of his interest in Darwin.

Notes

*   KCKP refers to King's College Keynes Papers. The catalogue numbers refer to Cox, 1995. *CW* refers to the *Collected Writings of John Maynard Keynes*, published by the Royal Economic Society, 1970–1989.
1.   KCKP, UA/6/15.
2.   Nevertheless, notwithstanding sociobiology's mistakes, such models are not without value. As noted earlier (see Chapter 2, Note 22), writers like Susan Rose-Ackerman have drawn attention to the importance of certain traits, such as 'heroism', in social evolution, and that this needn't be restricted to genetic explanations, as in Wilson. A much earlier student of entomology, Maurice Maeterlinck (see, e.g., his *The Life of the Bee*) was similarly convinced that in humans as well as in other species, 'loyalty, courage ... have always been the

very law of life' (Maeterlinck, 1914, p. 188), whatever the precise mechanism of operation.

3. In an address to the British Association for the Advancement of Science.
4. 'The Present Disorders of the World's Monetary System' (typescript for a series of lectures given by Keynes in Michaelmas Term, 1920). KCKP, UA/6/24/1–66 (quoting p. 27). See also Skidelsky (1992), pp. 45–6.
5. KCKP, UA/6/9/22–3.
6. F. Galton, *Inquiries into Human Faculty and Its Development* (London: Macmillan, 1883).
7. *Eugenics Review*, Vol XXXVIII, No.1 (April 1946), pp. 39–40.
8. KCKP, OC/3/46.
9. KCKP, OC/2/185.
10. This is in Keynes's notes for his talk (KCKP, PS/6/223–4), not in the printed version in the *Eugenics Review* (see Note 7). One specific title mentioned by Keynes is *The Art of Travel*. He doesn't mention Galton's earlier work, *Travels in South Africa*, but if he was telling the literal truth he presumably owned that as well. To provide some balance to perceptions of Galton, who has no doubt suffered from a very bad press in the decades since 1946, it is perhaps worth noting Darwin's reference to some of Galton's observations in this work and elsewhere concerning the apparent survival value of gregariousness in African wild cattle and other species (see Darwin, n.d., p. 477; Galton, 1889, pp. 19, 39).
11. KCKP, OC/4.
12. KCKP, PP/90. Jim Moore, personal communication, 13 April 1998.
13. See G. Darwin (1909). There are a number of photographs of ancient Egyptian monuments in Keynes's papers (KCKP, PP/85/15), taken by Keynes during a holiday in Egypt in 1913. He periodically reviewed books about ancient Egypt and other cultures (e.g. Christopher Dawson's *The Age of the Gods* [Murray, 1926] and Sidney Smith's *Early History of Assyria to 1,000 B.C.* [Chatto & Windus, 1928]; *CW*, XXXVII, pp. 287–91). Keynes was also deeply interested in prehistory, writing in support of efforts to preserve Stonehenge and other sites (Keynes, 1938a), and drawing listeners' attention to anthropological works such as Louis Leakey's *Adam's Ancestors* and Miles Burkitt's *The Old Stone Age* (in a 1936 radio broadcast, *On Reading Books* – KCKP, A/36/35–43). Virginia Woolf was very impressed with Keynes's ability 'to explain flints and the age of man' during a visit to Tilton in August 1935 (Skidelsky, 1992, pp. 509–10), and all in all, it is easy to conclude that these various activities represented different expressions of Keynes's general fascination with human nature and evolution.
14. KCKP, UA/24; *CW*, XXII, pp. 726–7; Richard Darwin Keynes to author, 29 May 1996.
15. J.M. Keynes (1943), 'Leonard Darwin (1850–1943)', *Economic Journal*, 53, 438–9.
16. *New York Times Book Review*, 3 Oct. 1915, p. 352.
17. KCKP, OC/2/13.
18. KCKP, UA/6/9/22–3.
19. G. Keynes to J.M. Keynes, 2 Sept. 1908. KCKP, PP/45/167.
20. KCKP, TP/D/276–86 ('Darwin').
21. KCKP, PP/55.
22. There is a summary of Keynes's speech in Gilbert E. Jackson and Philip Vos, *The Cambridge Union Society, Debates, April 1910–1911* (London: J.M. Dent and Sons, Ltd., 1911), which reads (p. 86): 'Mr Keynes could not at all agree that the previous speaker's [Lord Robert Cecil's] arguments against the efficiency of a socialistic organisation of government were valid. He did not consider that committees were inefficient. It was difficult to believe so when we saw that a great part of the industry of this country was carried on by joint-stock companies, which were a very good example of committee management. The noble Lord had cited Nelson as a shining example of the success of individualism. But

Nelson was certainly an official, a servant of the State, and he was not efficient from motives of material self-interest, but because it pleased him to do his 'job' as well as possible; and the speaker believed that most public men were actuated by the same kind of motive'. In 1913 Keynes had lunch with Beatrice Webb (for whom he had much greater intellectual respect than he had for Sidney), which he described as a 'deep spiritual experience' (Skidelsky, 1983, p. 241 and conversation with the author).

23. It should be mentioned that Athol Fitzgibbons (1988, Chapter. 10) has made a strong case for Keynes's basic sympathies with socialism, and it is perhaps worth noting that as late as 1924 he could sketch an article titled 'Prolegomena to a New Socialism'. Keynes's sketch (KCKP, L/24) appears to have eventually become his printed lecture, *The End of Laissez-Faire*.

24. Margot Asquith to J.M. Keynes, n.d.. KCKP, EJ/6/4/70. In 1893–4 Marshall and Mann were fellow commissioners in a Royal Commission on Labour. See Groenewegen (1995), and *Fourth Report from the Royal Commission on Labour with Minutes and Digest of Evidence before the Commission Sitting as a Whole, Appendix and Indices, 1893–94* (Irish Universities Press series of British Parliamentary Papers – Industrial Relations, Vol. 43, Shannon, Ireland: Irish Universities Press, 1970).

25. B. Tillett, *Environment and Character* (Christchurch, N.Z.: 'Lyttleton Times' Press, 1898), pp. 1, 9. (Tillett's pamphlet was originally published by the Labour Press, Manchester, in 1896.)

26. D. Robertson, review of E. Pataud and E. Pouget (1913), *Syndicalism and the Co-operative Commonwealth*, Oxford: The New International Publishing Co., in the *Economic Journal*, **23**, (Sept. 1913), pp. 420–2. While clearly unsympathetic to the book's philosophy, Robertson nevertheless describes it as a 'refreshing' work, insofar as 'At last we are told with some approach to definiteness what two, at least, of those who profess and call themselves Syndicalists really do want, and how they propose to get it'. Robertson noted that 'Tom Mann and "grand old comrade Kropotkin" ... appear to reserve the right to differ on ... important points'.

27. KCKP, UA/1/1.

28. Ibid.

29. KCKP, PP/57/1/1.

30. Keynes (1924), p. 318.

31. See, e.g., his *The Theory of Knowledge* (which Keynes also owned [KCKP, TP/D]), *Development and Purpose* and *Mind in Evolution*.

32. KCKP, PS/3/11–30(27). The outcome of these gatherings was a book, *Britain's Industrial Future* (Ernest Benn Ltd, 1928), whose authorship, according to a list of names after the title page, included Keynes, Lloyd George and Hobhouse. The book is said to draw upon the 'great researches of Mr. and Mrs. Sidney Webb' (p. 78). It notes, under the chapter heading 'Business Efficiency', '...it is true, we think, that there is much remediable inefficiency in British industry; and that particularly in the long-established industries there is often a wrong tradition – individualism instead of co-operation, secretiveness instead of publicity, neglect of marketing, indifference and often hostility to research' (p. 127). This is reminiscent of H.G. Wells's *Clissold* and *New Worlds for Old*. Indeed Keynes wrote to Wells about the book in January 1928 (Skidelsky, 1992, p. 265). Robert Skidelsky (1992, pp. 265–7) notes that Keynes's original draft for a contribution on 'The Financial and Industrial Structure of the State', which was intended to provide a general framework for the whole book, and which suggested that '"evolution" was tending to convert private companies into public or semi-official boards', was largely omitted from the final version.

33. Marshall to Keynes, 14 Jan. 1922. KCKP, RP/4/29. Marshall's point in this letter, and in *Money, Credit and Commerce*, is very important, and pivotal for the arguments in this and in my earlier chapter. A few pages further on (p. 264) in

MCC Marshall writes: 'Egyptian bas-reliefs suggests that the *individual* man of the present time is not very much more capable, physically and intellectually, than were many of his ancestors thousands of years ago'. (To which he adds: 'But in the modern age men *collectively* are able to compel Nature so to work in their service that the average material well-being of a vast population is far higher than was possible formerly ... This result is due mainly to organisation' – which calls to mind the arguments of Blake et al. [1966] cited in Chapter 2) To his first sentence Marshall attaches the following footnote: 'This notion was impressed on me by my father in the British Museum seventy years ago'. As indicated above (Note 13), Keynes, too, was interested in ancient Egypt and other early cultures (see also *A Treatise on Money* [Keynes, 1930], Vol. II, pp. 150–1) and noted in the MS for 'Economic Possibilities for Our Grandchildren': 'The absence of important technical inventions between the prehistoric age and comparatively modern times is truly remarkable. Almost everything which really matters and which the world possessed at the commencement of the modern age was already known to man at the dawn of history. Language, fire, the same domestic animals which we have today, wheat, barley, the vine and the olive, selected and evolved for human use, the plough, the wheel, the oar, the sail, leather, linen and cloth, bricks and pots, gold and silver, copper, tin and lead – and iron was added to the list before 1000 BC. – money, banking, statecraft, mathematics, astronomy, and religion. There is no record of when we first possessed these things. At some epoch before the dawn of history – perhaps even in one of the comfortable intervals before the last ice age – there must have been an era of progress and invention comparable to that in which we live today'. (KCKP, PS/4/36–7).

Nothing discovered since Keynes penned these lines (in 1928) substantially affects his argument. Specialists may disagree about precisely when modern humans replace Neanderthals in the fossil record, though the general consensus seems to be by around 34,000 years BP (Before Present) (see R. Leakey, 1995, and Lewin, 1998), but apart from one or two anthropologists (e.g. Robert Foley of King's College, Cambridge, who appears to believe that some kind of genetic change in humans is needed to explain the beginnings of agriculture), and seemingly most sociobiologists (who want to explain everything by genetics), most authorities are agreed that our species, *Homo Sapiens*, with all our collective capacity for dealing with our environment and attending to our economic needs, had biologically evolved by the time of, say, the execution of the cave paintings at Altamira, Lascaux and elsewhere (from around 20,000 years BP – see Laming, 1959). That is to say, all important human 'evolution' since that time has been a cultural phenomenon – in at least some sense a 'Lamarckian' rather than a Darwinian process (but see Part II of this volume). Any talk of 'macromutations' etc. in economics must be in a purely metaphorical sense. Interestingly, one of the first people to recognise the antiquity of modern humans was Alfred Russel Wallace, the co-founder of 'Darwinism' (he coined the word – see his 1890 book by that name). In 1878 – the year before the discovery of the Altamira paintings – Wallace wrote: 'The most important difference between [modern] man and such of the lower animals as most nearly approach him is undoubtedly in the bulk of the development of his brain, as indicated by the form and capacity of the cranium ... . Yet the oldest-known crania (those of the English and Cro-Magnon caves) show no marks of degradation. The former ... is (to use the words of Prof. [T.H.] Huxley) "a fair average human skull". ... The latter are still more remarkable, being unusually large and well formed. Dr. Pruner Bey states that they surpass the average of modern European skulls in capacity, while their symmetrical form without any trace of prognathism, compares favourably ... with many civilised nations of modern times. ... This conclusion is supported and enforced by the nature of many works of art found even in the oldest cave-dwellings, such as the numerous carvings and drawings representing a variety of animals, including horses, reindeer, and even a mammoth, executed with considerable skill on bone, reindeer-horns, and mammoth tusks' (Wallace, 1878, pp. 286–7). Louis Leakey, in *Adam's Ancestors*, one of the books recommended by Keynes, refers to 'the post-Mousterian Palaeolithic cultures of Europe, which [are] known to be made by men of *Homo sapiens* type' (p. 113) – a view recently reiterated at a conference in Gibraltar (see *Nature*, 8 Oct. 1998, pp. 539–40).

34. KCKP, UA/4/2.
35. Ibid.
36. This is an expansion of Keynes's (1908) Fellowship dissertation. See Fitzgibbons (1988), and also O'Donnell (1989).
37. KCKP, TP/D.
38. F. Darwin (1887), Vol. III, pp. 45–6.
39. One can of course argue that this interest went further than Darwinism, taking in the views of earlier philosophers, such as in David Hume's *Treatise on Human Nature* (which is in Keynes's library). Yet such works can also be seen to have provided much of the raw material for Darwin's theories. Hume's volumes, for example (which in fact Darwin cites – Darwin n.d., p. 480), contain paragraphs like this one: "Tis evident, that sympathy, or the communication of passions, takes place amongst animals, no less than among men. Fear, Anger, Courage and other affections are frequently communicated from one animal to another, without their knowledge of that cause ... Everyone has observed how much more dogs are animated when they hunt in a pack, than when they pursue their game apart; and 'tis evident this can proceed from nothing but from sympathy' (Hume, 1739, Vol. 2, pp. 214–5).
40. In an interesting paper, my attention to which was drawn by Robert Skidelsky, Paul Krugman (1996), who describes himself as a 'neo-Keynesian', takes a strongly individualist position which is a useful counter to some of the more overly enthusiastic semi-socialist versions of Keynes's ideas currently on offer, as reflected, for example, in the recent headline in the *Australian Financial Review* (29 Oct. 1998) which reads 'Leftist leaders lean backwards to J.M. Keynes' – a reference to the recent election of socialist politicians like Gerhard Schroeder in Germany. Krugman cautions that 'Economics is about what *individuals* do [Krugman's emphasis]: not classes, not "correlations of forces", but individual actors' – which is reminiscent of R.F. Irvine's argument, cited in Chapter 2, that in economics 'the centre of interest must always and everywhere be men ... red blooded men and women, driving through as best they could' (and indeed reminds one of Keynes's warning against the over-use of abstractions quoted in Note 29 to that chapter). Krugman discusses the writings of important contemporary evolutionary theorists such as John Maynard Smith and William Hamilton, and emphasises that even at the 'collective' level of evolution it is the individual organism that is the focus of selection. At the same time however, Krugman perhaps goes a little too far in his efforts to provide a corrective, and overstates the genetic component ('evolutionary theory [is] in some circumstances best thought of as genes "trying" to propagate as many copies of themselves as possible'). It is interesting, though, that in the final paragraphs of his paper Krugman leaves open the possibility of the inadequacy of a strictly genetic explanation of 'altruistic' behaviour, as in this example: 'When a bird sees a predator, it issues a warning cry that puts itself at risk but may save its neighbours (see also Chapter 2, Note 9); the reason this behaviour "works", we believe, is that many of those neighbours are likely to be relatives, and thus the bird may enhance its "inclusive fitness". But why doesn't the bird issue a warning only its relatives can hear? Well, we just suppose that isn't possible'. On Keynes's positioning somewhere between market and socialist economics, see also Bortis (1998).

PART II

6. Is Social Evolution Lamarckian or Darwinian?

Geoffrey M. Hodgson[1]

Is social, economic or cultural evolution 'Lamarckian' in some literal or metaphorical sense? Leading economists such as Jack Hirshleifer (1977), Herbert Simon (1981), Richard Nelson and Sidney Winter (1982), Friedrich Hayek (1988), Christopher Freeman (1992) and J. Stanley Metcalfe (1993) have claimed that it is (Hayek and Simon are both Nobel Laureates). Other prominent social theorists such as Karl Popper (1972), William McKelvey (1982), John Gray (1984), and Robert Boyd and Peter Richerson (1985) have likewise accepted that social evolution takes a 'Lamarckian' form. Is this widespread view correct?

If so, a possible problem arises. The prevailing wisdom in biology is that Lamarckian ideas are untenable, at least in the biotic context. This raises a question of theoretical inconsistency between biology and the social sciences. Can we be Lamarckians in the social sciences and Darwinians in biology? Is there a contradiction here? Can we be Protestants and Catholics at the same time?

Answers to these questions depend on the precise definitions of the terms involved. What does Lamarckism mean? Lamarckism is typically associated with the principal proposition that acquired characters can be inherited. Accordingly, variations of type occur largely through adaptations to the environment rather than random mutations. This meaning of Lamarckism shall be adopted here.

The term 'Darwinism' is no less problematic. It is often associated with the denial of the central Lamarckian proposition. However, detailed examination of its usage reveals a wider and more accommodating meaning. The answer to the central question of this essay depends in large part in the clarification of what is meant by 'Darwinian'.

The received wisdom that social evolution is 'Lamarckian' has seemingly received a major theoretical challenge from modern Darwinists. In the early 1980s Richard Dawkins (1983) coined the term 'Universal Darwinism'. Subsequently, the idea that some basic Darwinian principles apply to a very wide range of phenomena, from psychology to cosmology, has been taken up by a number of authors. If 'Universal Darwinism' applies to the social sciences as well, then this may be seen as an objection to lingering ideas of

'Lamarckian evolution' in that sphere. In fact, David Hull (1982) had already rejected some prominent versions of 'Lamarckian' social evolution on theoretical grounds. His position was later endorsed by Daniel Dennett (1995, p. 355n.) in an influential and popular work. As a result of these developments, the term 'Lamarckian' may seem to be erroneous or redundant in the social as well as in the biological domain.

Some theorists attempt to avoid this question by arguing that social or economic change has little or nothing to do with biological evolution. Several social scientists have argued that biological analogies or metaphors are of little relevance to the social sciences.[2] From the other side of the boundary, prominent natural scientists such as Stephen Jay Gould (1996) have protested against any export of biological metaphors or theories to the social domain. Some possible combinations of views are presented in Table 6.1.

Table 6.1: Some possible and prominent doctrinal combinations.

Combination	(1)	(2)	(3)	(4)
Biotic Evolution	Darwinian	Darwinian	Darwinian	Lamarckian
Social or Cultural Evolution (literally or metaphorically)	Darwinian	Lamarckian	Neither Darwinian nor Lamarckian	Lamarckian
Prominent Proponents[1]	Dennett Hull	Boyd, Gray Hayek Hirschleifer Metcalfe McKelvey Nelson Popper Richerson Winter	Gould A. Rosenberg Schumpeter Witt	Spencer

1. In some cases the position of a proponent may be simplified or interpolated. For example, social theorists do not always make their position on Darwinism in biological evolution clear, and in some cases the adherence to 'Lamarckism' in social evolution is indecisive or ambiguous. The primary purpose of this table is to show the diversity of apparently conflicting views, not to investigate each individual's conception in detail.

Clearly, Table 6.1 does not exhaust all the possibilities. If there are three options in each domain – Darwinian, Lamarckian and neither – then there are nine possible combinations overall, but we do not need to show them all. The table shows four prominent stances. With regard to social evolution, no distinction is made in the table between the literal or metaphorical adoption of an evolutionary theory. To some extent, this additional distinction is explored later in this article. Overall, even if we regard Lamarckism as untenable in biology (thus excluding combination (4)), there are still remaining and important differences of view to be resolved.

There is another reason why Table 6.1 does not describe the many possible variants. In both biology and economics the concept of self-organisation has become popular, and some would claim that it constitutes a new approach or paradigm (Depew and Weber, 1995; Hayek, 1988; Kauffman, 1993; Prigogine and Stengers, 1984; Witt, 1997). This leaves the question open whether self-organised systems are themselves objects of selection in some broader, phylogenetic evolutionary process. It is beyond the scope of this article to discuss this further. We simply note that Kauffman, for one, promotes such a possibility (Lewin, 1992, pp. 42–3). For him, self-organisation is a precondition of natural selection. But he still has natural selection in his story. Evolution is 'emergent order honored and honed by selection' (Kauffman, 1993, p. 644). The question, then, is what kind of selection process we are talking about? In this essay we attempt to answer this question in the social and cultural domain.

Some people fail to ask this question. Consider combination (3) in Table 6.1. Notably, some dismissals of biological metaphors in the social sciences are based on misunderstandings. For instance, some social theorists suggest that any flirtation with biology would place the theorist on the slippery slope to biological reductionism, in which social phenomena would be explained *entirely* in biological terms. True, biological reductionism is a flawed social doctrine, and is widely regarded as open to ideological abuse. But that is not necessarily what is being proposed.

Much of the exploration is at the level of analogy or metaphor. It is not fully appreciated that all sciences embody metaphor, and often, perhaps unavoidably, these metaphors have a naturalistic ambience (Black, 1962; Hesse, 1966; Klamer and Leonard, 1994; Lewis, 1996; Maasen, 1995). Furthermore, it is not always understood that such metaphors are not only unavoidable but also necessarily inexact – otherwise they would not be metaphors. Such misunderstandings conspire with the now-waning, twentieth-century orthodoxy in the social sciences that all connections between biology and the social sciences, and between biotic and social phenomena, should be broken. A denial that social evolution is Lamarckian or Darwinian is sometimes a coded way of saying to any biologist: 'get thee beyond the social sciences; thou hast nothing to add to our story'.[3]

Inescapably, however, social phenomena are situated in nature, and involve human beings. Humans, in turn, are the outcome of processes of biological evolution, just like other species. Human consciousness and intentionality are also an outcome of biological evolution. The social and the economic worlds interact with the natural, and sometimes with deleterious effects on the ecosystem. On the other hand, it can be accepted straightaway that the social sciences address properties and phenomena not found at the biological level. Consequently, the social sciences are not reducible to biology or ecology. But that does not mean that we can rest content with theories in one domain that are inconsistent with those in another. The specificity of some social properties is not an excuse to sever all connections with the biotic domain. Indeed, given current concerns about the possible damage to nature caused by human economic activity, it would be wise to maintain and explore these interconnections.

This raises the question of the compatibility or otherwise of theories of social or economic evolution with the accepted understanding of the processes of biological evolution. One of these questions is whether social evolution is Lamarckian. If so, what are the units and mechanisms of social evolution involved?

It will be shown that, contrary to widespread opinion, even in mainstream biology a limited version of Lamarckism is consistent with a modern and full-blooded Darwinism. Furthermore, some fully Darwinian processes may appear to have Lamarckian characteristics at another level. The Universal Darwinist position of David Hull (1982) does not undermine this proposition. While Hull rejects both literal and metaphorical Lamarckism in social evolution this is centred on the meme concept and the use of ideas or beliefs as the analogue of the gene. It thus has limited generality. When habit is seen as an alternative analogue to the gene in the social domain, a limited notion of Lamarckian social evolution is consistent with Darwinian principles.

Some Philosophical and Terminological Preliminaries

Emphatically, in asking whether social evolution is Lamarckian or Darwinian, it is not being proposed that all sciences can or should be reduced to one. It is not being proposed that biology can be reduced to physics, as suggested by some molecular biologists. It is also not being proposed that the social sciences can be reduced to biology, as some extreme sociobiologists have suggested. Complete explanatory reduction of one level to another 'lower' level is ruled out in principle, in part because of problems of complexity and intractability (Wimsatt, 1980; Hodgson, 1993). As Popper (1974, p. 260) has argued: 'hardly any major reduction in science has ever been *completely* successful: there is almost always an unresolved residue left by even the most successful attempts at reduction'. Especially in the real and complex world, a central problem with reductionism is analytical intractability. Attempts to explain one level entirely in terms of another inevitably involve oversimplification.

Reductionism, in which all the phenomena at one level are explained entirely in terms of those of another, is impossible and untenable. But this does not mean that some phenomena cannot be explained in terms of entities at a lower level. Indeed reductive explanations of this type are essential to science. But reduction and reductionism are not the same thing. Reductionism involves the injunction that everything at one level should be explained in terms of another. Examples of reductionism are the views that all social phenomena should be explained entirely in terms of individual volitions, or entirely in terms of the biological characteristics of the individuals involved, or that biology should be reduced to chemistry, or to physics.

Dennett's (1995, pp. 80–3) condemnation of the sin of 'greedy reductionism' thus creates confusion, because reductionism by its very nature is gluttonous. According to Dennett, those that are guilty of this sin 'underestimate the complexities, trying to skip whole layers or levels of theory in their rush to fasten everything securely and neatly to the foundation' (p. 82). However, such persons are not simply guilty of the sin of greed, but also of haste and sloppiness. All reductionism is greedy. Recklessness is an optional extra to add to this generally unsuccessful credo.

There is an important and additional reason for ruling out the reductionist doctrine that everything must be explained in terms of its constituent units. This is the existence of emergent properties.[4] Crucially, reductionism is countered by the phenomenon of emergence. As Tony Lawson (1997, p. 176) has explained: 'an entity or aspect is said to be *emergent* if there is a sense in which it has arisen out of some "lower" level, being conditioned by and dependent upon, but not predictable from, the properties found at the lower level'.

An example of an emergent property is colour. Colour derives from the properties of atoms and molecules. However, carbon atoms are not black, sulphur atoms are not yellow and a single copper oxide molecule is not green. Colour is an emergent property of these entities, just as a 'social atmosphere' is a property of a gathering of people. 'Self-organising' systems also display properties that are not found in their components (Prigogine and Stengers, 1984; Kauffman, 1993). We cannot deduce the emergent property from the constituent elements of the phenomenon. By this argument, we find in the social domain properties that are not explicable in terms of biology or physics. This means that the social sciences have a degree of autonomy from the natural.

Crucially, the concept of emergence is necessary to sustain any account of distinctively cultural evolution, such as in memetics, dual inheritance theory and so on.[5] Why is this so? The concept of meme, like that of the dual inheritance or coevolution of genes and culture, depends crucially on imitation. But how is imitation itself explained? A true reductionist would have to attempt to explain acts of imitation in terms of the behavioural dispositions in the biological genes. If they are so explicable then the basic idea of cultural evolution must be abandoned, for the simple reason that the notion of culture dissolves into its constituent biotic or other elements. There would be no barrier to the reductionist imperative that imitation and culture must themselves be explained in terms of biology. In general, however, such explanations prove to be too complex and intractable. In this case, does this mean that the scientific project of explanation must be abandoned? Fortunately, with the concept of emergence, science may proceed, by focusing on emergent properties at higher levels. The very idea of a social science that is not itself reducible to biology, depends upon a notion of social evolution that can proceed without necessarily changing the human genes.[6] On the basis of their emergent properties, irreducible features of culture can be retained. Accordingly, a notion of cultural evolution can be sustained.

However, the importance of the concept of emergence to social science in general, and to theories of cultural evolution in particular, is not sufficiently appreciated. The concept is hardly touched upon in the literature on both cultural inheritance and memetics. Nevertheless, to put it bluntly: without the concept of emergent properties there is no possibility of any autonomous social science that is consistent with scientific understanding in the physical and biological sciences. Emergent properties endow the autonomous categories of the social science with their reality and meaning. Without emergent properties in the social domain, social science becomes reducible to biology.[7]

The existence of emergent properties undermines biological and other forms of reductionism. However, it gives no excuse for the opposite error: that is, to sever all connections between biology and the social sciences. We observe an interconnected reality outside ourselves. It involves many elements, including physical matter, living organisms and human relations. Different sciences address different levels or parts of this reality. Nevertheless, theories and explanations at one level must be consistent with those at another. Social phenomena are not explicable in terms of the laws of physics. But they must be consistent with those laws. Similarly, biology is unable to explain crucial social phenomena. But that does not mean that we can ignore the processes of evolution or ecological constraints. Emergent properties give no escape from what we may term as the Principle of Consistency: explanations in one domain have to be consistent with explanations in another, despite the examination of different properties and the deployment of different concepts.

Accordingly, the question of the Lamarckian or Darwinian nature of social evolution cannot be avoided. However, both Lamarckism and Darwinism are somewhat plastic terms, without unanimity of definition. Let us first attempt to delineate what is meant here by the term 'Lamarckism'. First, it is not necessary to maintain that 'the biology of Lamarck' and 'Lamarckism' are the same thing; just as the term 'Keynesian' does not always, nor even typically (Leijonhufvud, 1968), comply with 'the economics of Keynes'. For much of the twentieth century, 'Darwinism' has been seen as a theory opposed to the 'Lamarckian' doctrine of the inheritance of acquired characters. If that is the case then Darwin himself was not a 'Darwinian'. In the *Origin of Species* and elsewhere, Darwin (n.d., pp. 63, 104, 185) repeatedly considered the possibility of the inheritance of acquired characters. Keynes, it could be said, was not a Keynesian; and Darwin himself was not a strict Darwinian in an overly-restrictive but widely-used modern ('neo-Darwinian') sense.

Having made this point, we are not required to do a detailed textual exegesis of the writings of Jean Baptiste de Lamarck.[8] It shall simply be established that Lamarck believed in the inheritance of acquired characters. Indeed, in his *Zoological Philosophy* of 1809 he elevated this notion into a 'law', writing, with emphasis as in the original:

> *All the acquisitions or losses wrought by nature on individuals, through the influence of the environment in which their race has been placed, and hence through the influence of the predominant use or permanent disuse of any organ; all these are preserved by reproduction to the new individuals which arise, provided that the acquired modifications are common to both sexes, or at least to the individuals which produce the young* (Lamarck, 1984, p. 113).

Although Lamarck was not the first to promote this idea, and was far from alone in doing so, 'Lamarckism' in common usage today generally involves one principal proposition: that the inheritance of acquired characters is possible and significant.

Note also the importance of 'the influence of the environment' in Lamarck's conception. Essentially, Lamarck's notion of evolution is driven by environmental changes rather than by the (genetic) variety within a population. In Lamarckism, organisms adjust continuously as if attempting to reach harmony with their environment. On this point the contrast with Darwin is clear. Lamarck argued that variation was a function of the environment, but for Darwin 'variation was present first, and the ordering activity of the environment ("natural selection") followed afterwards' (Mayr, 1982, p. 354). For Lamarck, the environment was the key agent of change.

In contrast, Darwin developed the view that intergenerational change resulted from a combination of renewed variation and environmental selection. For Darwin, variety is the evolutionary fuel. Nevertheless, as we shall see below, there are fully Darwinian theories that see behavioural adaptations as driving some evolutionary processes. There is nothing in Darwinism that necessarily commits us to seeing variation as entirely 'random' in origin. Whether its source is haphazard or guided in some way will depend on the circumstances, and will be a matter of empirical investigation rather than doctrinal conflict.

A question within Lamarckism is the role of intention or volition in driving the presumed adaptations to the environment. This raises the issue of the causal status of intentionality or will. The position of Lamarck himself is far from clear on this question. In some of his writings he stressed the role of volition in causing adaptations. In many passages it is excluded or downplayed. Furthermore, as Ernest Boesiger (1974) argues, Lamarck was a materialist rather than a causal dualist: he saw intention or volition as rooted in material causes. However, the compatibility or otherwise of human purpose with physical or materialistic causality would require full-length discussion in its own right. Hence we shall address questions of will or purpose only tangentially, or when they are called for directly. The term 'Lamarckism' here will be primarily associated with the proposition that acquired characters can be inherited.

Particularly from a historical perspective, the identification of the essence of 'Darwinism' is no less problematic (Hull, 1985; Depew and Weber, 1995). Later in this essay an attempt will be made to identify Darwinism in terms of some core characteristics. It will be argued that Darwinism involves a detailed, causal, step-by-step, understanding of evolution based on the features of variation, inheritance and selection. This causal schema is the central element that links Darwin and the modern Darwinians. Darwinian evolution occurs when there is some replicating entity that makes imperfect copies of itself, and these do not have equal potential to survive. The genetic constitution of that replicating entity is known as the 'genotype'. The characteristics of the organism are the 'phenotype'.

At the core of Darwin's theory is an insistence on causal explanation. If organisms are volitional, then Darwinism would require that volition itself has to be explained in evolutionary terms (Hodgson, 1999c). Darwinism attempts to provide a detailed explanation of the evolution of complex phenomena, without recourse to any *deus ex machina*.

In addition, some biologists go further, and associate Darwinism with the denial of the possibility of the inheritance of acquired characters. This combined doctrine is often referred to as 'neo-Darwinism'. However, as noted above, Darwin himself presumed such a Lamarckian possibility. It is thus rather restrictive to associate Darwin's name with the denial of a doctrine that he repeatedly entertained.

There are further reasons for adopting a broad rather than a narrow definition of Darwinism. These are elaborated later below, but we can make the point briefly here. When Dawkins and others use terms like 'Universal Darwinism', they do not in principle exclude the possibility of the inheritance of acquired characters, even if it is absent from biotic life on Earth. The empirical discovery of some acquired character inheritance would not be seen by them as a refutation of Darwinism. What they would insist is that the Darwinian explanation of evolution – based on inheritance, variation and selection – is more compelling and complete than any of its rivals.

In his attack on Lamarckism, August Weismann (1893) proposed a 'barrier' between the organism and (what we now call) its genes. Such a barrier would rule out the Lamarckian inheritance of acquired characters. For the reasons given above, it is best not to build the Weismann doctrine into the definition of 'Darwinism' used here. As elaborated in more detail below, Darwinism is defined here as a broader doctrine, involving variation, inheritance and selection, and insisting on step-by-step causal explanations of evolutionary processes. The word 'Weismannism' can be taken to mean the denial of the possibility of the inheritance of acquired characters. The Weismannian version of Darwinism is described as 'neo-Darwinism'. The three definitions to be used here are summarised in Table 6.2 below.

Table 6.2: Definitions of three doctrines

Term	Definition
Darwinism	A causal theory of evolution in complex or organic systems, involving the inheritance of genotypic instructions by individual units, a variation of genotypes, and a process of selection of the consequent phenotypes according to their fitness in their environment.
Lamarckism	A doctrine admitting the possibility of the (genotypic) inheritance of acquired (phenotypic) characters by individual organisms in evolutionary processes.
Weismannism (or neo-Darwinism)	A doctrine denying the possibility of the (genotypic) inheritance of acquired (phenotypic) characters by individual organisms in evolutionary processes.

The modern neo-Darwinism conception of evolution is portrayed in Figure 6.1 below.[9]

Figure 6.1: Neo-Darwinian (Weismannian) evolution

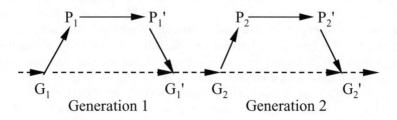

In Figure 6.1, G_1 represents the population of genotypes in the first generation. These genotypes instruct the formation of the population of phenotypes P_1. These phenotypes interact and mate. Some die. The surviving adult population is P_1'. Associated with this surviving population is the revised gene-pool G_1'. They give birth to the next generation, with a sexually recombined, and possibly also mutated, population of genotypes G_2. The whole process repeats, indefinitely. The solid lines indicate the causal relationships of organism development (ontogeny), natural selection (phylogeny) and so on. The broken lines indicate the persistence of genetic information through time within the 'vehicles' of the organisms. The genetic information may alter along the course of the broken line, but, according to the Weismann doctrine, only as a result of the differential survival and alteration of the population of phenotypes.

Figure 6.2: Lamarckian evolution

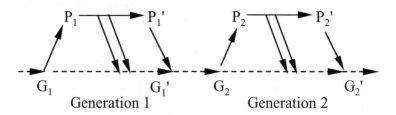

Figure 6.2 illustrates the Lamarckian doctrine of the inheritance of acquired characters, again cast in a modern framework. (Lamarck, like Darwin, was unaware of the nature of the genes.) Again, the symbols G_i, G_i', P_i and P_i' refer to the pool of genotypes and phenotypes in the population.

Lamarckism presumes that characters acquired during the development of the phenotype – from P_i to P_i' – may alter the genetic information by other than differential survival of a population of phenotypes. The twin arrows indicate the supposed Lamarckian causal connection from phenotype to genotype. The result is that Lamarckian evolution can result in significantly greater genetic change, from G_i to G_i'. Genetic change can result not simply from differential survival through natural selection but also through the inheritance of acquired characters. This also can result in more significant genotypical and phenotypical changes from generation to generation. Hence Lamarckian evolution can be much 'faster' than the Weismann doctrine would allow.

Darwinism and Lamarckism in Biology

The basic Darwinian principles – of variation, inheritance and selection – have been applied with considerable persuasiveness and explanatory success. Darwin's theory was not primarily about destinations or outcomes, but a causal theory of the process of evolution itself. What makes the Darwinian approach so powerful is its concern with the detailed, step-by-step, and 'algorithmic' explanations of causal processes.[10]

Of course, most modern biologists reject the possibility of the inheritance of acquired characters in the biotic realm. A major problem for Lamarckism in biology is to render the inheritance of acquired characters consistent with what is known about the genetic code. There are good reasons why organisms have evolved in such a way that their acquired characters are very unlikely to lead to an alteration of their genes. The genetic coding has to be protected from most outside influences. Otherwise the valuable genetic information – the product of millions of years of struggle, testing and evolution – would get contaminated or lost. For this reason the genetic information has to be largely inert and unreactive. It is argued that this is a reason why the Weismann barrier has evolved. The biologist Conrad Waddington (1969, p. 369) later made a similar point about the preservation of the genetic code: 'If it was capable of being changed by all sorts of environmental influences, of the kind which exert natural selection on the organisms, it would soon be reduced to a jibbering nonsense'.

To make Lamarckism work, acquired characters must be inherited in the genetic code, without chaotic damage to it. The DNA program would have to be changed in a meaningful and effective way to reflect the characters acquired, so that they could be passed on to the next generation. This presumes that the environment acts like an expert computer software redesigner, somehow understanding the complex interconnections between each piece of coding. Such a degree of detailed, complicated and fortuitous reprogramming is unlikely to happen in the haphazard turmoil of nature.

However, 'Lamarckism' remains of interest among small groups of biologists. For instance, there is a minority view that the inheritance of acquired characters may be possible in a restricted set of circumstances, such as the transfer of acquired immunities from mother to child (Steele, 1979; Ho and Saunders, 1984; Jablonka et al, 1992; Steele et al, 1998). It is not the job of the social scientist to adjudicate in this debate. Biologists themselves will have to sort this matter out. It is a matter of causal explanation and expert empirical enquiry into real phenomena. The social scientist would reasonably take an interest in this investigation, but she does not have to place any reputational bets on the scientific outcome.

In contrast, the more general theoretical and philosophical presuppositions of Lamarckism or Darwinism should be subject to close scrutiny by the social scientist. Some of the problems involved do not depend upon the precise mechanisms of reproduction that we find in Earthly life forms, based on DNA. It is at this general philosophical and theoretical level that consistency across the social and biological domains must be obtained.

Let us consider some further problems at this theoretical level. Lamarckians assume that the source of new characteristics, that are acquired and then passed on, is the organism's adaptation to its environment. Richard Dawkins (1983, 1986) explores a problem with this Lamarckian assumption. He writes: 'It is all very well inheriting acquired characteristics, but not all acquired characteristics are improvements. Indeed, the vast majority of them are injuries' (Dawkins, 1986, p. 299). It is necessary to explain why disadvantageous acquired characters do not cumulate into extinction. It is also necessary to explain why some acquired characters are improvements.

For example, we acquire thicker skin on our hands and feet because we put these surfaces of the body to greater use. The Darwinian explanation of this is as follows:

> Skin that is subject to wear and tear gets thicker because natural selection in the ancestral past has favoured those individuals whose skin has happened to respond to wear and tear in an advantageous way. ... The Darwinian maintains that the only reason even a minority of acquired characters are improvements is that there is an underpinning of past Darwinian selection. In other words, the Lamarckian theory can explain adaptive improvement in evolution only by, as it were, riding on the back of the Darwinian theory. (Dawkins, 1986, p. 300)

Dawkins's argument is persuasive. Essentially, Lamarckism lacks an explanation as to why there is a propensity to inherit improvements rather than impairments. But note: if Lamarckism is simply defined as the admission of the possibility of the inheritance of acquired characters, then Dawkins's argument does not refute Lamarckism. What Dawkins shows is that some Darwinian mechanism of natural selection is a necessary complement of any viable Lamarckian theory. Darwinism and Lamarckism would thus dovetail together. However, as Dawkins demonstrates, the complementarity is asymmetrical. Any viable Lamarckism requires Darwinism as a prop, but the reverse is not true.

Dawkins's argument earmarks a problem that must be addressed and resolved in any Lamarckian framework. It is the problem of the inheritance of acquired impairments. It shall be raised again below when we discuss the application of Lamarckian ideas to the socioeconomic domain.

There is another theoretical and philosophical problem concerning the Lamarckian notion of will or volition. There must be a causal explanation of why organisms seek to adapt to their environment. In an attempt to fill this gap, Lamarckism presumes a voluntarism of will. But the origin of this will itself remains unexplained. A causal explanation of why organisms strive for advantage or improvement is lacking. In short, Lamarckian theory has another gaping hole in it that has to be filled by a Darwinian or other explanation. Darwinism explains why organisms seek to adapt to their environment in terms of the production of random variations of genotype, leading to different behaviours, some of which involve successful adaptations. Darwinism thus points to an evolutionary explanation of the very origin of will of purpose itself.[11] Even if acquired characters can be inherited, Lamarckism may again require Darwinism as an explanatory crutch.

Having noted serious theoretical problems within exclusively Lamarckian explanations, we move on to explore some ways in which residual versions of Lamarckism may persist even within a Darwinian framework, and without posing a threat to it. Indeed, a much looser version of 'Lamarckism' lingers even within modern biology. It is raised here because it is highly relevant to the discussion of the broad compatibility or otherwise of Lamarckism or Darwinism, across both biology and the social sciences. It is important to consider this carefully because these ideas are not, and were not designed as, a challenge to Darwinism. In fact they were originally developed as a buttress to Darwinian theory.

In the 1890s, two biologists, James Baldwin in the USA and C. Lloyd Morgan in Britain, independently addressed the problem of explaining a sufficiently rapid pace of evolution within a Darwinian framework. This was a pressing problem at the time, because a prominent Lamarckian objection to Darwinism was that evolution would happen too slowly and haphazardly without the inheritance of acquired characters. The Lamarckians claimed that the allegedly 'blind' and 'random' principles of Darwinism could not explain the rate and effectiveness of biotic evolution.[12]

Baldwin (1896a) and Morgan (1896) developed and published in the same year an argument that showed how evolution could be hastened without the inheritance of acquired characters. Morgan was relatively unlucky, for the phenomenon acquired the name of the 'Baldwin effect'. But, in absolute terms, Baldwin was unlucky too, for as Darwinism became ascendant after the 1930s, over-cautious thinkers dismissed the Baldwin–Morgan arguments because they seemed to smack of Lamarckian heresy. Ironically, however, the Baldwin–Morgan theories had been devised to rebut Lamarckism and rescue Darwinism. Some time later, the British Darwinian biologist Waddington revived and refined the argument. There are technical differences between Waddington's notion of 'genetic assimilation', Morgan's argument and the Baldwin effect. I shall gloss over these, and concentrate on Waddington's theory.[13]

Since Weismann, Darwinians have doubted the possibility of the inheritance of acquired characteristics. But this does not rule out the inheritance of the capacity to acquire particular characteristics. The ability to be fortuitously adaptable, or to learn, can be inherited, without any threat to the Darwinian framework. As Waddington (1969, p. 373) argues:

> Natural selection has built into all the more highly evolved organisms some capacity for reacting to stress in ways which tend to make the organism more effective in dealing with it. Such responses can be considered as a very generalized form of learning. It is clear enough that responding to a stress in this way would be useful to the organism and would therefore be favoured in natural selection.

In other words, natural selection may not simply lead to the development of species which are more adapted to their environment, but also to different capacities to respond by further adaptation to future changes in the environment. After Waddington, similar ideas have been developed by John Campbell (1987) and Christopher Wills (1989). The central thrust of the arguments of a sizeable group of Darwinian biologists is that 'natural selection will favor traits that enhance the possibility of further evolution'. This reveals 'evolvability to be the greatest adaptation of all' (Depew and Weber, 1995, p. 485).

Returning to the previous illustration: if we do manual work, then the skin on our hands thickens. However, our children will not inherit skin of extra thickness. Nevertheless, we do pass on, through our genes, the capacity to grow thick skin in response to manual work. Over time, considering the population as a whole, natural selection may favour those with a genetic disposition to grow thicker skin more readily. Accordingly, an acquired character is not inherited directly. But through natural selection the capacity to acquire that character becomes enhanced in the population as a whole. As Waddington (1975, pp. v–vi) puts it:

> [A]lthough an 'acquired character' developed by an individual is not inherited by its individual offspring, a character acquired by a population subject to selection will tend to be inherited by the offspring population, if it is useful ... [G]enotypes, which influence behaviour, thus have an effect on the nature of the selective pressures on the phenotype to which they give rise.

All this is consistent with Darwinism. There is no breach of the Weismann Barrier. To check this, we zoom in to observe the processes of acquisition of thick skin: we see that an adult does not pass on the acquired attribute of thick skin to its offspring. The infant's skin is thin and vulnerable. It will stay so, unless the hands are used. At this micro level, the Weismann Barrier is apparently intact, and there is no whiff of Lamarckian heresy.

Figure 6.3 shows this. The pace of evolutionary advance is more rapid, as in the Lamarckian process illustrated in Figure 6.2. However, there is no Lamarckian mechanism involved and the process is identical to the neo-Darwinian one shown in Figure 6.2. At the level of the individual organism there is no direct influence of phenotype upon genotype.

Figure 6 3: Genetic assimilation

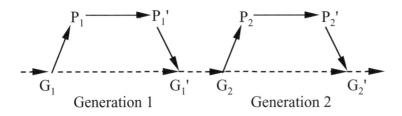

But let us change our viewpoint. Instead of observing micro-transmission, we zoom out to observe the population as a whole. Instead of the proverbial trees, we now see the forest. New and contrasting properties emerge at this level. Because the capacity to acquire harder skin increases through time, we observe at the population level that harder skin spreads more rapidly and widely among the population. And – here comes the crunch – at the species or population level these acquired capacities and characteristics are, in a sense, 'inherited'. However, the acquired characteristics are not transmitted from an individual to its offspring. For that reason, the word 'inherited' is used with a slightly different meaning in the penultimate sentence. If we view the population as if it were a single individual, then the acquired character is 'inherited' from one generation to the next. Through time, some things are acquired and 'passed on' within that population. But we are now using the words 'inheritance' and 'individual' as metaphors, and with a slightly changed meaning. It is important to point this out, in order to avoid any slippage or imprecision in the use of terms. Nevertheless, the population-wide view does give us a different picture. Emergent properties are revealed. At the population level, properties and processes emerge that have quasi-Lamarckian characteristics but which strictly do not involve Lamarckian inheritance at the level of the organism.

To use another metaphor, consider the method of painting known as pointillism, developed by the French painter Georges Seurat in the 1880s. Small, closely juxtaposed dots or strokes of pure colour were deposited on the canvas. Seen from a distance, these points produce the illusion of the solid forms and intermediate colours of people and landscape. At the micro level, there is nothing but separate points of pure colour. At the macro level there is a sense of complete and continuous form. The meanings and representations in paintings are emergent properties, not present in the points at the micro level. This results in an apparent but resolvable 'contradiction' between isolated points at one level and solid forms at another.[14]

In a similar manner, Waddington's theory of genetic assimilation produces an apparent contradiction between Darwinian processes at the micro level and the Lamarckian 'inheritance' of acquired characters for the population as a whole. However, the contradiction is apparent, not real. There is no contradiction, even within biology, between the quasi-Lamarckian notion of genetic assimilation and the principles of Darwinism. This does not in any way undermine Darwinism, nor give victory to any lingering group of Lamarckians, as Waddington and others have made repeatedly clear. What it does show, however, is that the layered ontology of complex systems and the existence of emergent properties makes the pattern of causal laws much more complicated than any dogmatic reductionist would admit or imagine.

Furthermore, the Waddington story should warn us about being over-hasty in applying the label 'Lamarckian' to social or cultural evolution. What might look like Lamarckism from a distance might not actually be so at the micro level.

The existence of emergent properties would support the possibility of different kinds of evolutionary processes at different ontological levels. The example of genetic assimilation also suggests such a possibility. It also warns us of the complications involved in addressing two levels at once. We can be ambitious with analogies, but ultimately we have to be careful about details. Above all, the Principle of Consistency requires that theories and explanations at a higher level do not overthrow or contradict those at a lower level. Waddington's theory of genetic assimilation exhibits this feature.

For some, however, the idea of 'Universal Darwinism' may be seen as a challenge to this relatively tolerant outcome. If Darwinism has universal explanatory power, why complicate the story by adding still more, different, types of explanation? This is one of the questions that must be addressed in the following sections of this essay.

Universal Darwinism

Apart from examining the 'effect' named after him, Baldwin (1909) was one of the first to argue that the Darwinian principles of natural selection applied not simply to biology but also to mental and social evolution. Like William James and Thorstein Veblen, Baldwin was an early pioneer of the idea that Darwinism had a wider application than to biology alone. However, the term 'Universal Darwinism' was probably first coined much later, by Dawkins (1983). Dawkins argues that if life existed elsewhere in the universe, it would follow the Darwinian rules of variation, inheritance and selection. The crux of this issue has been discussed already: even if there was a very different system of replication, including one that allowed the inheritance of acquired characters, a coherent account of the evolutionary process would still require the key elements of the Darwinian theory. As long as there is a population of replicating entities that make imperfect copies of themselves, and not all of these entities have the potential to survive, then Darwinian evolution will occur.

As such, Darwinian evolution is not tied to the specifics of genes or DNA: essentially it requires some replicating entity. On planet Earth, we find that DNA has the capacity to replicate. But other 'replicators' may exist, on Earth and elsewhere. One relevant example is the propensity of human beings to conform and imitate, making the replication of habits and ideas a key feature of human socio-economic systems. 'Universal Darwinism' is not a version of biological reductionism or 'biological imperialism' where an attempt is made to explain everything in biological terms. On the contrary, 'Universal Darwinism' upholds that there is a core set of general Darwinian principles that, along with auxiliary explanations specific to each scientific domain, may apply to a wide range of phenomena.

As a result, Universal Darwinism is not an 'imperialistic' doctrine in the manner of the 'economic imperialism' of neoclassical economists such as Gary Becker (1976) or Jack Hirshleifer (1982).[15] Such 'imperialisms' involve the claim that a wide range of phenomena can be explained completely and exclusively in terms of a single set of principles.[16] By leaving an opening for domain-specific, auxiliary explanations, Universal Darwinism does not necessarily involve such a claim.

Accordingly, in his key chapter on 'Universal Darwinism', Henry Plotkin (1994, Ch. 3) considers a number of Darwinian-type selection mechanisms. He discusses the early suggestion, made by Darwin himself, that 'the struggle for life' may be going on among such entities as the words and grammatical forms of human language, as well as among organic life. Darwin (n.d., p. 324–5) hinted that languages may evolve like species. As another example of the extension of 'natural selection' to different entities, Plotkin cites the proposal of William James (originally made in 1880) that ideas themselves replicate and produce random variations, upon which social and natural circumstances select the survivors (James, 1897, p. 247).[17] Such a notion is now familiar to us in the form of the 'evolutionary epistemology' of Karl Popper (1972), Donald Campbell (1974a) and others.

Plotkin also places within his framework of 'Universal Darwinism' the ideas of 'neural Darwinism' pioneered by Gerald Edelman (1987). Furthermore, he also brings in the immune system. In these cases there is a selection process working on a regenerating variety of replicating units, be they lymphocytes (in the evolution of the immune system) or neural connections (with neural Darwinism). He makes the point that what is being proposed is not merely an evolutionary analogy or metaphor but the existence of multiple processes that are actually evolutionary, and they are evolving in accord with basic Darwinian principles of variation, replication and selection.

It is important to re-emphasise that in making Darwinian evolution universal, Dawkins, Plotkin and others do not attempt to explain everything in biological terms. The alleged universality of Darwinian mechanisms does not mean that the process involved is always that of genetic variation and selection. Furthermore, when genetic evolution does exist, this does not rule out additional evolutionary processes, acting on different entities, at different ontological levels. Plotkin (1994, p. 101) himself proposes 'a hierarchically structured evolutionary theory' in which there are different units of selection at each level. Plotkin's anti-reductionism is explicit. He explicitly rejects the notion that evolution at a higher level can be explained entirely in terms of evolutionary processes at a lower level:

> What saves intelligent behaviour from such a [genetic] reductionistic account is the presence of selectional processes in the mechanism of intelligence. As long as the secondary heuristic operates, even if in only small part, by Darwinian processes involving unpredictable generation of variants, then the products of that secondary heuristic, intelligent behaviour, cannot be reductively explained by genetics or genetics and development. (Plotkin, 1994, p. 176)

We could explore 'Universal Darwinism' even further than Plotkin. More than a century ago, the American philosopher Charles Sanders Peirce proposed in 1898 that the laws of nature themselves evolve (Peirce, 1992). This idea is being further developed by physicists today, involving the argument that key physical constants take the values they do because alternative universes in which the constants took different values failed to survive (Smolin, 1997). What could be more universal than to see the universe in which we live as a result of a Darwinian process of selection among alternative universes? Here, it seems, Universal Darwinism triumphs by making Darwinism play God.

The theistic allusion is not intended as an invitation for ridicule. As with God, there is something both wondrous and worrying about universal theories. The Darwinian theory is extremely powerful, because it is the only adequately detailed causal account of the evolution of complex systems, including organic life. It has the quality – to use another metaphor – of the 'universal acid' (Dennett, 1995) dissolving every theoretical receptacle into which it is placed. Seemingly, as a theory, it cannot be contained. Instead it apparently provides an encompassing framework within which all lesser theories are placed.

We have to leave these cosmological questions to the physicists. Coming back down to earth, the universality or otherwise of Darwinism is not something that can be resolved by mere social scientists. What is important for the social scientist to note is this: the notion of Universal Darwinism itself provides no alternative to a detailed explanation of the particular emergent properties and processes at the social level.

It is important to establish another conclusion here, before we move on. The work of Dawkins, Plotkin and others on 'Universal Darwinism' shows that the terms 'Darwinian' or 'Darwinism' are each being used prominently in two senses rather than one.[18] One sense is more restrictive than the other. The less restrictive sense is that 'Darwinian' processes involve variation, inheritance and selection. The more restrictive sense would also exclude the possibility of the inheritance of acquired characters. This is the Weismannian version of Darwinism: it is alleged by most biologists to apply to organic life. As noted above, Weismannism and Lamarckism are logically incompatible. But, in general, and more broadly, Darwinism and Lamarckism are not. In this sense we investigate the possibility that social evolution can be consistent with some notion of Lamarckism, which does not overthrow Darwinism in the biological domain. We explore this possibility in more detail in the remainder of this essay.

Hull's Rejection of Lamarckism in Social Evolution

Having found some breathing space for a version of Lamarckism within a (Universal) Darwinian framework, it is useful at this stage to consider an attempt to exclude Lamarckian ideas from social evolution. David Hull's

(1982) article is a rare challenge to the notion that social evolution can in any sense be Lamarckian. Hull argues that 'sociocultural evolution' is Lamarckian in neither a literal nor a metaphorical sense. He attacks the proponents of Lamarckian social evolution with two arguments, of which the first can be dealt with more briefly.

Hull emphasises that intentionality plays a major role in human social evolution, but he regards the use of the Lamarckian label as misleading, even in this respect. Hull (1982, p. 312) writes:

> The trouble with terming sociocultural evolution 'Lamarckian' is that it obscures the really important difference between biological and sociocultural evolution – the role of intentionality. In sociocultural evolution, Lamarckian correlations exist between the environmental causes and the conceptual effects, but the mechanism responsible for these correlations is not the least Lamarckian. Rather, it is the conscious striving of intentional agents.

The key claim here is that Lamarckism excludes intentionality. However, Lamarck himself did not completely exclude a role for intentions, even in the evolution of non-human species. In the text of a lecture given in 1800, Lamarck wrote:

> [T]he bird of the shore that dislikes swimming, and which none the less needs to approach the water to find its prey, is continually exposed to sinking in the mud; but, wishing to avoid the immersion of its body, its feet will get into the habit of stretching and lengthening. The effect of this, for those birds which continue to live in this manner over generations, will be that the individuals will be raised if on stilts, on long naked legs, that is to say legs bare of feathers up to the thigh and often beyond. (Lamarck, 1984, p. 415)

In this passage, Lamarck clearly sees an adaptation resulting from the volitions of the bird. Any suggestion that Lamarck himself completely excluded intentionality in evolution would thus be mistaken. However, such suggestions play a very minor role in his writings. Overall, Lamarck stressed habit much more than conscious will (Burkhardt, 1984, pp. xxx–xxxi).

When it comes to Lamarckism, as opposed to the writings of Lamarck himself, it is much more difficult to belittle the role of intentionality. Lamarck's own views and those of the many subsequent 'Lamarckian' biologists are not identical. In embracing the category of intentionality, many 'Lamarckians' went much further than Lamarck. Furthermore, by promoting versions of vitalism, some Lamarckians elevated the notion of intention into a distinct category of causality. Hull's denial of a concept of intention in what he describes as 'Lamarckism' is thus misleading.[19]

Let us consider the second and more substantial of Hull's arguments. He criticises both 'literal' and 'metaphorical' notions of Lamarckian social evolution. For him, the processes of social evolution cannot literally involve the key Lamarckian idea of the inheritance of acquired characters. Hull (1982, p. 278) considers the question of social learning, arguing that 'social learning is not an instance of the inheritance of acquired characters'. For him, it is more like infection or contagion. Unlike a disease, learning can be beneficial, but Hull suggests that a similar mechanism of contagion takes place. For example:

> [A] mother can transmit syphilis to her unborn child. Such transmission is congenital, not hereditary, and for this reason is no more an example of the inheritance of acquired characteristics than is the transmission of fleas. In order for acquired characteristics to be literally *inherited*, the genetic material cannot be bypassed. ... In order for sociocultural evolution to be Lamarckian in a literal sense, the ideas which we acquire by interacting with our environment must somehow become programmed in our genes. (Hull, 1982, p. 309)

There is no feasible way in which the ideas we acquire by learning can lead to the reprogramming of our own biological genes. (Although ideas can, for instance, affect our choice of sexual partner and thereby influence the genes of our offspring.) Accordingly, social evolution is not literally Lamarckian: it does not involve Lamarckian processes at the individual, biological level. Hull is right in this respect. But the validity of this conclusion simply flows from the established argument in biology that there is no way in which an organism can inherit an acquired character. In the passage quoted above, Hull simply uses the word 'literal' to mean 'biological'. By this token, and given the prevailing view in modern biology, any 'literal' sense of Lamarckism must be excluded, in any context. Hull's critique of the notion that social evolution is 'literally' Lamarckian is correct, but simply by virtue of the fact that biological evolution is not Lamarckian.

We may agree with Hull that social evolution is not Lamarckian in a 'literal' or biological sense. But the question of whether social evolution is Lamarckian in a 'metaphorical' sense remains. When Hull criticises the idea that social evolution is 'metaphorically' Lamarckian, it is important to understand the type of analogy that he criticises in this respect. Hull takes it for granted that the unit of cultural evolution is the idea or meme. He concentrates on memetic versions of sociocultural evolution, neglecting other sociocultural theories that have been described as 'Lamarckian'.[20]

With this specific version of sociocultural evolution in mind, Hull (1982, p. 311) argues that 'ideas are analogous to genes, not characteristics'. Hull thus rejects the notion that something like Lamarckian transmission is involved. For him, the inheritance of acquired ideas or memes is not an instance of the inheritance of acquired characters, because ideas and memes are analogous to genes, not characteristics.

Furthermore, for Hull, the idea itself does not acquire characteristics. Hence there is no parallel to the genotype–phenotype distinction: there is no idea-genotype that helps to determine a distinguishable idea-phenotype. Given these assumptions, there is indeed a problem with the Lamarckian analogy: 'In order for sociocultural evolution to be Lamarckian in a metaphorical sense, conceptual genotypes must be distinguishable from conceptual phenotypes and the two must be related in appropriate ways' (Hull, 1982, p. 309).

Hence, for Hull in his 1982 paper, social evolution is in no sense Lamarckian. 'At the metaphorical level, however, a consistent story can be told for sociocultural evolution being Darwinian' (Hull, 1982, p. 311). Two years later, Hull (1984b, p. lx) modified his position. At first he repeated his earlier argument that

> memes (or ideas) are the analogs of genes, not characters. Social learning is an example of the inheritance of acquired memes and not an example of the inheritance of acquired characters.

He then continued:

> Learning from experience is a better candidate for Lamarckian inheritance in sociocultural evolution. While baking a cake, a cook may make a mistake and use sour cream instead of sweet milk ... he or she might alter the recipe accordingly. ... When we learn from experience, conflicts between our ideas and their applications cause us to change our memes. If such applications count as part of our conceptual phenotype, then sociocultural evolution is in this sense Lamarckian. (ibid.)

This is a much more accommodating position than he took in his 1982 essay. He goes on, however, to express reasonable 'doubts as to whether the ability to learn from experience and pass on knowledge to others as a form of Lamarckian inheritance is all that informative'.

Hull's (1982, 1984b) discussions of Lamarckism in the social domain are based on a narrow notion of culture as ideas or memes. Working in the same framework, Susan Blackmore (1999, pp. 61–2) rightly argues that whether memetic evolution is Lamarckian or not depends on whether, respectively, it is meme-as-behaviour or meme-as-instructions that is being copied. Copying-the-product brings the possibility of inheritance of acquired modifications to the outcome, whereas copying-the-instructions does not; any alterations in behaviour or outcome will not be passed on, because it is the instructions, not the outcomes, that are being replicated.

Blackmore then goes on to argue that the transmission of some memes involves the copying of behaviour by imitation while others involve the copying of instructions. Accordingly, her devotion to the concept of the meme leads her to an agnostic conclusion on the central issue here. In fact,

Blackmore (1999, p. 62) concludes that 'the question "Is cultural evolution Lamarckian?" is best not asked'. The question is thus evaded. However, despite her wishes, the question will not go away. In fact, Blackmore is led to an evasive conclusion because she does not probe more deeply into the notion and mechanics of such terms as 'copying' and 'instruction'. Indeed, the concept of the meme is itself ambiguous. The literature on memetics suffers from some confusion concerning the casual use of 'information' or 'ideas' as the analogue of the gene.[21]

The casual identification of memes with ideas has a crucial defect. The nature of ideas and the causal mechanisms by which ideas lead to behaviour are not spelt out. It is simply assumed that one leads to the other. As a result, in a very real sense, memetics is insufficiently Darwinian: it does not identify the detailed, causal mechanisms involved.

Habit as a Cultural Analogue to the Gene

An earlier tradition of evolutionary thinking in the social sciences saw the analogue of the gene in the social sphere as habits, rather than information or ideas. These were the pragmatist philosophers such as Charles Sanders Peirce, William James and John Dewey. American institutional economists such as Thorstein Veblen (1919) and John Commons (1934) built their ideas on these pragmatist foundations.

The pragmatists argued that the interpretation of information and the following of instructions depend crucially on ingrained habits of cognition, thought and behaviour. They are established through custom, practice and habit. Mere codifications or declarations are not enough. As Peirce (1878, p. 294) put it: 'the essence of belief is the establishment of habit'. Ingrained habits of thought and behaviour are necessary to unlock information, so that it can help form part of the motivational fuel for human agents.

Habits are defined as self-actuating propensities or dispositions to engage in particular responses or forms of action. All ideas and beliefs are built upon habits, but the reverse is not always true. Some habits arise from instincts, not ideas. Writers such as Plotkin (1994), Margolis (1994) and Murphy (1994) have argued that habits are an essential foundation for even the most deliberative and rational thoughts.[22] In turn, acquired habits are founded upon inherited instincts. Accordingly, habit is a bridging element between, on the one side, the biological and, on the other, the psychological and social domains.

As well as habit, the concept of tacit knowledge is an important section of this bridge. In a classic work, Michael Polanyi (1967) showed that ideas and deliberations depend on an essential, tacit substratum, which in principle cannot entirely be made explicit. This, in turn, rests on a lower substratum of inherited instinct. In many respects, Polanyi's argument that human deliberation must be placed in its evolutionary and physiological context is redolent of the earlier work of instinct psychologists such as James (1890) and the institutional economist Veblen (1899, 1914, 1919).[23] Although the modern literature on memetics makes a bold attempt to place ideas and culture in an evolutionary perspective, it can often be criticised for ignoring the tacit and habitual substratum of all ideas and beliefs. By Polanyi's canon, much of the literature on memetics is not evolutionary enough.

A habit is an adaptation. The capacity to acquire habits parallels the aptitude for learning. Acquired habits can be passed on by the imitation of the behaviour of others. Some have described this as 'Lamarckian'. But the acquisition of those habits is also ruled by Darwinian principles at the biological level. In any theory of cultural or memetic evolution, it is necessary to understand both the nature and the evolution of the unit of culture – or meme – itself. Otherwise, the meme or unit is left in explanatory mid-air. Given this, disentangling the Lamarckian and Darwinian features of social and biological evolution is no longer an option, nor a matter that can be avoided. It is essential to any theory of cultural or memetic evolution and for understanding how such a process relates to biological evolution.

Habits are not themselves behaviour, they are dispositions or propensities. They are thus closer by analogy to the genotype than to the phenotype. Accordingly there is a strong *prima facie* case for considering habits as units of cultural inheritance. We pursue this argument in the next section.

Darwinism and Lamarckism in Social Evolution

In discussing the mechanics of evolution, Dawkins (1982) makes a useful distinction between replicators and vehicles. A replicator is an entity of which copies are made. In the biotic world, an organism is not a replicator, because alterations in it are not passed on to subsequent generations. In evolutionary processes, individual or group selection is about the selection of vehicles. Gene selection is about the selection of replicators.

Similarly, Hull (1980, 1981, 1988a) states that there are two ingredients involved in any form of selection at any level. For selection to occur, there must be both 'replicators' and 'interactors'. Hull's concept of replicator is identical to that of Dawkins. For both authors, a replicator is an entity that passes its structure directly in replication. However, Hull's concept of 'interactor' is slightly different from Dawkins's 'vehicle'. For Hull (1981, p. 31), interactors are 'entities that produce differential replication by means of directly interacting as cohesive wholes with their environments'. Hull's concept and definition is preferred here, because of its emphasis on interaction with the environment as well as the relative cohesiveness of the unit.

Dawkins and Hull rightly argue that much of the debate about units of selection confuses these two items. In the biotic world, genes are the replicators and organisms are the vehicles/interactors. Using these terms, let us now recapitulate the basic differences between Darwinian and Lamarckian evolution.

Genes are like chunks of read-only memory, carrying coded instruction systems directing the growth and behavioural propensities of the organism. Genes are carried within the organism (that is, the 'vehicle' or 'interactor') of which they are a part. The organism produces the 'seeds' of new organisms, carrying copies of its own genes and the instructions within them. These genes program each seed to interact with its environment to help create a new organism from the seed.

Evolution is Darwinian in the narrow, Weismannian sense if the genetic memory is strictly read-only, with the additional possibility of a small number of copying errors or mutations. Accordingly, there is little or no change in the genes of the seed compared to the genes of its parents, even if the adult organisms differ substantially as a result of growth in, and adaptation to, different environments. Changes occur through the natural selection of the fitter organisms in the prevailing environment.

Evolution is Lamarckian (in the sense of the acceptance of the possibility of the inheritance of acquired characters) if the genetic memory is not read-only, and can be modified to embody any characters acquired by the organism as it adapts to its environment. Changes in a population occur through natural selection of the fitter organisms in the prevailing environment, and through advantageous acquired adaptations being passed on via the genes to succeeding generations. As explained above, Lamarckism relies on Darwinism as a prop to explain the adaptive behaviour of the organism in its environment and to overcome the problem that some acquired characters may be impairments.

Consider the two most important rival understandings of the 'unit of culture' or 'meme' addressed above: ideas versus habits. The plausibility of Lamarckian or Darwinian analogies will be considered in each case.

In the 'culture as ideas' version, ideas are regarded as coded instructions that somehow (in a manner that is not adequately explained) direct the growth and behaviour of the organism. Ideas are carried within the organism (that is, the 'vehicle' or 'interactor') of which they are a part. The human organism makes progeny through biological reproduction, and through socialisation, within the family or community, makes copies of some of its own ideas. Although ideas do not themselves 'produce the organisms of which they are a part' (Hull, 1982, p. 311), neither, at the literal and biological level, do the genes alone 'produce the organisms of which they are a part'. Both ideas and genes can help to produce the organism, in interaction with its environment. Crucially, some ideas help human offspring to interact with their environment to create new organisms.

Is this version of cultural evolution a Lamarckian process? The answer depends primarily on whether ideas themselves are seen as modifiable as a result of behaviours and experiences not themselves encoded in prior ideas. In principle they are. Hence a Lamarckian possibility must be admitted. Although some ideas are difficult to modify and resistant to change, the possibility of Lamarckian alterations and consequent transmissions cannot be excluded. As Lamarckism is here defined in terms of the possibility, rather than the necessity, of acquired character inheritance, then this version of cultural evolution can be deemed Lamarckian.

Consider the second analogical possibility: habits as genes. Habits are acquired and imprinted instruction systems made up of instruction elements that direct the growth and behaviour of the organism. Habits are carried within the organism (that is, the 'vehicle') of which they are a part. The human organism makes progeny through biological reproduction, and through imitation of behaviour, largely via socialisation within the family or community, it makes imperfect copies of some of its own habits in its progeny. These habits dispose each descendant to interact with its environment, eventually and possibly to create a new adult human organism from its seed. A Lamarckian possibility seems to emerge here because the replication of habits proceeds by the replication of behaviour, rather than of the 'software' of the habits themselves.

Although habits are analogous to genes, the mechanisms of replication and transmission are very different. Unlike the replication of DNA, habits do not directly make copies of themselves. Instead they replicate indirectly. They impel behaviour that is, in turn, consciously or unconsciously imitated by others. Eventually, this copied behaviour becomes rooted in the habits of the imitator, thus transmitting from individual to individual an imperfect copy of each habit by an indirect route.

Especially when transmitted in codified form, ideas may seem to replicate more directly than habits. Written documents can be readily copied. This may partly account for the popularity of the ideas-as-genes analogy. However, it rests on a positivist view of knowledge. Ideas do not replicate on their own. Ideas are replicated through the existence of common concepts and habits of thought.

It is largely through the strong propensity to imitate that habits are acquired. Clearly, what is required in the habits-as-genes version of cultural evolution is an explanation of the propensity to imitate or conform to the behaviour of others. One strong possibility is that the propensity to imitate is instinctive, and this instinct has itself evolved for efficacious reasons among social creatures (James, 1890; Veblen, 1899; D. Campbell, 1975; Boyd and Richerson, 1985). The habit-based version of cultural evolution may thus require a (Darwinian) biological explanation to be complete.

Figure 6.4: Lamarckian social evolution

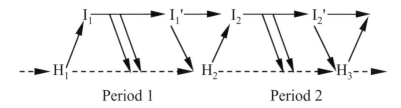

Period 1   Period 2

Figure 6.4 illustrates the Lamarckian process of social evolution. The phenotypic level, from I_1 to I_2' – and so on – is the level of manifest behaviour and social institutions. Each 'period' can be seen as the lifetime of the individual. There is no close analogue of mating or sexual recombination. The twin arrows show the effects of imitation, conformity and institutional constraints on the formation of new and changed habits. Although the picture is significantly different from both Figure 6.1 and Figure 6.2, it is Lamarckian in the sense illustrated in Figure 6.2, in that there is a downward effect from the higher to the lower level, in addition to the differential selection and survival within the population of institutions.

At this point a further important distinction must be established. There are two types of arguments against the notion of Lamarckian social evolution: theoretical or empirical. They are quite different. As we have seen, Hull (1982) rejects Lamarckian social evolution on theoretical grounds. According to him, the very concept is misleading and misconceived. In contrast, Michael Hannan and John Freeman (1989, pp. 22–3) argue that Lamarckian selection processes are unimportant in the population ecology of social organisations. In their view, selection takes place around deeply embedded rules. New adaptations modify organisations only at a higher and more superficial level. This is an empirical rather than a theoretical rejection of Lamarckism, because it is based on a factual claim concerning the evolution of organisations. Hannan and Freeman may be right or wrong, but in no case does their argument imply that Lamarckian social evolution is impossible in principle. This distinction between theoretical and empirical critiques of Lamarckian social evolution further complicates the picture.

Let us sum up. If an acquired characteristic can affect the social equivalent of a gene then social evolution can be described as Lamarckian. If ideas are analogous to genes then there is no compelling reason to assume that acquired characteristics change the program of instructions in the idea. In which case Lamarckism would not apply. However, if behaviour is programmed by habits, and imitations of behaviour establish new habits, then acquired characteristics become incorporated in habits and Lamarckism may apply. These comparative points are summarised in Table 6.3.

The upshot of this discussion is that there is a basis to describe social evolution as Lamarckian, in the sense of admitting the possibility of the inheritance of acquired characters. Research into the degree to which this possibility is realised is a matter of empirical enquiry. However, to repeat a general theoretical point made earlier, Lamarckism must always rely on Darwinism as a complement. Because it is an incomplete explanation of an evolutionary process, Lamarckism can never substitute for Darwinism. Any Lamarckian inheritance of acquired characteristics does not in any way, or at any level, undermine Darwinism. According to the prevailing view in biology, biotic evolution is exclusively Darwinian: here the Weismann barrier rules out Lamarckism. Genetic assimilation in biology is Darwinian, but it involves at the population level something that looks like – but strictly is not – Lamarckism. Social evolution is Darwinian and can also be Lamarckian. At this level, the two dovetail together.

This leaves an outstanding problem that must be addressed and resolved in any Lamarckian framework. As noted above, Lamarckism lacks an explanation as to why there is a propensity to inherit improvements rather than impairments. Consider this problem in the social domain. It has been argued that habits are typically replicated by behavioural imitation. But imitation is not always slavish or automatic. People are selective; they make choices. Some behaviours will not be imitated because people will see them as deleterious, or whatever.

There is nothing in principle that rules out the imitation of detrimental behaviours. The Aztec and Mayan civilisations probably stagnated partly because of their appetite for human sacrifice. The modern military–industrial complex may yet lead to the nuclear or ecological ruin of our civilisation. Even in biology, there is nothing in evolution that suggests that the outcome is always beneficial or optimal (Hodgson, 1993). Once we escape from Panglossian conceptions of evolution then this possibility of decline or extermination can be admitted. But this is not the central issue here. Essentially, the Lamarckian problem of the inheritance of acquired impairments requires us to explain why people choose to imitate one set of behaviours rather than another. On this point, Lamarckism requires further

Table 6.3: Is there Lamarckian inheritance in biotic or social evolution?

	Replicator	Interactor or Vehicle	Phenotype	Can There Be Lamarckian Inheritance?
Definition ⇒ Genotypic Units ⇓	An entity that passes its structure directly in replication.	Vehicle for replicator that, as a cohesive whole, interacts with its environment, resulting in differential replication.	Phenomenal form and behaviour of interactor or vehicle. Outcome of the interaction between genotype and environment.	Lamarckism involves inheritance from generation to generation of a character acquired by the interactor or vehicle.
Genes	Genes replicate via sexual recombination, with occasional mutations.	An organism.[1]	The organism and its behaviour.	No – An acquired character cannot modify the replicator, due to the Weismann barrier.
Ideas	Ideas replicate via imitation of codifiable instructions, with possible mutation.	An individual or group.[2]	The behaviour of individuals or groups.	It depends whether or not the ideas themselves can be modified as a result of behavioural experiences.
Habits	Habits replicate indirectly, via behavioural imitation, with possible mutation.	An individual or institution.[3]	Individuals and institutions: their constitution and behaviour.	Yes – Because habits are replicated through behavioural imitation. Without direct replication of the habit itself, any acquired behaviour can modify the replicator.

1. Possibly groups are also interactors or vehicles. This depends on the verdict on the group selection controversy. We do not need to go into this debate here. For discussions see Hodgson (1993), Sober (1984b) and Sober and Wilson (1998). See also Laurent's introductory chapter in this volume.

2. The admission of groups as interactors or vehicles is also controversial. Notably, Hayek (1988) emphasised groups and not simply individuals as units of selection.

3. Note Veblen's (1899, p. 190) definition that 'institutions are, in substance, prevalent habits of thought with respect to particular relations and particular functions of the individual and of the community'.

theoretical explanation. It is not principally a matter of evaluation of outcome.

Any answer to this question must involve a theory of social agency. It must show the basis on which imitative choices are made, and the causal mechanisms involved. As noted above, Lamarckism does not itself provide such an explanation. Whether or not Darwinism is of help here is a matter of dispute. Evolutionary psychologists argue that it is (Plotkin, 1994). At a minimum, a theory of human agency must be consistent with our understanding of the biological evolution of the human agent. What is also clear is that Lamarckian theory does not provide a complete explanation of social evolution. The statement that social evolution is Lamarckian is thus generally inadequate rather than necessarily wrong. John Maynard Smith (1988, p. 61) has rightly pointed out: 'Cultural evolution is commonly said to be Lamarckian rather than Darwinian, but there has been surprisingly little effort to work out a precise theory of its principles'. Even at the most general and sketchy level, there are large gaps in the Lamarckian story that the social scientist is obliged to fill. Lamarckism, as such, may provide little help in filling them.[24]

Conclusion

Social evolution conforms to the basic Darwinian principles of variation, inheritance and selection. Consistent with the notion of 'Universal Darwinism', social systems embody the same fundamental Darwinian mechanisms as other complex, evolving systems. But also, social evolution has the additional and 'Lamarckian' feature of the inheritance of acquired characters. It is quite wrong, therefore, for evolutionary economists to distance themselves completely from either Darwinism or Lamarckism. In general, and broadly interpreted, the two are compatible. But it also has to be recognised that the Darwinian principles are more fundamental, because Lamarckism itself always relies on Darwinian props.

Where biotic and social evolution differ is that we find a Weismann barrier in the former, but not obviously nor necessarily in the latter. But, as is well known, even Darwin himself was unaware of its existence.

Furthermore, discourses on 'Universal Darwinism' establish a sense of 'Darwinian' evolution that is more general than the specifics of genes, DNA and Weismann barriers. Accordingly, social scientists are mistaken if they reject the Darwinian analogy in the social domain for the reason that evolution therein is different from biological evolution. Of course it is different. But the analogy is relevant at a more general and basic level because of the 'universal' features of complex, evolving systems. D.

Campbell (1965, p. 24) made the point some time ago that the appropriate analogy for social evolution is not biotic evolution, but the more general processes of evolution of complex systems 'for which organic evolution is but one instance'.[25] Such a general conception of evolution would be close to the broad notion of 'Darwinism' discussed above. The formulation of this conception would inevitably rely on biology, alongside other materials, for inspiration. Biological metaphors are useful materials, if used critically and unslavishly, with which to help construct such a more general theory.

The question is not whether social evolution is either Lamarckian or Darwinian but: 'Can social evolution be Lamarckian without contradicting Darwinism?' It has been argued here that the answer is 'yes'. Social evolution must be consistent with the presuppositions of 'Universal Darwinism' but these do not exclude the possibility of the inheritance of acquired characters at the social level.

This position should lead us to examine the causal details behind variation, inheritance and selection within societies. Of course, the precise details of social and genetic evolution will differ: habits are not nearly so durable as genes, the social context of selection is less stable, social imitation may prevail over random mutations of habit, the generative sources of variety in the social domain may not be so great as in the biotic, and so on. But nevertheless they are all subject to the most general principles of 'Darwinism' as defined here.

We have reached a position that was not earmarked among the options in Table 6.1.[26] Biotic evolution is Darwinian. Social evolution can be Lamarckian; it is also Darwinian in some broad or 'universal' sense. This position is also consistent with Weismannian evolution at the biotic level. Apart from Veblen (1899, pp. 192, 248; 1904, p. 369 and note) – who accepted the cultural inheritance of acquired traits but also the methodological superiority of Darwinism even in the social sciences – there have been very few proponents of this doctrinal combination hitherto. If the argument in this chapter is correct, this neglected possibility is the only one that is generally viable.

Having reached this conclusion, the remaining question is to consider, along with Hull (1984b) and others, whether these labels are really useful, especially outside biology. Here the case for the use of 'Darwinism' is much stronger than 'Lamarckism', even in the social context. Darwinism connotes a detailed causal examination of ongoing processes through time, based on the principles of variation, inheritance and selection. This is a much more substantial package than one that merely involves the possibility of acquired character inheritance. When we are talking of social evolution, not only is it important to insist that Lamarckism does not exclude the possibility of Darwinian ideas, but also – in the broad but powerful sense used here –

Darwinism is a much more useful and substantial label even at the social level.

Furthermore, a 'post-Darwinian' social science, as envisaged by Veblen (1919), would involve a major paradigm shift. It would involve a detailed examination of causal processes and the resolution of the problem of intentionality and agency in the social context. In contrast, a Lamarckian theory of social evolution does not necessarily involve a departure from the existing menu. The challenge for social scientists, as it was for Veblen over 100 years ago, is to develop explanations of human institutions and social structures that are consistent with the Darwinian paradigm. This does not mean that Darwinism provides all the answers; but that it is a powerful theory of widespread consequences, which cannot be overthrown or ignored by social science.

Notes

1. The author is extremely grateful to Markus Becker, John Foster, David Hull, Thorbjörn Knudsen, John Laurent, John Nightingale, Peter Richerson, Mikael Sandberg and many others for extensive discussions and critical comments on preceding drafts of this paper. The paper was first presented at New School University, New York, on 28 October 1999.
2. Penrose (1952) is a classic early statement of this view, although, in personal conversation with the author shortly before her death in 1996, she became much more sympathetic to evolutionary analogies in economics. Several self-proclaimed 'evolutionary' economists have also been sceptical or dismissive of the value of biological analogies in economic analysis. See, for example, Schumpeter (1954, p. 789), De Bresson (1987), Witt (1992, p. 7), Ramstad (1994) and Rosenberg (1994a).
3. For critical reflections on the split between the social sciences and biology see Hirst and Woolley (1982), Degler (1991), Weingart et al (1997), Hodgson (1999a).
4. The concept of an emergent property was established by Morgan in the 1890s (Hodgson, 1998d).
5. For discussions of cultural or memetic evolution see Blackmore (1999), Boyd and Richerson (1985), Brodie (1996), Dennett (1995, Ch. 12), Durham (1991), Lynch (1996) and Rose (1998).
6. The flawed and now unfashionable idea that socioeconomic evolution works principally by modification of the human genotype was promoted by Spencer and Marshall. Spencer (1881, pp. 400–1) argued that 'society cannot be substantially and permanently changed without its units being substantially and permanently changed ... social evolution ... is limited by the rate of organic modification in human beings'. Likewise, the economist Marshall (1923, p. 260) wrote: 'Economic institutions are the products of human nature and cannot change much faster than human nature changes'. The arguments of C.L. Morgan, and especially Veblen, had the explicit objective of explaining social evolution in terms that did not require changes in the human gene-pool (Hodgson, 1998b). Nevertheless, there are genuine but complex connections between human nature and what may be possible in terms of human social organisation and development; for a discussion, see Chapter 2 in this volume by Laurent.

7.   Prior to Morgan's development of the concept in the 1890s, social scientists often relied on devices such as the metaphor of society as an organism. By identifying such an object of analysis, a place for social science was retained. However, the organism metaphor is widely criticised for its defective and inadequate depiction of the relationship between individual agency and social structure. Similar objections have been raised against various structuralist and holistic developments in twentieth century social science. In contrast, a social science based on the concept of emergence provides a means of avoiding the defects in these approaches.

8.   For discussions of Lamarck's ideas and their impact see Boesiger (1974) and Burkhardt (1977, 1984). Although his position has often been misinterpreted, Lamarck did believe that the inheritance of acquired characters is possible. In fact, the idea of acquired character inheritance was widespread at the time and Lamarck adapted it from others (Burkhardt, 1977, 1984). Lamarck also believed that organisms – in an upward drive towards perfection – become progressively more complex. Similar ideas were promoted by Spencer, and they survive in some quarters today.

9.   Diagrams of this type are found in Lewontin (1974), Boyd and Richerson (1985), Durham (1991) and elsewhere. The author also acknowledges the inspiration of unpublished work by Thorbjörn Knudsen.

10. The useful metaphor of Darwinian evolution as an algorithm is deployed in Dennett (1995). The same emphasis on the detailed and processual nature of Darwinian evolution is found in the writings of the institutional economist Veblen (1904, p. 369 and note): 'Darwin set to work to explain species in terms of the process out of which they have arisen, rather than out of the prime cause to which the distinction between them may be due. This is the substance of Darwin's advance over Lamarck, for instance'. However, where Dennett and Veblen differ is that Dennett fails to deploy any concept of emergent properties, and thus lapses into reductionism. In contrast, Morgan and his concept of emergence (Hodgson, 1998b) influenced Veblen. Nevertheless, Veblen's use and apprecation of the vital importance of the concept of emergence was inadequate.

11. As Veblen (1934, p. 80) put it in 1898: 'By selective necessity he [the human] is endowed with a proclivity for purposeful action'.

12. Morgan (1896) and Baldwin (1896a, 1909) also addressed the problem of accounting for the even more rapid pace of cultural evolution, in a manner consistent with Darwinism. I have argued elsewhere that Morgan's thoughts on this matter were crucial for Veblen and the development of institutional economics (Hodgson, 1998b).

13. Morgan's argument depends upon a notion of the organism making an 'intelligent choice'. But this choice is itself inadequately explained by natural selection. The Baldwin effect depends upon the luck of fortuitous mutation after habits are established. In contrast, Waddington's genetic assimilation works through progressive selection of the appropriate capacity to respond to stress. See, for example, Dennett (1995, pp. 77–80), Hardy (1965, pp. 161–70), Maynard Smith (1975, pp. 303–7), Piaget (1979, pp. 14–21), Richards (1987, pp. 480–503).

14. The mind handles the detail by pattern recognition and 'chunking', discussed by researchers into cognitive psychology, artificial intelligence and elsewhere. Such chunking is often indispensable to make sense of a complex system, but at the cost of a loss of some precision and predictive power. For a stimulating discussion of chunking and the problem of 'levels of description' see Hofstadter (1979). Related themes are discussed in Cohen and Stewart (1994).

15. Hirshleifer (1982, p. 52), for example, thus favours an '"Economic imperialism" – the use of economic analytical models to study all forms of social relations rather than only the market interactions of "rational" decision makers'. It is based on the assumption that: 'All aspects of life are ultimately governed by the scarcity of resources'.

16. For a critique of 'economic imperialism' see Udéhn (1992).
17. James's remarkable 1880 essay 'Great Men and Their Environment' (reprinted in James, 1897) not only sketches an evolutionary epistemology, it also contains a powerful critique of Spencerian evolution. He attacked what today would be called cultural determinism, with a plea for the retention of a notion of individual agency. Furthermore, glistening within are the nugget ideas of bounded rationality (p. 219), cumulative causation (p. 227) and path dependent evolution (p. 238). James pioneered the notion – by 1898 affirmed by Veblen (1934, p. 79) – that laws and explanations in the social and biotic domains must be consistent with each other.
18. See Hull (1985) for an extensive discussion of the problems of identifying the essence of 'Darwinism' from the perspective of the history of ideas.
19. Also misleading in some respects is my own earlier treatment of this issue. Hodgson (1993) insufficiently differentiated the views of Lamarck himself from those of later Lamarckians. Accordingly, I failed to note the very limited role of volition or intention in Lamarck's own writings, despite its widespread use by later Lamarckians. In general, my mistake was to identify Lamarck too closely with the Lamarckian tradition. Hull (1982) made the opposite error: the Lamarckian label was identified too closely with the personal ideas of Lamarck. Hodgson (1993) also failed to explore in sufficient detail the core characteristics of Darwinism as identified in this present essay.
20. Many of the prominent and non-memetic statements that social evolution is 'Lamarckian' – such as those cited earlier in this essay – appeared after Hull's article. This may partly explain his one-sided concentration on the memetic version of social or cultural change, as prompted by Dawkins (1976).
21. Regrettably, the contemporary enthusiasm for 'memes' and 'memetics' far outstrips the achieved degree of clarity and consensus concerning such core categories. A meme has been variously described as a unit of cultural imitation (Dawkins, 1976), a unit of information residing in a brain (Dawkins, 1982), units of culturally transmitted instructions (Dennett, 1995), an influential and replicable unit of information in the mind (Brodie, 1996), actively contagious ideas (Lynch, 1996), or behavioural instructions stored in brains and passed on by imitation (Blackmore, 1999).
22. See also the arguments in Hodgson (1997a, 1998a).
23. See also the discussion of evolutionary psychology in Plotkin (1994).
24. On this issue, see also Nightingale (2000).
25. In his fascinating book on cultural evolution, Durham (1991, p. 187) dubs this insight 'Campbell's Rule'. In a useful development of the argument, Cziko (1995) describes the acknowledgement of such a 'universal selection theory' as 'the Second Darwinian Revolution'.
26. However, some of the researchers listed in the table may also argue that social evolution is both Lamarckian and Darwinian. For example, as well as describing it as Lamarckian in their 1985 book, Boyd and Richerson (1992) also argue that it is Darwinian.

7. Nesting Lamarckism within Darwinian Explanations: Necessity in Economics and Possibility in Biology?

Thorbjørn Knudsen[1]

The role of Lamarck in the social sciences seems to mirror that of Darwin in biology. In biology, it is an established fact that evolution is Darwinian. Even if the implications of Darwin's theory were not unlike those of Lamarck's, Darwin's claims have been systematically substantiated by empirical studies to an extent that has been impossible to ignore: Darwin's theory is today universally held by modern biologists. Neo-Darwinism has been so successful that one of its pillars, the central dogma, is commonly thought an unassailable truth. According to the central dogma, information can flow from the genetic code to protein but never in the reverse direction.[2]

Against this view, the immunologist Ted Steele has been the lone maverick who in the last twenty years has advocated the possibility of Lamarckian selection in biology. Steele's book, *Somatic Selection and Adaptive Evolution*, caused a temporary stir in the beginning of the 1980s but was soon forgotten when it turned out that his argument could not be supported by empirical evidence (Cronin, 1991). However, Ted Steele and co-workers continued to develop their theory of Lamarckian inheritance through the 1990s and have recently summarised their views in *Lamarck's Signature* (1998).[3]

For the biologist, the most important implication of Steele et al. (1998), if taken seriously, is undoubtedly the theoretical possibility that the central dogma may be violated by the molecular processes involved in immunological response. Their book highlights a crucial difficulty for the natural-selection explanation of immunological response, that of timeliness. For the social scientist it is worth noting that they present their Lamarckian theory as limited, consistent with, and nested within, a Darwinian explanation.[4] Not only is the possibility of the co-existence of Lamarckian and Darwinian explanations opened but the indicated nested relationship also suggests that Darwinian evolution is necessary to guide Lamarckian evolution.

For the social scientist, the crucial importance of this claim lies in the rejection of the strong biological reductionism which spread during the 1970s and 1980s (Plotkin, 1988) in favour of a view acknowledging the social level as distinct from and yet dependent upon the biological level. This was argued by Castoriadis (1987), Hodgson (1993, 1999a, 1999b), Monod (1971), Morin (1974, 1990, 1992) and others.[5] The possibility that a Lamarckian explanation can co-exist with a Darwinian one also suggests a resolution of much futile discussion in the social sciences which assumes that Lamarckism implies rejection of Darwinism and vice versa.

Moreover, as will be argued in the ensuing, the nesting of Lamarckian selection within a Darwinian explanation is also necessary in economics to solve a fundamental but largely ignored problem associated with Lamarckism.[6] Without the stable baseline provided by immutable genes, there is no guarantee that the 'right' level of immutability is present. According to what may be termed the baseline problem of Lamarckism, genes lose track of evolution if their carrier, in response to environmental stimuli, changes them too often.[7] Since it is widely held that economic evolution is Lamarckian, this issue poses a severe problem in need of solution. Steele et al.'s (1998) idea of nested Lamarckism may point to such a solution, if a viable analogy that abides by the structure of the Darwinian explanation can be devised. Against prevailing views that economic evolution is demonstrably Lamarckian, we outline a possible Darwinian theory of economic evolution, referred to as Local Emulative Selection. It provides the necessary guidance for the Lamarckian theory to be convincing as an explanation of the evolution of complex organisational forms.

The premise of the present work is that any evolutionary explanation in economics that aspires to account for unpredictable evolution should strictly abide by the structural requirements of Lamarckian or Darwinian explanations. This may be termed the Structural Equivalence Principle. However, it is commonly accepted that social evolution in general, and in economics in particular, is Lamarckian. Therefore, most economists are likely to limit their use of Darwinian explanations to a loose inspirational metaphor for the expression of competitive forces. In fact, most economists view the possibility of a truly Darwinian explanation in much the same light as the biologist considers Lamarckism; at best, a misguided idea. Due to what is referred to as the baseline problem, however, any Lamarckian explanation, including those in economics, needs Darwinian guidance. Thus, the main argument of the present work is that the possibility opened by Steele et al. (1998), of nesting Lamarckism within a Darwinian explanation, is worth exploring in view of the need to solve the baseline problem.

Before entering into the argument, it is important to be clear about what is, and what is not, involved in the claim of the necessity for Darwinian guidance. First, we believe that there are a number of distinct differences between the social and the natural realm. Therefore, and emphatically, we do *not* imply that social evolution is guided by biological evolution in a narrow deterministic sense. However, social evolution should be consistent with and not contradict what we know about biological evolution. Second, what is meant is that any theory that aspires to account for unpredictable evolution needs to abide by the Structural Equivalence Principle. Moreover, the structural equivalent of Darwinian selection is necessary for any reasonable explanation of the evolution of complex forms such as the human eye or the modern business corporation. Nonetheless, many aspects of cultural and economic evolution seem obviously Lamarckian. For the time being we will attempt to resolve the need for Darwinian guidance by proposing an explanation nesting the Lamarckian within the broad Darwinian framework. This argument may be viewed, if one wishes, as an expression of Universal Darwinism (see Plotkin, 1994).

Accounting for Unpredictability Requires Lamarck or Darwin

Broadly, a distinction can be made between genetic and developmental evolutionary explanations. It is further common to divide genetic explanations into two branches: (1) phylogenetic explanations, including Darwinian and Lamarckian explanations, and (2) ontogenetic or unfolding explanations. Since the focus of the present work is on Darwinian and Lamarckian theory, we are primarily concerned with the subset of genetic explanations referred to as phylogenetic.[8]

The central distinguishing feature between genetic and developmental explanations is their explanatory structure. In genetic explanations a crucial distinction is introduced between an underlying code and the behavioural entity which is 'programmed' by the code. The structure of genetic explanations, therefore, encompasses two layers. By contrast, developmental explanations, such as the recent theories of stage-wise development towards ecological sustainability, typically conflate these two layers. Briefly, we shall point out that a layered structure is necessary if we wish to account for unpredictable evolution, suggesting that developmental explanations are not very useful. Moreover, it will be indicated that both developmental and ontogenetic explanations leave too much of the evolutionary process unexplained.

That is, we are left with only two alternatives, the ones originally devised by Lamarck and Darwin. Consequently, evolutionary explanations in economics that aspire to account for unpredictable evolution must abide by the explanatory structure shared by both. As will be pointed out in conclusion, we further need to consider the possibility of constrained Lamarckism in the sense that a Lamarckian explanation may be nested within a Darwinian one. Returning to genetic explanations, we shall provide a broad description of the code and its relation to the organism or agent. Since it is the assumptions about the relation, or more precisely the information flow, between the code and its carrier that differentiates modern Darwinism from Lamarckism, this is essential background to what follows. As will be pointed out in the following, the only distinction between the structure of Lamarckian and Darwinian explanations is the assumptions regarding the information flow between the code and its carrier. While a Darwinian carrier can never change its underlying code, the Lamarckian can. Otherwise, the two explanations are identical.

The code provides the instructions which, dependent upon environmental triggers, unfold into the properties which allow the agent to interact with other agents within a specific context. In biology, the layered theoretical structure corresponds to empirical reality, the code to genes, and the interacting entity to the organism. It is further important to emphasise that the relation between the code and its carrier is not deterministic. The code contains a wide range of potentials, which are gradually triggered by environmental cues through the organism's unfolding in maturation. According to Jacob (1985), the code provides any normal child with the potential to grow up in any community, to talk any language, to accept any religion and any set of social conventions. The code installs the conditions that allow the child to react to environmental stimuli, to seek and find regularities, to memorise regularities and to recombine regularities (Jacob, 1985). In this sense it works very much like a recipe for a mince pie. Although all mince pies have shared features they are also unique and none are quite like my grandmother's. In short, any organism is programmed by the genetic code; however, it is programmed to learn (Jacob, 1985).

In biology, the code is contained in the genes in terms of a specific sequence of nucleotide bases which make up the DNA molecule. In economics, matters are less settled but there seems to be wide agreement that Nelson and Winter's (1982) idea of routines as the economic analogy to genes is useful. In both instances an underlying code acts as a recipe for the development of an entity (organism or agent) and its capacities. Evolution, then, can be explained in terms of two subprocesses: (1) changes in the code due to recombination and mutation, i.e., genetic response, and (2) changes in the code due to migration, death and differential reproductive success, i.e., phenotypic selection. Note that changes in the code refer to the distributional properties of social or biological populations. Given enough time, the accumulated changes in the code due to these two processes are enough to account for the evolution of very complex entities such as the human eye.

One of the great attractions of phylogenetic explanations is that very little is left to exogenous events. Even mutation, the main source of new variety and unpredictability, is a genetic phenomenon generally caused by events within the mutating DNA. By contrast, developmental explanations depend on a large unexplained exogenous component, the change from one stage to the next. Ontogenetic, or unfolding, theories confine their explanation to the outcome of the interaction of the environment with the genetic imprint received by the organism at birth, or founding in the case of a business firm. Unfolding explanations leave the genetic imprint unexplained, with no way to comprehend changes in the code. In phylogenetic explanation, not only do we attempt to explain the growth of the organism and the development of communities of organisms, but also we explain the code itself, as pointed out in the previous paragraph.

Figure 7.1 shows these differences schematically.[9] The unexplained component, X, is largest for developmental theories, smaller for ontogenetic theories and smallest for phylogenetic theories. When the task is *post hoc* reconstruction of the possible processes which may account for the evolution of a particular trait or character, this is a great attraction. Why? Because otherwise there are likely to be too many degrees of freedom in explanation, too many equally possible stories which may fit the evidence. Put differently, when the task is to account for unpredictable evolution, which can be defined as changes in the state space of a population's defining characteristics caused by mutation, a phylogenetic explanation is to be preferred since its contenders are not up to the task. We are then left with two alternatives, the Lamarckian or the Darwinian explanation, and the task of specifying their structural equivalents in the social realm.[10] Consequently, any evolutionary explanations in the social realm that aspires to account for unpredictable evolution should abide by the structural requirements of either a Lamarckian or a Darwinian explanation, as outlined in Figure 7.1. This may conveniently be termed the Structural Equivalence Principle.

The ensuing section argues the case for this principle as a criterion for valid evolutionary theory in economics. It begins with a brief historical introduction of the classical Lamarckian and Darwinian explanation in biology and then identifies the structure and content of their modern counterparts. Subsequently, the Structural Equivalence Principle is applied to economics. The question is whether it is useful to do so, given the difference in the explanatory content of economics compared to biology.

Figure 7.1, Structural characteristics of evolutionary explanations[1].

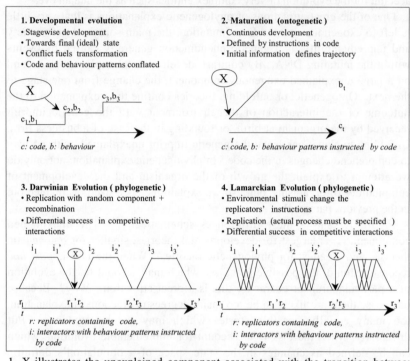

1. **Developmental evolution**
 • Stagewise development
 • Towards final (ideal) state
 • Conflict fuels transformation
 • Code and behaviour patterns conflated

c: code, b: behaviour

2. **Maturation (ontogenetic)**
 • Continuous development
 • Defined by instructions in code
 • Initial information defines trajectory

c: code, b: behaviour patterns instructed by code

3. **Darwinian Evolution (phylogenetic)**
 • Replication with random component + recombination
 • Differential success in competitive interactions

r: replicators containing code,
i: interactors with behaviour patterns instructed by code

4. **Lamarckian Evolution (phylogenetic)**
 • Environmental stimuli change the replicators' instructions
 • Replication (actual process must be specified)
 • Differential success in competitive interactions

r: replicators containing code,
i: interactors with behaviour patterns instructed by code

1. X illustrates the unexplained component associated with the transition between stages or cohorts (generations). In movement from the developmental through the ontogenetic to the two phylogenetic explanations, an increasing amount of the transition process is endogenised. Therefore, the unexplained component X is largest in developmental explanations and smallest in phylogenetic explanations.

Lamarckism and Darwinism: Questioning Received Wisdom

Lamarck for Biology?

Clearly not. The prevailing view in modern biology is that Lamarckian inheritance for a number of reasons is thoroughly invalidated. As we shall see, recent work, against prevailing views, attempts, at least in a limited sense, to reopen the case for Lamarckian inheritance. Since the modern idea of Lamarckian inheritance is a much modified version of Lamarck's own work, we shall provide some background.

We first turn to Lamarck's theory of evolution and describe how it presented a revolution in thought, a bold break with the creationist view that the social neither could, nor should, be viewed as a development of the natural. His theory, as Darwin's, encountered strong resistance from commonly held views, providing remarkable evidence of a gene-like immutability in the ideas directing cultural evolution, including, in a broad sense, technological and scientific progress. Lamarck propounded the then untenable view that life forms evolved from the simple to the increasingly complex and perfect. He also provided a perfectly legitimate theory of evolution through adaptation. According to Mayr (1982), Lamarck's was a theory as legitimate as Darwin's, with the misfortune that its premises turned out to be invalid.

We next turn to Darwin's theory and its break with tradition. The implications of Darwin's theory were not unlike those of Lamarck's. In sharp contrast to Lamarck's claims, however, Darwin's were systematically substantiated by empirical observation to an extent that they were impossible to ignore. As it turned out, Darwin's theory won out and is today universally accepted by modern biologists. In fact neo-Darwinism has been so successful that one of its pillars, the central dogma, is commonly thought an unassailable truth. In order to evaluate one of the few well-founded recent claims to the contrary, we briefly introduce neo-Darwinism in its modern gene-centred form. A complete overview is not intended, only enough to describe what is of interest to the present paper, the possibility of Lamarckian inheritance in biology. Our focus, therefore, is limited to Weismann's barrier and the central dogma in modern biology: the molecular barrier that prevents Lamarckian inheritance. Finally, the most important reasons for the modern biologist's negative view of the possibility of Lamarckian inheritance are reviewed.

Lamarck's Legacy

Jean-Baptiste Pierre Antoine de Monet de Lamarck (1744–1829) settled upon an academic career after an injury forced him to abandon a military career.[11] His early academic enthusiasms were for botany and meteorology; however, his scientific work, including his evolutionary theorising, are best viewed as facets of the pursuit of a comprehensive naturalist philosophy. His first masterpiece was the definitive French flora, published in 1779 by the government (Lamarck, 1779). Lamarck was lucky enough to receive patronage from Georges, Comte de Buffon (1707–1788), the director of the Jardin du Roi in Paris. Buffon helped Lamarck secure his first job as an assistant in the Botanical Department of the natural history museum and later engineered Lamarck's election to the Académie Royale des Sciences. Most of his working life was spent at the Jardin du Roi, benefiting from its natural history collections. Lamarck published papers in a wide range of academic fields, including chemistry, physics and meteorology; however, most were coolly received. Moreover, Lamarck lost sympathy because he refused to abandon views that opposed what were then seen as important scientific advances. Sadly, at his funeral, Georges Cuvier, Lamarck's famous opponent and colleague at the museum, used the occasion to turn the customary 'eulogy' into ridicule of much of Lamarck's work, partly a warning to those who indulged in scientific speculation relating to evolutionism. The two major points of critique were weak empirical support for his (vertical) evolutionism and the attribution of will to animals. The latter point is a popular misconception of Lamarck's views based on a misreading of his use of the term '*besoin*', to mean 'want' rather than 'need', as Lamarck intended it to do. The first critique was later repeated by Charles Lyell, Darwin's mentor, who strongly opposed the destruction of the border between the natural and the social implied by Lamarck's evolutionism.

During the 1790s, Lamarck developed his intimately linked theories about the nature of living things and the physical world. Drawing on studies of the fossil record, he became convinced that the environment influenced the development of the organism and, in contrast to common views at the time, that the species had not evolved once and forever but gradually over time. Focusing on Lamarck's contribution to evolutionary biology, it is worth noting that his contribution as an outstanding invertebrate zoologist and pioneering systematist was later entirely and unjustly ignored due to the refutation of his theory of inheritance of acquired characters.

Lamarck's name is invariably associated with the latter theory, the idea that, for example, the blacksmith's son inherits his father's strong arm. This idea was not original to Lamarck; in fact it had been commonplace for centuries before Lamarck. Later, most of those who did not read Lamarck in the original believed that Lamarckism simply meant the idea of the inheritance of acquired characters. As Mayr (1982) notes, it is a curious fact that Lamarck received both credit and blame for a concept that was universally held at his time. Against popular views to the contrary, the contribution of Lamarck did not lie in coining the concept of acquired inheritance; rather, according to Mayr (1982), Lamarck signifies the first breakthrough for evolutionism. It must be emphasised that evolutionism was a radical and controversial break with the received world-view at the time, that all life owed its existence to an omnipotent Creator. This is one reason it took yet another fifty years after Lamarck for evolutionism to be widely accepted. Another reason is that Lamarck's ideas were poorly substantiated by empirical evidence. It took Darwin to deliver a proper empirically substantiated theory of evolution. Nevertheless, according to Mayr (1982), it cannot be ignored that Lamarck was the first to systematically: (1) emphasise the fact of evolution, a theory of process that broke with the prevailing steady-state theories at his time; (2) provide a mechanism of evolution, i.e., inheritance of acquired characters; and (3) take primary interest in adaptation, albeit in terms or the transformation of species from lower to higher forms over time. The kernel of Lamarck's biological philosophy, including the famous idea of acquired inheritance, was set out in his *Zoological Philosophy* and later elaborated in his *Natural History of Invertebrates* (Burkhardt, 1995; Jordanova, 1984):

> 1st law: In every animal which has not passed the limit of its development, a more frequent and continuous use of any organ gradually strengthens, develops and enlarges that organ, and gives it a power proportional to the length of time it has been so used; while the permanent disuse of any organ imperceptibly weakens and deteriorates it, and progressively diminishes its functional capacity, until it finally disappears.
> 2nd law: All the acquisitions or losses wrought by nature on individuals, through the influence of the environment in which their race has long been placed, and hence through the influence of the predominant use or permanent disuse of any organ; all these are preserved by reproduction to the new individuals which arise, provided that the acquired modifications are common to both sexes, or at least to the individuals which produce the young. (Lamarck, [1809] 1984, p. 113)

Lamarck's idea of soma to germline information flow was formulated in these two propositions set out in an elaborate system of natural philosophy (Jordanova, 1984).[12] As previously mentioned, the idea of soma to germline influence was commonplace in the eighteenth century and before. Nature, it was thought, was a harmonious system, a divine creation. Before Lamarck, embryos were thought to be preformed by their divine maker. No more than a small stimulus was necessary for their predestined unfolding to take place. Lamarck rejected this idea in favour of the view that reproduction and subsequent development of the organism both involved giving life to formless matter. The organism came with potentials, a capacity for growth to be invoked in a specific environment. Therefore, according to Lamarck, the development of organs and faculties were linked to their use and disuse. This idea was accepted by Darwin (1868), as was Lamarck's idea that everything which had been acquired during the organism's lifetime was transmitted to the next generation, subject to the condition of common parents.[13] However, Darwin objected to Lamarck's transformism, the view that life necessarily would evolve into higher and more complex forms (Darwin, 1868).

In other words, while Darwin accepted Lamarckian inheritance, he rejected the commonly held contemporary view, espoused by Lamarck, that organisms would evolve in stages towards higher, more complex and perfect forms. In biology this view was earlier referred to as the theory of recapitulation.[14] It has a long history and can be seen as an early attempt to give human beings, the supposedly highest life form, a more conspicuous role in the divine maker's otherwise perfect order. According to the original theory of recapitulation, the 'choice' of the organism was one of accepting the Maker's invitation to commence evolution into higher life forms. This idea is the basic organising principle for the theory of the natural order presented in *Zoological Philosophy*, in which nature endows organisms with a set of faculties (feeding, growing, multiplying and preserving organically produced progress). By transmission of these faculties to all individuals organically reproduced throughout time, Lamarck (1984, p. 130) suggests that the 'living bodies of all classes and orders have been successively reproduced'. Although Lamarck does not use the actual term 'recapitulation,' it is clear that this is the idea which underlies his classification of animals into six distinct stages of increasing perfection.

In sum, Lamarck's theory of evolution may be seen as a bold break with the creationist view, universally held at his time, which implied that the social could not be viewed as a development of the natural. His premises and their implications (Plotkin, 1994, pp. 26–7) turned out to be invalid and unable to be supported empirically. Nonetheless, the logic of his theory of evolution by adaptation from simple to complex and perfectly adapted organisms remains legitimate. Whether he made evolutionary thinking itself more legitimate, thereby providing Darwin's ideas, fifty years later, with a more fertile environment, remains a moot point.

Darwin: Natural Selection as the Motor of Evolution

While Darwin was not the first to suggest that species are not created but evolve, he was the first to present a coherent and convincing argument, with evidence, that could stand against the commonly held view that nature, including the species, is created by some external force and then placed in the world to commence its predestined movement. Thus it should be pointed out that Darwin's theory of the evolution of species built upon contrasting and complementary ideas important at his time; ideas which themselves reflect a descent with modification induced by the selective forces of history. Important and well-documented influences on Darwin, apart from that of economist Thomas Robert Malthus in September 1838, include, among others, Lamarck, the ornithologist John Gould, Gilbert White, the parson naturalist of Selbourne, the natural theologian Paley, the German plant geographer Alexander von Humboldt, the geologist Charles Lyell, and, through him, proponents of the theory of embryonic recapitulation such as Friedriech Tiedemann and Johann Meckel (Mayr, 1982; Richards, 1992; Worster, 1994).[15] The economists Bernard Mandeville, Adam Smith and Charles Babbage seem to have influenced Darwin's thought (Hodgson, 1994).[16] Nonetheless, Darwin's theory of the evolution of species by natural selection radically broke with tradition because it discarded previous ideas of creation by an omniscient external force.

Furthermore, Darwin's theory seems to mark a point of bifurcation where biology and economics part tracks. At Darwin's time, the concepts of nature and the economy were overlapping, both referring to a natural order established by some external force or Creator. In early economics such notions are reflected in Physiocrat thinking and in the concept of a natural order present in Adam Smith's theory, and still present in the economic concept of equilibrium. In early biology it was common to refer to 'the economy of nature,' some sort of economising principle which both reflected and served to uphold the harmonious natural order.[17] The concept of a natural order was the foundational concept of Carl von Linné's classification system and can be found in later works such as the climax theory coined by the Danish biologist Eugenius Warming. However, Darwin's theory of natural selection, together with the revival of Mendelian genetics after 1900 (see Campbell, 1984), meant that the concept of a natural order resting upon externally given principles eventually was evicted from biology in favour of evolutionary theory. Thus Darwin's work marks a bifurcation of economics and biology in terms of foundational concepts guiding research. Equilibrium is the foundational concept of economics. It reflects the Arcadian idea of a natural order. The Darwinian concept of natural selection was the new idea adopted in biology.

Darwin's conversion to evolutionism was gradual, but his development of the idea of natural selection that followed seems to be the outcome of an extraordinarily intense intellectual effort between July 1837 and September 1838 (Mayr, 1982). As the title *On the Origin of Species* indicates, Darwin was primarily interested in diversification (horizontal evolution), the multiplication of species. It is, however, a curious ambiguity in the *Origin* that natural selection, the driving force of 'vertical evolution', for Darwin seems to explain also 'horizontal' evolution (Mayr, 1982). Whatever the reason, it is to natural selection as an explanation for evolution that we now turn.

It is a well-known fact that Darwin's theory from the end of the nineteenth century up until the 1940s went out of favour. As Cronin (1991) notes, Darwinism was commonly castigated for hindering scientific progress by insisting on asking the wrong questions. As it turned out, Darwin's theory had implications much wider in scope than anticipated at the time of its contrivance. As noted by Nobel Laureate Jacques Monod (1997), the predictive contents of the selective theory of evolution were much richer than Darwin himself ever knew. In fact, they were rich and broad enough also to be of interest as explanation for evolution in the social world. In the following, we shall focus on the modern Darwinian theory of evolution by natural selection as it appeared after the synthesis between classical Darwinism and Mendelian genetics. It is important to note, as indicated by Monod (1997), that Darwin's original formulation of evolution by natural selection still stands; however, there has been a change in focus from the organism-centred view of classical Darwinism to the gene-centred view of neo-Darwinism (Cronin, 1991).

Natural selection was defined by Darwin as, 'the preservation of favourable variations and the rejection of injurious variations' (Darwin, n.d. [1872], p. 64; cf. Durham, 1991, p. 12). Over the years it has been redefined to its current meaning, the differential reproduction of genotypes. Natural selection involves two independent processes: genetic transmission and epigenetic phenotype–environment interaction. This entails a description of the state space of the genotype, the phenotype, genetic and epigenetic processes and the crucial link between genetic and epigenetic processes. Commonly, the focus is upon the processes of variation, fitness and heredity. Endler (1992) provides this useful definition of natural selection:

> 'Natural selection' can be defined as a process that occurs if and only if these three conditions are present: the population has (a) variation among individuals in some attribute or trait (phenotypic variation); (b) a consistent relationship between that trait and mating ability, fertilising ability, fertility, fecundity, and/ or survivorship (fitness variation); and (c) a consistent relationship, for that trait, between parents and their offspring, which is at least partially independent of common environment effects (inheritance). (Endler, 1992, p. 220)

According to Endler (1992), if these three conditions are met, then one or both of the following outcomes will occur:

(1) the trait frequency distribution will differ among age classes or life-history stages to an extent beyond that expected from ontogeny (growth and development); (2) if the population is not at equilibrium, then the trait distribution of all offspring in the population will be predictably different from that of all parents, beyond that expected from conditions (a) and (c) alone. Conditions *a* (phenotypic variation), *b* (fitness variation), and *c* (inheritance) contain all of the biology, and the process (outcomes 1 and 2) results purely from probability and statistics – the correlated effects of the biological conditions ... . (Endler, 1992, p. 220)

Thus defined natural selection is ahistorical; it only depends upon 'current ecological and genetic conditions'. Crucially, evolution (cumulative genetic changes) may or may not happen in consequence of natural selection as it is explained only partially by natural selection. Furthermore, natural selection does not necessarily give rise to evolution because an evolutionarily stable equilibrium may be reached dependent upon history as well as natural selection (conditions a, b and c). Two classes of more restricted uses of the term natural selection are identified by Endler (1992): (1) alternative subprocesses (such as mortality selection and sexual and non-sexual selection), and (2) component or sequential processes. This level of description will largely be evaded here. It should be noted, however, that we, in order to illustrate the difference between natural selection and Lamarckian selection, find it useful to split natural selection into two independent subprocesses: (1) genetic change between generations (genetic response) and (2) phenotypic change within generations (phenotypic selection). The bridge between this decomposition of natural selection and Endler's (1992) general definition is straightforward:

> In terms of the general definition of natural selection, phenotypic selection requires conditions (a) and (b) for natural selection. The response is the genetic change that occurs as a result of phenotypic selection in combination with the genetic system, which requires condition (c) for natural selection; it is the between-generation change in trait distributions after phenotypic selection. ... If there is no inheritance (condition c), the process of natural selection cannot occur. (Endler, 1992, pp. 222–3)

Notably, Endler (1992) defines the phenotype and *not* the genotype as the unit of selection. Natural selection may be described as the two independent subprocesses of differential survival (phenotypic selection) and perpetuation of phenotypes to the next generation which requires inheritance (genetic response). Furthermore, natural selection is ahistorical and involves the two independent subprocesses of differential survival and inheritance. Evolution works in terms of variation accumulated over time in both of these subprocesses.[18] In the following we turn to the reason why natural selection, according to the central dogma in modern biology, involves an insurmountable barrier that prevents information from flowing from soma to germ cells. It is this barrier, postulated by the German biologist August Weismann in the 1880s, which allows the separation of natural selection into phenotypic selection and genetic response.

Weismann's Barrier and the Central Dogma in Biology

This section explains what in biology is known as Weismann's barrier and its modern equivalent, the central dogma, which states that information can flow from DNA and RNA to proteins but never in the reverse direction. In the ensuing we shall examine recent claims put forward by Ted Steele and co-workers challenging the central dogma. In order to do this, this section provides the necessary background in terms of a rough description of the genetic machinery.[19]

According to modern biology, information can flow from germline to soma cells, never in the other direction. The Weismann barrier between germline and soma refers to the claim that the germ line is independent of changes from within the body and, therefore, protected from such changes. Weismann based his claim on compelling evidence, the fact that parental mutilations cannot be inherited. For example, mice are not born with a shorter tail even if their forebears' tails have been cut for twenty generations or more. The general claim, if true, means that no changes in the organism can alter the germline cells and, consequently, acquired characteristics cannot be inherited. When the blacksmith develops big muscles, his son will not benefit by inheritance and his daughter need not be worried about unfitting looks. Moreover, the difficulty in explaining the preferred difference in inheritance between son and daughter disappears. In terms of the interactor–replicator framework, the claim is that interactors cannot, ever, change the code contained in replicators.

In its modern form Weismann's barrier translates into the central dogma which states the following relation between genes and soma cells: DNA <-> RNA -> protein. The genetic code is contained in DNA and RNA molecules. Through a rather complex process the genetic code is translated into protein. According to Ted Steele and co-workers' 'somatic selection theory', Weismann's barrier can be selectively penetrated, at least in theory. That is, sometimes there is a two-way relation between DNA, RNA and protein. We shall evaluate this claim below. In order to do this, it is necessary, however, to provide some detail of the genetic translation machinery.

The Modern View of the Genetic Translation Process

The general idea is as follows. DNA contains the genetic code. Mediated by RNA, through a process known as transcription, the DNA code translates into protein chains. The DNA <–> RNA relation works very much like a tape-recorder. In both directions, information can be edited as well as transmitted. By contrast, the RNA –> protein relation is one-way, like a record-player. To explain further, a few facts established by molecular genetics have to be stated.

DNA is the molecule which contains the genetic code. The code contains information in sequences composed of four building blocks, the nucleotide bases, A (adenine), T (thymine), C (cytosine), and G (guanine). The four building blocks can be thought of as a genetic alphabet of four letters. A sequence, or strand, of DNA is composed of this alphabet, arranged in triplets, groups of three letters, each specifying an amino acid. In 1953, Watson and Crick discovered the structure of the DNA molecule, the famous double helix which combines two complementary strands of paired nucleotide bases (A pairs with T and C pairs with G). Genes, it is believed, consist of sections of these strands, thousands to millions of paired bases in length. Since the possible combinations of a strand consisting of one million of the four nucleotide bases are many times the number of atoms in the known universe, it should, as noted by Maynard Smith and Szathmáry (1999, p. 8) 'provide an adequate basis for continued evolution'.

Chemically, RNA resembles DNA with the minor difference that the nucleotide T is replaced with the functionally equivalent U (uracil). However, there is an important structural difference. Whereas DNA is made of two strands of complementary bases, RNA is (usually) single stranded. Since the double strands of DNA are complementary, the molecule holds a strong structural basis for error-correction absent in RNA. The significance of this difference lies in the fidelity of DNA replication.

When DNA is replicated, the structure of the double helix provides the basis for an elaborate error detection and correction process. The new DNA is formed as a replica of a DNA template which is read by a chemical 'copying machine'. During formation of the new DNA strand, it is constantly checked for errors. The key to this elaborate error detection process is the double helix. The new strand of DNA immediately starts to form complementary bases (A–T and C–G) to produce a double helix and by comparison of the two strands, incorrect base pairs are immediately detected, in which cases error correction ensures that they are deleted and substituted with a correct base pair. Due to this error detection and correction procedure, the error rate in DNA replication is extremely low ($<10^{-9}$) whereas RNA replication is considerably more error prone ($10^{-3} - 10^{-4}$).[20] The reason for this difference lies in the single stranded RNA molecule which, in contrast to the double helix, does not provide the means for elaborate error detection.

In genetic translation, RNA blueprints are made of selected stretches of a DNA sequence, referred to as transcription, followed by a process where the RNA blueprint serves as a template for protein synthesis. More precisely, the RNA blueprint serving as a template (mRNA) consists of codons, amino acids which consist of three letters of the genetic alphabet (A, U, C, G). A new protein is formed by 'reading' the RNA template three letters at a time, resulting in complementary copies (anti-codons) which are attached to the growing protein. Since RNA is involved in protein synthesis, the error rate is equal to the one observed in RNA replication ($10^{-3} - 10^{-4}$).

We can now state the content of the central dogma with more precision: genetic information only flows from DNA and RNA to protein – never in the reverse direction. DNA and RNA can be copied from DNA and RNA templates. In genetic translation, information can flow from the genetic code, the DNA, to RNA. This process is referred to as transcription. The inverse process, reverse transcription, was first predicted by Howard Temin in 1959[21] and met an initial stormy reception when it was presented to a wider audience (Temin, 1964). The existence of reverse transcription was confirmed in the 1970s (Baltimore, 1970; Temin and Mizutani, 1970) and is today widely recognised as an essential process in the replication of retroviruses (e.g. HIV) and other cellular events (Coffin et al., 1997).

The discovery and confirmation of reverse transcription in a sense opens half of Weissman's barrier. According to the central dogma in modern biology, the remaining half is still an insurmountable barrier; information can never flow from protein to RNA or DNA.[22] As we shall see in the ensuing, Ted Steele and co-workers have devised a theory, the 'somatic selection theory', which challenges this dogma. The core idea involves the possibility of production of free DNA copies from RNA templates of viruses. If it can be shown that such free DNA copies can, at least partly, be integrated into the genetic DNA code, Weissman's barrier is broken. Before turning to Steele et al.'s (1998) claims, we shall briefly evaluate the standing of Lamarckism in modern biology.

The Possibility of Lamarckian Inheritance

Before Weismann, Lamarck's idea of development through use and disuse of bodily organs coupled with inheritance, stated in his 1st and 2nd laws (in *Zoological Philosophy*), was widely accepted and it is a historical fact that Darwin and his grandfather Erasmus Darwin before him assumed the idea. Part of the evidence is contained in Darwin's (1868) theory of Pangenesis, published nine years after the *Origin*. According to Steele et al. (1998), it is a curious fact that this seminal contribution, allegedly due to the embarrassment involved in Darwin's recourse to Lamarckian heresy, is often expunged from the scientific literature by neo-Darwinist hardliners. Whatever the reasons for the neglect of the Lamarckian in Darwin, it is important to note that a modern claim of Lamarckian inheritance in biology involves a much modified version of the idea. It is to the possibility of Lamarckian inheritance in its modern form that we now turn. Briefly, we shall note that the idea of Lamarckian inheritance is the only alternative to Darwinian selection and that it cannot easily be dismissed as false. We shall further invoke a distinction between direct Lamarckian inheritance involving information flows in the 'wrong' direction, from protein to RNA and DNA, and indirect Lamarckian inheritance involving mediation from cultural inheritance.

The battle in modern biology has concerned the possibility of violating the central dogma, but notwithstanding a few claimed cases of possible direct Lamarckian inheritance (see e.g. Maynard Smith, 1989), the theoretical possibility of direct Lamarckian inheritance has not yet been supported by empirical observation. Although no one disputes the possibility of cultural mediation of Darwinian selection, it has been widely agreed for some time now that Lamarck's theory is thoroughly refuted in the biological sphere. One of the leading texts in evolutionary biology provides a succinct summary of the case:

> By the 1930s and 1940s, many other scientists [besides Weismann] had done experiments that led to a total rejection of Lamarckian inheritance. By this time, Mendelian genetics had developed, providing a foundation for the variational principle that Darwin's theory required. Subsequently, molecular genetics demonstrated that changes in DNA are translated into differences in proteins. No mechanism is known whereby changes in proteins (or in other constituents of the body, other than nucleic acids) can alter the information encoded in the DNA. (Futuyama, 1998, p. 232)

Note that the case for Darwinism rests on a formidable body of empirical evidence which, since Weismann conducted his experiments, all seems to refute Lamarckian inheritance. It is no wonder that the case for Lamarckian inheritance has remained firmly shut for some time. It should be noted, however, that Futuyama's (1998) balanced statement opens a theoretical possibility that can never be refuted, that a hitherto unknown mechanism may be found that demonstrates protein-induced changes in DNA.

Dawkins (1996a) is less shy in passing judgement. In a number of works Dawkins (1982, 1989, 1996a) developed three very powerful arguments that seem to completely demolish Lamarckism. The first argument is simply that the assumption of inheritance of acquired characteristics seems to be inconsistent with all known empirical evidence in all life forms studied by biologists. The second argument states that this just confirms a logical necessity. The principle of acquired characteristic *has* to be false in any life form that relies upon an epigenetic recipe in a period of unfolding or embryonic development, i.e., in most life forms on earth, but not necessarily in Mars-folks. Why? Because the genetic code, as described above, works like a 'recipe'. Particular environmental cues trigger a subset of a much wider range of potentials. Therefore, the organism only represents one of an arbitrarily large set of possible configurations contained in the code. The insurmountable difficulty for Lamarckian inheritance is that the characteristics acquired by the organism are a very small subset of the entire code. Yet, when these characteristics are passed on, the entire code should somehow be altered. Clearly, this could only happen if the code worked like a blueprint so that the genes mapped one-to-one on the organism. But it doesn't and they don't. As Dawkins (1996a) explains:

> We can no more imagine acquired characteristics being inherited than we can imagine the following. A cake has one slice cut out of it. A description of the alteration is now fed back into the recipe, and the recipe changes in such a way that the next cake baked comes out of the oven with one slice already neatly missing. (Dawkins, 1996a, p. 298)

Having raised two formidable difficulties for Lamarckism, Dawkins (1996a) then deals the death blow. Even if the assumptions of Lamarckian theory were not true, it is, for two different reasons, incapable of explaining the evolution of adaptive complexity. First, the vast majority of acquired characteristics are injuries. Therefore, if all characteristics were inherited, each generation would not be starting afresh but increasingly be encumbered by accumulated decay and injury of previous generations. To avoid this, the organism needs discrimination based on a history of its environment. Provided the environment does not change too fast, discrimination is readily provided by Darwinian selection. To equip organisms with foresight equalling the cumulated memory of generations seems a bit strained. It seems even more strained to equip the organism with the ability to build organs of the complexity of an eye through sheer use. As Dawkins (1996a) notes, the lens is transparent and corrected against spherical and chromatic aberration. To make Lamarckian inheritance responsible for such achievement amounts to the claim that the lens will improve because it is used, because light passes through it, etc. Clearly, the story is incredible whereas the Darwinian alternative provides a simple and straightforward explanation. Since good eyesight is often a matter of life and death for any animal, any improvement in eyesight no matter how tiny will be seized upon by Darwinian selection. Given a sufficient number of generations, the consistent accumulation of slight improvements may eventually result in very complex and refined structures such as the eye. In conclusion Dawkins (1996a) notes:

> So, it isn't that Lamarckism is a rival to the Darwinian theory that happens to be wrong. Lamarckism isn't a rival to Darwinism at all. It isn't even a serious *candidate* as an explanation for the evolution of adaptive complexity. It is doomed from the start as a potential rival to Darwinism. (Dawkins, 1996a, p. 303, emphasis in original)

In her brilliant book on the unsolved Darwinian puzzles of altruism and sexual selection, Cronin (1991) uses the arguments developed by Dawkins (1982, 1989, 1996a) in a very powerful rebuttal of Lamarckism. Cronin (1991) observes that Lamarckism, despite its early rejection in biology and its less than persuasive arguments, has had an enduring attraction. Cronin (1991) offers a number of reasons: (1) a feeling among biologists, among others Sir Peter Medawar, that a response mechanism on the part of the organism was missing in the Darwinian theory, (2) that Lamarckism would lend an order to evolution that Darwinism has been felt to lack,[23] (3) that Darwinism excludes mind, and (4) that Lamarckism offers hope of a better future. For these and more reasons, Lamarckism is still in vogue despite its clear rejection in biology on empirical grounds. Cronin's (1991) rebuttal of Lamarckism goes further, however, in following Dawkins's argument that even if Lamarckism had not (yet) been rejected on empirical grounds, it would have to be rejected on the basis of its limited explanatory power. The Lamarckian explanation can simply not do the job of explaining the evolution of complex biological forms such as the human eye. Cronin's (1991) arguments are convincing and, as will be argued in the ensuing, point to the need for considering the role of Darwinian explanation in evolutionary economics. Otherwise, how could we explain the evolution of complex organisational forms in terms of the process through which they emerged? Despite Cronin's (1991) powerful rejection of Lamarckism, her final verdict is more balanced than Dawkins's (1996a).[24] If Lamarckian mechanisms are to go anywhere, they must ride on the back of Darwinian achievements.

Maynard Smith (1989), one of the leading figures in modern evolutionary biology, and an acknowledged influence on Cronin (1991), seems to go even further in his assessment of Lamarckism:

> First, it is not so obviously false as is sometimes made out. Secondly, it is the only alternative to Darwinism as an explanation of the adaptive nature of evolution. (Maynard Smith, 1989, p. 8)

Maynard Smith (1989) then proceeds to review some contexts in which the neo-Darwinist picture is 'dubious or actually false', including cell differentiation, changes in gene amplification, cortical inheritance in ciliates and cultural inheritance.

In sum, both Maynard Smith (1989) and Cronin (1991), in contrast to Dawkins (1996a), open at least the theoretical possibility that a Lamarckian explanation might work in certain circumstances. In the ensuing section we shall present a modern biological version of nested or selective Lamarckism developed by Ted Steele and co-workers. Subsequently, we shall turn to the social realm and argue that the problems which plague Lamarckian explanations in biology point to the necessity of nesting Lamarckian explanations in economics within a theory that abides by the structure of Darwinian explanations.

Ted Steele and Co-workers' 'Somatic Selection Theory'

Recently, a modern molecular view of Lamarckian inheritance was articulated by biologist Ted Steele. The hypothesis developed by Steele (1979) opened at least a theoretical possibility that Weismann's barrier could be crossed. Roughly, the claim was that acquired immunological tolerance could be inherited. More precisely, Steele (1979) proposed a mechanism to explain the genetic evolution of antibody variable genes (V–genes) via a soma-to-germline gene feedback loop. This mechanism, if it existed, would allow for the creation of new genetically variant animals in response to foreign microbial invaders from the external environment. That is, it provides a plausible hypothesis for Lamarckian inheritance based on contemporary molecular knowledge. According to Cronin (1991), Steele's (1979) claims created a temporary stir in the beginning of the 1980s but lost attraction since they were not sustained on further investigation. Now, after twenty years of research, Steele and co-workers are back with a new book.

Steele et al.'s (1998) arguments in favour of Lamarckian inheritance encompass the following themes: (1) showing the theoretical possibility of selective penetration of Weismann's barrier, that, at least in association with immunological changes, a plausible mechanism can be pointed out where protein changes translate into RNA and DNA changes; (2) establishing that the proposed mechanism of selective penetration of Weismann's barrier not only is possible in principle but also is consistent with all known empirical evidence; and (3) making the case that not only is selective penetration possible in theory and consistent with empirical evidence, it is also compatible with Darwinian natural selection and necessary as an addendum to explain some peculiarities associated with the immune system.

Since Steele et al. (1998) state their case on the basis of advances in modern molecular biology, it is tough going for a social scientist. Also, it is the business of the biologist, not a social scientist, to pass judgement on their claims. The detail and complexity involved, unfortunately, should prevent any attempt by a layman who wanted to do so. Nevertheless, much can be learned from their argument which is of relevance also to the student of evolution in the social realm, notwithstanding the wider implications of the social dynamics involved in the reception of their work. In consequence, only a very rough outline of the work of Steele et al. (1998) is presented, and the focus will be on its wider implications. In particular, we shall note that it seems worthwhile to consider the possibility that limited Lamarckian inheritance consistent with Darwinian selection may be at work in the social realm.

The Immune System: Directed Mutations

As aforementioned, the discovery and confirmation of reverse transcription opens half of Weissman's barrier, but according to the central dogma in modern biology the remaining half is still an insurmountable barrier. Information can never flow from protein to RNA or DNA. However, according to Steele et al. (1998), free DNA copies can be produced from RNA templates of viruses. If it further can be shown that such free DNA copies under some circumstances can be integrated into the genetic DNA code, Weissman's barrier is broken.

The point of departure for Steele et al. (1998) is the known fact of the immune system's capacity to come up with a timely response to threats by novel infectious diseases despite its limited repertoire of antibodies. All immune systems can: (1) respond to virtually any antigen by the capacity to make an enormous repertoire of antibodies, (2) mount an enhanced memory response when challenged by an antigen a second time and, (3) maintain self-tolerance. In the 1960s it became apparent that the genome could not contain a sufficiently wide array of coding necessary to account for the repertoire of the immune system. In consequence, the possibility of somatic response was considered and, according to Steele et al. (1998), solved the problem. The possibility of somatic mutation clearly solves a problem of speed, or comprehensiveness, by allowing the immune system to come up with the necessary response to even unknown antigens fast enough. According to Steele et al. (1998), it is possible that free-floating DNA during this process may be altered and subsequently incorporated in the genome by a process of reverse transcription. Moreover, this theoretical possibility should be consistent with all the available evidence.

To repeat, it is not the job of the social scientist to evaluate these claims.[25] Some of the implications of Steele et al.'s arguments, however, may be relevant also for the social sciences. Importantly, Steele et al. (1998) open the possibility of nesting Lamarckism within a Darwinian explanation. They do not claim that their theory refutes the general validity of Darwinian theory. The claim is more limited: that Lamarckian selection working under the guidance of natural selection may play a limited but crucial role during immune responses. The possibility that an environmental signal (the antigen) may create a response which is subsequently integrated into the genome clearly violates the central dogma. It is important to note, however, that they view this as a selective mechanism of Lamarckian inheritance, nested within, and otherwise consistent with, natural selection.[26] The genetic variation caused by somatic mutation is, they assert, subsequently acted upon by natural selection. That is, an immune system which is able to acquire the free-floating DNA and incorporate it into the germline DNA code may have been selected for by natural selection.

This possibility of nesting Lamarckism within a Darwinian explanation should be of interest also to the social scientist. Why? Because the Darwinian explanation is demonstrably successful in accounting for evolution of very complex forms such as the human eye. The Darwinian explanation has solved what may be termed the baseline problem. However, natural selection may be too slow in responding to very fast change by virtue of the absence of information flows between organisms and genes. Consequently, the possibility of having Lamarckism in economics guided by an explanation which has the structural properties of Darwinian selection seems to be worth considering. Before considering this, however, we shall evaluate the role of Darwinian explanations in economics.

Darwin for Economics?

A distinction between neoclassical and heterodox approaches in economics should be made plain. Heterodox economics encompasses a swarm of distinct and more or less conflicting approaches, including new and old institutionalists, Marxists, post-Keynesians and Austrians. While huge differences in assumptions, theoretical emphases and methodology separate the various different heterodox approaches, a shared overlap is their emphasis on dynamics. Thus, it is not uncommon to hear the claim among critics of mainstream economics that neoclassical theory fails to deal with dynamics. As Hamilton (1953) pointed out long ago, this claim is simply dubious, since neoclassical theory, notwithstanding recent developments in game-theory, is surely concerned with change and dynamics in price and quantity, albeit in an equilibrium framework. The issue is not *if* neoclassical theory deals with change, it is *how* – and the difference between neoclassical theory and institutional approaches must be found in their concepts of change (Hamilton, 1999).

Broadly caricatured, neoclassical theory typically views change sequentially in comparative static terms, as moments of discontinuity caused by exogenous forces followed by reactions which re-establish equilibrium. That is, only one part of the economy changes, and it does so abruptly in response to independent forces. By contrast, the institutional and evolutionary economist is concerned with change in terms of the process which is its cause and holds 'the economy is at all times undergoing a process of cumulative change, and that the study of economics is the study of process' (Hamilton, 1999, p. 17). What Hamilton (1999) originally pointed to in 1953 was the inadequacy of unqualified use of change as a distinction between institutional economics and neoclassical economics.[27] That is, the oft-used distinction between statics and dynamics cannot separate heterodoxy and mainstream economics without further qualification.

As an example, consider Harrod's (1939) use of the term 'Dynamic Theory' to introduce his growth theory, which combined the use of the multiplier and accelerator in an equilibrium framework. Despite an initial promise to do the opposite, both Harrod and Keynes, according to Shackle (1967), failed to deliver a theory of cumulative change and returned to the respectability of 'equilibrium'. Since Myrdal's early works presented a theoretical framework ready at hand, Shackle (1967) viewed this failure as unwillingness to embrace novelty in the form of uncertain expectations. Or consider Schumpeter's definition of dynamics offered as an extension of, but not an alternative to, Walras and Marshall:

> ... throughout this book [Schumpeter, 1954], Dynamics means exclusively analysis that links quantities pertaining to different points of theoretic time ... and not the theory of evolutionary processes that run their courses in historic time: it is practically coextensive with sequence analysis and includes period analysis as a special case (Schumpeter, 1954, p. 1160).

Schumpeter saw this form of dynamic considerations as a genuine new beginning, a crossing of the Rubicon which leaves 'the main body of economic theory on the "static" bank of the river' (Schumpeter, 1954, p. 1160). He was, further, very careful to point out that static theory should enter as a special case of a future general economic dynamics, pointing to Samuelson (1947, Part II) as a promising step in that direction.[28] There is no doubt that Schumpeter (1954) embraces dynamics and yet rejects the notion that economics should be studied as a process of cumulative change. The qualification provided by Hamilton (1999), however, was that institutional and evolutionary economics is a novelty-embracing study of a cumulative process. Despite promising beginnings, Harrod (1939) failed to do this, and Schumpeter (1954) explicitly rejected the possibility.

Recently, Hodgson (1999a) included novelty as the most fundamental criterion in a taxonomy of evolutionary economics and supplied anti-reductionism and biological metaphor as additional criteria to cut across the confusingly wide variety of approaches that come with the term 'evolutionary economics'. Briefly, he insists on novelty as a fundamental ontological criterion to be embraced by a worthwhile evolutionary approach; however, in addition, emergent properties, and thus a layered ontology, must be recognised. Therefore, Hodgson (1999a, Chapter 6) advocates a novelty-embracing anti-reductionist institutional wing of evolutionary economics as a worthwhile alternative to neoclassical theory and the more limited evolutionary approaches which crop up with increasing frequency. Accepting the implications of Hodgson's (1999a) classification, the previous discussion seems to indicate something further. When novelty is embraced and actually shows itself on the scene, it was previously argued, an explanatory structure which reduces the unexplained must be sought out, i.e., the Structural Equivalence Principle must be observed. In the above, two possible and quite similar alternatives were presented which fulfilled this requirement: Lamarck's and Darwin's theories. In addition, these come with a layered ontology which may easily be expanded to the explanatory task at hand.

The argument is that unpredictable evolution calls for the minimisation of the explanatory weight carried by exogenous variables in order to reduce the number of alternative explanations that, *post hoc*, may fit the evidence. If this is accepted, only the explanatory structure of Lamarckian and Darwinian theory are contenders to account for unpredictable evolution since they minimise the role of exogenous variables. Put differently, when evolution is unpredictable because novelty frequently changes the defining characteristics of the state space of interest, the explanation must be Lamarckian or Darwinian. This point is apparently not widely recognised.

By contrast, it seems to be widely believed that economic evolution is Lamarckian. This was not always the case. Over 100 years ago, when Veblen (1898) introduced the evolutionary perspective into economics as a challenge to the contemporary mainstream, his appeal was to Darwinism.[29] In his remarkable article, Veblen characterised mainstream economics as a pre-evolutionary science, explicitly rejecting its mechanistic approach, and appealed to Darwinian theory as a proper scientific foundation for further theoretical development. What Veblen had in mind was 'development of a theory of a cumulative sequence of economic institutions stated in terms of the process itself' (Veblen, 1898, p. 77). Although the promise never was quite fulfilled by Veblen, or his immediate followers, he provided an important and early contribution that explicitly acknowledged a Darwinian foundation as an alternative to the mainstream and castigated the latter's mechanistic foundation. Since then, it has repeatedly and convincingly been argued that classical economics, conceived in the eighteenth century, received a Cartesian and Newtonian imprint at birth (see e.g. Hamilton, 1953; Hodgson, 1993; Mirowski, 1989). Apparently, this imprint was a set of instructions which, since then, with remarkable gene-like fecundity and fidelity, has replicated itself.

At the time of Veblen's appeal to Darwinian theory, it was in retreat and largely remained so till the 1940s. Moreover, in the first half of the 20th century the evolutionary framework in economics lacked clear equivalents to notions such as variety, fitness and adaptation (Metcalfe, 1998) still to be developed in biology. In this period mainstream economics was simultaneously strengthened by the theoretical and methodological developments in the interwar period which Shackle (1967) characterised as 'an immense creative spasm'. Thus, when Alchian (1950) reintroduced Darwinian evolution into economics, the appeal was to 'natural selection,' and the intention seemed to be reinforcement of, rather than challenge to, mainstream theory. Darwin had become a dirty word in the social sciences, tainted by the 'Social Darwinist' episode which had abused the evolutionary perspective and regrettably associated it with reactionary and racial viewpoints (Hodgson, 1993). Ideology rather than scientific evidence was the source of the move away from biology in the social sciences (Degler, 1991). When economists and social scientists today look to biology for inspiration, it is, with a few exceptions (e.g. Hannan and Freeman, 1989), to Lamarck they turn, definitely not Darwin (Nelson, 1995).[30] And when references are made to 'natural selection,' as Alchian (1950) did, the phrase is used as metaphor in a rather loose sense to denote differential survival.[31] Although the flavour of economic natural selection, or better, survivor selection, is Darwinian, it must be emphasised that the idea is very different from its more precise and sophisticated use in modern biology.[32] Confusingly, in economics Darwin's name turns up more often than Lamarck's; however, it is primarily associated with economic natural selection and everyone seems to agree that social evolution is Lamarckian.

By 1950 Darwin had lost his appeal in the social sciences, and it has never been regained, which may partly explain why the term 'natural selection' rather than Darwinian selection was used as metaphor when the evolutionary framework reappeared in economics in the 1950s.[33] Indeed, it is a great irony that the resurgence of the evolutionary framework in economics associated with Alchian (1950), Boulding (1950), Downie (1958), Hamilton (1953), Nelson (1962), Penrose (1959), Salter (1960), Steindl (1952), Winter (1964) and others happened at a time when the prevailing negative atmosphere against Darwinism in the social sciences prevented appreciation of the biological conquests gained in the synthesis of classical Darwinism and

Mendelian genetics.[34] It is even more ironic that many contemporary economists persist in ignoring these conquests, and the subsequent 40-year development of constructs like natural selection, adaptation or fitness in biology. Even if Alchian (1950) can be excused, a more updated understanding of what is involved in the modern biological version of natural selection may help avoid some of the pitfalls Alchian suffered, pitfalls exposed by Penrose (1952).

Nonetheless, the idea that market processes, in a metaphorical sense, may work like natural selection is due to Alchian (1950), and was further developed by Winter (1964). In economics, 'natural selection' is used in a metaphorical sense to denote weeding out of the less efficient caused by competition for scarce resources. Economic natural selection is based on the variation, selection, heredity framework. Variation is introduced by the entry of new firms into competitive markets and selection refers to differential death, or perhaps migration, in terms of exit of the less efficient. Differential efficiency, in turn, can be explained by appealing to the introduction and disappearance of products (Boulding, 1993), processes (Nelson and Winter, 1982) and perhaps organisational forms (Hannan and Freeman, 1989). As pointed out by Penrose (1952), Alchian (1950), however, did not adequately address the problem of heredity or genetic transmission. Despite Nelson and Winter's (1982) important development of an analogue to genes, the conceptualisation of genetic transmission and its link to competitive market processes remains one of the most important unsolved problems for evolutionary economics (Knudsen, 1998a, 1998b).

In sum, the use of 'natural selection' in economics has a Darwinian flavour, although it is metaphorical and very different from its current meaning in modern biology. As March (1999, p. 103) explains, one of the major contributions of Malthus, and subsequently Darwin, had been 'to recognise the role of competition for environmental resources in tightening the control of the environment over the evolution of species'. The metaphorical use of 'natural selection' in economics and in organisation theory, originally introduced by Alchian (1950), relies on competition to play a similar role in 'selecting' the producers who, for some reason, are the most efficient, whether the reason be known or not. The efficient survive and the inefficient go bankrupt. This is the commonly used meaning of 'natural selection,' or survivor selection, in economics.

Given the assumption of relentless competition, the beauty and appeal of survivor selection is that 'evolutionary outcomes are implicit in the environment and are optimal' (March, 1999, p. 104). Therefore, as Friedman (1953) argued, the actual processes of adaptation can be ignored; given survivor selection, maximising is secured. As March (1999) further notes, however, the assumptions of efficient histories have long been suspect despite their widespread appeal. According to March (1999), uniquely required optimal outcomes are rarely realised in populations of business organisations due to complications such as path dependency, multiple equilibria, interactions among multiple actors, and co-evolution between actor and environment encompassing multiple nested layers of adapting units. Hodgson (1993) raises a number of related difficulties that must be overcome to avoid the Panglossian fallacy of assuming that efficiency or maximising behaviour necessarily follows survival. The mere unqualified assumption of a causal sequence between survival and efficiency (or maximising behaviour) is simply an empty statement, a circular argument of the worst sort (Simon, 1976). Moreover, the Friedman (1953) conjecture that economic natural selection produces maximising behaviour has been shown to depend on additional assumptions (see e.g. Schaffer, 1989; Blume and Easley, 1992; Luo, 1995).

In principle, it is possible that efficient or optimal outcomes are the consequence of survival, but it cannot be taken as datum. In each specific instance, it is necessary to point out exactly how this could be accomplished. Furthermore, as an antidote against parochial anthropocentrism in deciding whether or not evolution means progress, one of the leading textbooks in evolutionary biology notes that 'as far as we can tell, it is only by sheer accident that our ancestors escaped extinction' (Futuyama, 1998, p. 700). Indeed, it is now common among evolutionary biologists to conclude that progress or improvement in an objective sense cannot be found in evolutionary history (*ibid.*).

When this point is ignored, it is easy to see why economists associated with the mainstream such as Alchian (1950), Enke (1951) and Friedman (1953) embraced 'natural selection' in the belief that 'survival of the fittest' was guaranteed. As aforementioned, the use of the term 'natural selection' in economics simply refers to survivor selection, which by no means corresponds to the meaning of natural selection in biology. Oddly, the use of the term 'natural selection' in economics, also embraced by a few leading economists, should not in any way be taken as an indication of an association with Darwinism. This is a point also endorsed by most institutional and evolutionary economists. Economic evolution, according to both heterodox and neoclassical economists, is obviously Lamarckian. It is understandable that the abuse of Darwinian theory associated with 'Social Darwinism' carries a sentiment which still leads to habitual rejection of Darwin for economics. It is unfortunate, however, that the idea of Darwinian selection, in its modern form, is generally dismissed without further consideration of its possible advantages in accounting for unpredictable evolution.

Furthermore, it is not uncommon to find Darwinian selection rejected as inappropriate in the social realm without a clear indication of what is actually being rejected. If the rejection is of the idea that social processes are genetically determined, it is clearly well founded. However, no modern biologist in his right mind would suggest such a thing. As Cronin (1991), Dawkins (1996a), Jacob (1985) and others explain, genes work like a recipe rather than a blueprint. In each instance, the outcome depends on epigenetic relations, the complex interactions between organisms and their environment which results in the realisation of genetic potential through the period of maturation. Most rejections of the relevance of Darwinian selection in economics seem to suffer from the misunderstanding that genetic determinism is necessarily implied. However, as argued by Cronin (1991) and Durham (1991), the structure of Darwinian selection is sufficiently general to be translated into the social realm.

Since the structure of explanations which aim to account for unpredictable evolution must be either Lamarckian or Darwinian, and since the latter has the best empirical track record, it may be a good idea to reconsider its possible use in economics. But there are at least two additional factors which suggest that it is important to consider the theoretical possibility of an economic analogy to Darwinian selection: (1) as shown above, Lamarckian and Darwinian selection share an almost identical explanatory structure; and (2) the continuity problem in Lamarckian theory, which we have introduced as the 'baseline problem'. It is now the time to deal with this baseline problem. The way is then clear to illustrate how a Darwinian model of economic evolution can actually be devised.

Lamarckian Economic Evolution and the Baseline Problem

The survivor-selection view of economic natural selection is useful but very narrow. It does not provide the analogue to genetic replication necessary to account for evolution. The missing analogue to genes was provided by Winter (1964) and further developed by Nelson and Winter (1982), who suggested that routines may function as a code containing firm-specific productive knowledge.

As pointed out by Camic (1986), Hodgson (1993, 1999a) and others, the concept of routine, or habit, originates with the instinct psychology and pragmatist philosophy of William James and Charles Sanders Peirce (see e.g. James, [1923] 1977). Veblen (1919) introduced into economics the idea of relatively stable individual modes of thought and action sensitive to the common social context, habits. Moreover, he was the first to develop the idea that shared individual 'habits' define social institutions and that these institutions are the units of selection in an evolutionary story taking place in the social realm (see e.g. Hodgson, 1998a). Moreover, and crucially, Veblen (1914) saw that habits and instincts provide a bridge over the divide between the social and the biological realm. For Veblen (1914), instincts were inherited behavioural dispositions which gave rise to the automatic and immutable quality of social habits. Veblen (1914) uses biology to explain the emergence of stable individual habits and in turn argues that the commonality of stable habits across the generality of men gives rise to social institutions.[35] The story is explicitly evolutionary, and the mode of explanation genetic. For Veblen (1914), the habitual elements of human life are social analogues to genes which, through an unremitting and cumulative process, are the cause of a continued proliferation of institutions. Nelson and Winter (1982) much later developed a comparable theory of cumulative development of productive knowledge.[36]

For Nelson and Winter (1982), routines are repositories of productive knowledge that code for particular behaviour patterns. The idea derived from a number of empirical studies in the 1940s which showed the ubiquitous use of rules of thumb or behavioural programmes in decision making.[37] For example, it was found that decision-makers used mark-up price rather than literally maximising. March and Simon (1958) and Cyert and March (1963) further showed how behavioural programmes or rules of thumb serve as devices that help decision-makers allocate scarce attentional resources to the most important problems at hand.   Building on these behavioural foundations, Nelson and Winter (1982) devised the behavioural foundations of their evolutionary theory and provided a Lamarckian theory of economic evolution.

For Nelson and Winter (1982), routines are immutable over relatively long periods and instruct for stable behaviour patterns. Routines are firm-specific, and reflect a process of cumulative adaptation to a specific business environment.   By containing the code for stable firm-specific action sequences, the notion of routines is equivalent to the genotype, and stable firm–specific action patterns correspond to phenotypes. That is, Nelson and Winter's (1982) theory contains a 'genetic' explanation which is equivalent to the structure of the modern versions of Lamarckian or Darwinian selection. Furthermore, Nelson and Winter (1982) indicate how routines can be replicated through imitation and socialisation of newcomers. Therefore, we argue, routines have the necessary characteristics to serve as social equivalents of genes: they contain a relatively immutable code and they have the capacity to convey that code. It should be noted, however, that Nelson and Winter's (1982) story needs further development. In particular, the idea of external market-based economic natural selection needs to be reconciled with the much richer internal Lamarckian story of heritable routines (Knudsen, 1998a).[38] We shall leave this matter here and use Nelson and Winter's (1982) internal story to illustrate a much more fundamental problem of adaptation that all Lamarckian explanations remain saddled with.[39]

When the business environment changes, the firm needs to adapt its routines, but its immediate possibilities for adaptation are constrained by its productive knowledge stored in the existing routines. Recombination and perhaps 'mutation' of the existing routines develop new routines. Although it has not been widely recognised, an even stronger limit is implied by the immutable nature of routines. If routines are relatively immutable, it follows that only a subset of the total pool of routines that constitute the sum of the firm's productive knowledge will change in immediate response to the need for adaptation. An even stronger implication of the immutable nature of routines is that they are only altered if the need for adaptation is sufficiently strong.

It is enlightening to consider what would happen if all of the firm's routines were subject to change from the slightest shift in the business environment. Adaptation can be considered as the accumulated wisdom that results from a series of experiments across time. Unless these experiments use a baseline, it is impossible to provide estimates of the consequences of deviation from the last period's routines. Therefore, in the absence of a baseline, an additional experiment has no value. In Darwinian selection, immutable genes establish the baseline. By reference to the baseline contained in the gene pool, any new experiment provides the means of progress in existing knowledge. Thus, provided the environment does not change too abruptly, very complex structures, like the human eye, can be built in a series of experiments, each of which adds to an established baseline. Moreover, if the rate of irreversible environmental change is not too high, a baseline can be established which works very much like a moving average. In the absence of immutable genes, a baseline could not be established, and in the absence of a baseline, knowledge could not progress cumulatively.

The establishment of a baseline for the progress of knowledge through adaptation, then, provides a fundamental but ignored problem for the Lamarckian analogue of routines to genes. More generally, any Lamarckian explanation has to come up with a story that limits the genetic response to environmental change. The appeal to relative immutability is not enough since, in a Lamarckian explanation, there is no guarantee that the genes are not changed too fast. Put differently, when genes change against a background of environmental change, how do we explain the evolution of the right 'amount' of immutability? The obvious explanation would be Darwinian selection, which has no such difficulty since the level of immutability is absolute. Then, where does the baseline problem leave Lamarckian explanations of economic evolution?

Let us first note that a Lamarckian explanation has firm-specific routines as equivalents to genes and the individuals' firm-specific behaviour patterns as equivalents to organisms. While individuals carry routines, they are developed in a particular social setting, the business organisation. The explanation is Lamarckian because the routines may be changed in the lifetime of their carriers, the individual managers and employees. Whether they are changed deliberately or not does not change the fact that the explanation is Lamarckian.[40] When the need for adaptation arises due to change in the business environment, we have noted that some sluggishness is appropriate.[41] But the baseline problem is deeper. Not only is some level of immutability or sluggishness in response appropriate, it is crucial in order to establish the baseline without which progress is absent. Then, how do we explain the evolution of the appropriate level of immutability of routines? Without the appeal to an underlying Darwinian explanation, the Lamarckian problem of discrimination crops up. In biology, discrimination on the part of the carrier of genes is necessary to explain why the useful developments, such as the blacksmith's strong arm, should change the genes whereas the harmful developments, such as burns or scars, are not inherited. In face of the demands on information-processing capacity needed to discriminate, Lamarckism as a general explanation of evolution is untenable.

Clearly, as emphasised in recent developments in Austrian economics (see e.g. Loasby, 1991, 1998; Minkler, 1993), there is always a difference between *ex ante* and *ex post* managerial evaluation of various alternatives. Therefore, we can excuse our manager as a general source of discriminatory power necessary to solve the baseline problem. In other words, it seems necessary to appeal to an underlying Darwinian story to solve the baseline problem. Alternatively, we must appeal to divine intervention ensuring that the right level of immutability is always present, or assert that the evolution of institutions is only apparent. Since the latter alternatives are unpalatable, it seems obvious to look for a possible economic or social explanation that abides by the structure of Darwinian selection. Such an explanation is outlined in the following section. The concluding section then argues for the possibility of nested Lamarckian explanations in economics.

Local Emulative Selection: A Darwinian Model of Economic Evolution

What would a valid economic analogy to Darwinian selection look like? Consider the case of routines containing tacit knowledge, as emphasised by Nelson and Winter (1982) and many others (e.g. Loasby, 1998). Further, imagine that such tacit knowledge is important as a provider of the contextual framework that allows people to act. In fact, such a suggestion is supported by impressive evidence, as is the idea that tacit knowledge is transmitted among individuals in a process known as implicit learning (see e.g. Reber, 1993). Assume on these grounds that people in a productive unit develop a tacit understanding of their task through interaction with each other. Due to complexity, the tacit understanding is likely to be unique to each productive unit.

Let a manager choose the alternative he likes the most for replication and have this successful unit train the members of the new unit. If training means that members of our template for replication for some time engage in the actual work process together with the newcomers, then tacit knowledge is likely to be transmitted through implicit learning. Furthermore, it is likely that the transmission process leaves the newcomers with a modified version of the donors' tacit knowledge. In such a process, routines are tacit and relatively durable knowledge components that, like a recipe, instruct their bearers, the individuals in a productive team, in the automatic execution of appropriate action sequences. The selection process is managerial and evolution happens by 'descent with modification'. Depending on their adaptedness[42] to the managerial landscape, productive units are selected. When the firm expands, the well-liked units are more likely to be used as templates for replication.

In fact, what has just been described is essentially equivalent to evolution by natural selection in biology. The crucial point is that knowledge is tacit in the sense that it is outside the reach of consciousness and also immutable, at least for a relatively long period of time. This condition *per definition* effectively hinders the bearer of such knowledge from changing it. Knowing, but not being able to tell, is not enough since the knowledge components could be altered by deliberate effort. However, when the knowledge components are outside the reach of consciousness and are transmitted through implicit learning, which is also unconscious, there is an effective and complete separation between routines and their bearers. This alleged principle of evolution in economics by something very much like natural selection might be characterised by two attributes. First, it is emulative: the tacit knowledge contained in routines is transmitted through emulation. The use of the term emulation is meant to indicate that, in the actual transmittance, the newcomers copy tacit knowledge held by the unit selected for replication. The process takes time and the copy is likely to be imperfect. It is a modification. Second, the process is local. What enables the transmittance of tacit knowledge is a learning process where the members of the unit selected for replication train the newcomers. Since tacit knowledge effectively serves as an isolation mechanism between units, direct exposure through a prolonged period of training is needed to accomplish the transmittance of tacit knowledge. Without local and direct exposure, the story is not plausible. In fact, there is a double meaning of localness since the subject is tacit knowledge. Because the knowledge involved is developed in a specific setting, it is unlikely that it would work if the setting were significantly altered. Having the unit selected for replication transfer, tacit knowledge in unfamiliar surroundings is likely to be counterproductive since tacitness involves the development of a contextual framework in a specific locale.

To sum up the argument, it is indeed possible to devise an analogy to Darwinian selection, valid in the social world. Referring to its two primary characteristics, it may be termed *Local Emulative Selection*. Notably, Local Emulative Selection differs from cultural selection (see Durham, 1991) because the knowledge components in cultural selection are non-tacit. Also, the choice process considered in cultural selection is primarily conscious. It is important to note the difference since cultural selection is Lamarckian whereas Local Emulative Selection is Darwinian.

What has been suggested is a principle of social evolution that nevertheless abides by the structure of natural selection in biology. It should be emphasised, however, that this explanation should be viewed as an underlying process within which Lamarckian selection is nested. Even if the idea of Local Emulative Selection is only a conjecture, the persistence of habits of thought, evidenced in the case of Lamarck and Darwin and beautifully illustrated in economics by Shackle (1967), lends some credibility to the story. Moreover, the great attraction of such an explanation is that it solves the baseline problem. It does so by pointing to a mechanism through which the necessary Darwinian guidance is provided. This guarantees that economic evolution can seize upon the sample of events realised over time in a particular business environment. Immutability of routines, it is submitted, is an inherent property that is due to tacit knowledge. Moreover, the alleged tacit and immutable nature of some level of routines is consistent with the view that human capacities, including the conceptual apparatus associated with language, are themselves the outcome of biological evolution and yet distinctly evolving (Bickerton, 1990; Chomsky, 1986; Hocket 1960; Lieberman, 1991; Maynard Smith and Szathmáry, 1999; Monod, 1971; Morin, 1974, 1990, 1992; Pinker, 1994). As Maynard Smith and Szathmáry (1999) note, the analogy between the genetic code and language is remarkable. Therefore, it should not be too surprising to learn that tacit conceptual frameworks developed over a long period of time appear to be transmitted through a process that abides by the structure of Darwinian selection. At the very least, this possibility is rather convenient, as it not only solves the baseline problem, but also provides the Darwinian tree in which an apparently Lamarckian phenomenon may be safely nested.

Conclusion

According to Steele et al. (1998), their theory of Lamarckian inheritance is limited, nested within and otherwise consistent with natural selection. Because the Darwinian explanation is demonstrably successful in accounting for evolution also of very complex forms, it was argued that the possibility of nesting Lamarckism within a Darwinian explanation should be of interest also to the social scientist. Put differently, the Darwinian explanation solves the baseline problem that plagues its Lamarckian contender. However, natural selection may be too slow in responding to very fast change by virtue of the absence of information flows between organisms and genes. Therefore, the possibility of having Lamarckism in economics guided by an explanation that has the structural properties of Darwinian selection seems worth considering. As the brief review of the role of Darwinian explanations in economics indicated, however, there is some confusion in the use of terms such as 'Darwinian' or 'natural selection' in this discipline. The commonly held view is that natural economic selection denotes survivor selection. Taking Nelson and Winter's (1982) theory of 'internal' evolution of firm-specific routines as the Lamarckian point of departure, we illustrated the possibility of a Darwinian explanation within which it may be nested. Having argued for the necessity of solving the baseline problem without rejecting the role of Lamarckism in economic evolution, this solution seems worth pursuing in future research.

It is thus suggested that the possibility of an underlying Darwinian explanation guiding Lamarckian selection should be considered when accounting for social evolution. The sketch of Local Emulative Selection, where an underlying code containing productive knowledge is conveyed by experienced team members to newcomers, was suggested as a possible conjecture. When the code contains tacit knowledge, and the conveyance involves implicit learning where action sequences are unconsciously emulated, we arrive at one possible conceptualisation of what a Darwinian explanation might look like in the social realm. A possible alternative is a Lamarckian argument according to which the baseline problem is solved with reference to evolved immutability in the underlying code. Since this argument reduces to the untenable claim that whatever exists does so because it could not be otherwise, it must be rejected. A third alternative, corresponding to classical Lamarckism, might hold that changes in the underlying code will first have effect when the code is conveyed. This would be the case if there is replication before the change in the code affected its carrier or some inverse Weismann-barrier prevented that information flowing from replicators to interactors. Why a change in a code containing productive knowledge should not influence its carrier before the code is conveyed seems hard to understand, although not impossible in special cases. Also, if Steele et al. (1998) are correct, the change in the genetic code implied by their theory will surely affect its carrier whether it is conveyed to future offspring or not. Even if we abstain from evaluating the possibility of nested Lamarckism in biology, it seems necessary in the social realm since the alternatives are restricted to special cases or are rather dubious. In view of the baseline problem, it is thus suggested that Darwinian guidance is called for to explain evolution within the social realm, including within the intricacies of economic evolution.

According to the Structural Equivalence Principle presented in the first sections of this chapter, any evolutionary explanation in economics that aspires to account for unpredictable evolution should strictly abide with the structural requirements of Lamarckian or Darwinian explanations. The above discussion suggests that this statement should be further limited by adding the condition that any Lamarckian explanation should be safely nested within an overarching Darwinian tree. Accepting this idea would have profound implications for evolutionary economics as we know it, both in its verbal and its more formal incarnations.

Although limitations of space prevent more detailed consideration of these issues here, some general suggestions can be indicated. First, considering the more verbal representations of evolutionary economics, Nelson and Winter's (1982) multi-level selection argument may readily serve as a basis for devising a nested argument. One example has been presented, that of Local Emulative Selection in replication of routines which contain team-specific productive knowledge. Second, more formal representations, such as evolutionary game theory, would need to introduce a difference between potential and realised strategies in order to start considering games with a Lamarckian flavour embedded within a more general Darwinian one.

Notes

1. The author is very grateful for discussions with and comments from Geoffrey M. Hodgson, John Laurent and John Nightingale as well as inspiration from William B. Durham and James G. March. Any remaining errors were produced without any help.
2. See also the ensuing section, 'Weismann's barrier and the central dogma in biology'.
3. See also Steele et al. (1987, 1993, 1997).
4. Although other biologists have advocated maternal transmission of immunity (e.g. Anderson, 1995), we shall primarily focus on Steele et al.'s (1998) work. In the present work, the issue of Lamarckism in biology is considered because of its relevance for the social sciences, i.e., understanding what is involved in modern claims of Lamarckism in biology and how this may illuminate evolutionary theorising in the social sciences in general and economics in particular. Clearly,

there is no point in attempting a complete coverage in order to evaluate the biologist's claims of Lamarckian inheritance at the molecular level. This is a job for the biologist, not the social scientist.

5. For a defence of biological reductionism see Williams (1986). Plotkin (1988, 1994) provides compelling arguments against reductionism in biology. See Hodgson (1993, 1999a: Ch.6, 1999b) and Morin (1974, 1990, 1992) for the use of (hyper)complex emergent properties in a powerful defence of anti-reductionism in the social sciences.

6. Although the present chapter's treatment of the problems associated with the use of evolutionary explanations is general to the social sciences, we shall primarily focus on economics.

7. Whereas this point has been recognised in biology (see e.g. Cronin, 1991; Dawkins, 1982, 1989, 1996a, and Waddington, 1969) it has been largely ignored in economics.

8. See Hodgson (1993) for a comprehensive taxonomy with representative examples of developmental, ontogenetic and phylogenetic explanations.

9. In Figure 7.1, I have denoted two-way arrows in the schematic exposition of Lamarckian evolution. This implies that the change in the underlying code has effects within the lifetime of the interactor. Such two-way information flows are implied by Steele et al.'s (1998) Lamarckian theory (if they are right), and seems plausible in cultural and social evolution (see, e.g., Durham, 1991). Another possibility would be that the change in the underlying code first affected interactors in the next generation, i.e., there should be one-way arrows from interactors to replicators. This possibility corresponds to classic Lamarckism but is less plausible in social evolution.

10. This idea is also advocated by Witt (1996). Knudsen (1998a, 1998b) provides further arguments and illustrations.

11. The historical evidence in this section draws on Jordanova (1984), Burkhardt (1995) and Mayr (1982).

12. The 1st and 2nd laws in the *Zoological Philosophy* (Lamarck, 1984).

13. No implication of intellectual inheritance is intended, just the statement that both Lamarck and Darwin considered inheritance of acquired characters. As Mayr (1982) demonstrates, there is a great area of overlap in the set of ideas embraced by Lamarck and Darwin. Darwin's own assessment of Lamarck's work ranges from '… veritable rubbish' to '… the conclusions I am led to are not widely different from his; though the means of change are wholly so' (Rousseau, 1969, in Mayr, 1982, p. 358).

14. Here, I refer to the classical theory of recapitulation, according to which the embryo embodies ancestral structures so 'the ontogenetic stages recapitulate the adult stages of the ancestors' (Mayr, 1982, p. 215). The classical theory of recapitulation relies on the concept *scala natura*, the idea of a Great Chain of Being which goes back at least to Aristotle (Mayr, 1982). *Scala natura* refers to the idea that nature can be perfectly ordered according to a grand scale of perfection ranging from the most simple to the perfect being. Classical recapitulation saw *scala natura* and ontogeny as parallels and the belief was that the *scala natura* could be recognised in ontogeny, commonly referred to as the Meckel–Serrès law (Mayr, 1982). So, according to Etienne Reynaud Serrès and Johann Meckel, earlier types of existence towards the permanent stage of perfection could be recognised in the development of the embryos of higher beings. Later substitution of the term 'adult' for 'permanent stage' in the 1830s led to severe misrepresentation of the classical theory of recapitulation (Mayr, 1982). Eventually, the ideas associated with *scala natura* were forgotten and the classical theory of recapitulation was transformed through Darwin's re-interpretation of Serrès's, Tiedemann's and von Baer's ideas (Richards, 1992). It should be noted that even if Karl Ernst von Baer attacked Serrès's ideas, 'he shared more than enough of its assumptions with its advocates that Ernst Haeckel

could reasonably call upon von Baer in defence of both species evolution and recapitulation theory' (Richards, 1992, p. 99). Today, the biological theory of recapitulation usually refers to the epigenetic development processes involved in realisation of genetic potential as the embryo changes to the adult.

15. Serrès, Tiedemann and Meckel thought of evolution as recapitulation (in the classical sense, cf. note 14) and Lyell cited both Serrès and Tiedemann (Richards, 1992). Later, according to Richards (1992), Darwin received a strong impetus for his ideas of species change from classical recapitulation theory.

16. The many influences on Darwin from biologists and economists suggest that it is futile to enter the debate as to whether biology or economics has the upper hand. To argue, as Rosenberg (1994a, p. 385) did, that the terms of the trade 'are always in the direction from economics to biology and not vice versa' seems unbalanced. Well-known influences in both directions are too plentiful to favour such an interpretation, and more could be added. For example, it speaks in favour of economics that Darwin received support from economist Henry Fawcet in the years when his theory was under siege (Fishburn, 1995). On the other hand, an important influence on Malthus, who again crucially inspired Darwin, was Benjamin Franklin in his biological studies (Hirshleifer, 1977, p. 4, note 9). And so on.

17. In a review of a work titled *Elements of Natural History* in *The Anti-Jacobian Review and Magazine* for July 1802 (Vol. XII, pp. 238–46), the reviewer notes the author's use of the term 'economicks', writing: 'This term, *Economicks*, is not, in itself, improper. It is adopted by the Germans from the ancient Greeks. It implies "the principles of that prudence which is exercised in preparing and preserving things for the use of man, and in applying them to use with the smallest waste, and the greatest advantage possible". But, it is a technical term, almost peculiar, in the present time, to the Germans, and far from being peculiarly happy. The author would have done well, therefore, rather to have said "the science of Economy", or to have used a defining circumlocution, than to have at all introduced such a word as "Economicks" in his book'. Here we have, then, what would appear to be one of the first usages in English of the word that was to become 'economics', and, like 'economy of nature', in a natural history context. [Eds]

18. Changes in the phenotypic distribution because of differential survival, differential reproductive success and changes in genotypic distributions (caused by genetic recombination and mutation).

19. The topic is vast and very complex; therefore, only a very rough outline is provided here. It serves the purpose of providing some background for understanding what is involved in modern claims of Lamarckism in biology. For a more complete treatment, the reader is referred to standard texts in biology. See Futuyama (1998) for a general treatment and Li (1997) for a comprehensive description of the genetic machinery .

20. According to Maynard Smith and Szathmáry (1999).

21. First presented in Temin's thesis at Caltech, 1960 (Coffin et al., 1997).

22. According to Monod (1997), there is nothing surprising in the discovery of (RNA–>DNA) reverse transcription because it involves very simple molecular events, predictable from the basic principles of physical chemistry. Furthermore, Monod (1997) argues that reverse transcription does not open the remaining part of Weissman's barrier, because information could not possibly flow from the protein to the genome. Monod (1997) further asserts that 'in spite of some hesitation even by some very distinguished colleagues, I am ready to take any bet you like that this is never going to turn out to be the case'.

23. Cronin (1991) associates this point with Steele's (1979) book and argues that his claims of heritable acquired immunological tolerance created a temporary stir which was silenced by the fact that his claims were not sustained upon further investigation. Cronin (1991) further asserts that Steele's (1979) work was not

only explicitly inspired by, but also financed by, Arthur Koestler, who had an enduring commitment to Lamarckism and, according to Cronin (1991, p. 38), a perverse blind spot on Darwinism.

24. A similar statement can be found in Dawkins (1996, p. 300), that 'the Lamarckian theory can explain adaptive improvement in evolution only by, as it were, riding on the back of the Darwinian theory'. However, given what follows three pages later, it must be viewed as a rhetorical device, not an opening for the theoretical possibility of Lamarckism.

25. Even if Steele was initially rebuked by the scientific community for his heretical ideas, the emerging data over the past twenty years seem to provide some support for his hypothesis. According to Steele et al. (1998), there is now no doubt that the genes (made of DNA sequences) which encode for the proteins for recognition of foreign invaders (antibodies) undergo rapid somatic gene mutation as a result of being activated by the antigens of the invading infectious agent. Moreover, their theory is certainly not fantastic. However, they seem to suffer from a difficulty in presenting sufficiently convincing empirical evidence in support of their argument.

26. This is a conservative reading of Steele et al.'s (1998) argument. They also seem to open the possibility of the more far-reaching conclusion that Lamarckian selection may work hand in hand with Darwinian selection.

27. Hamilton (1999) uses the term 'classical' throughout.

28. Samuelson's (1947) dynamics, however, seems to have been influenced by Newtonian mechanics rather than Darwinian notions. Although Samuelson (1947) had borrowed material from Alfred Lotka's *Elements of Mathematical Biology* (Hodgson, 1993), Samuelson's (1947) ideas had little to do with biology *per se*. Rather they were, according to Hodgson (1993, p. 284, n. 8), 'mechanistic notions, common to physics, and have nothing to do with richer biological notions such as population thinking and time irreversibility'.

29. As Krabbe (1996) points out, traces of the influence of Darwinian thinking can also be found among proponents of the German Historical school, including Bücher (1893) and Schmoller (1900). However, the German Historical school was severely impaired by a developmental stage-wise view of evolution and the embrace of organicist metaphor. Thus, Veblen (1898) was the first economist to devise an evolutionary explanation where the outcome is explained in terms of the cumulative process through which it was brought about, i.e., a phylogenetic explanation.

30. See Hodgson (1999a, Ch. 5) for a detailed history.

31. As pointed out by Kay (1995), Friedman's (1953) famous defence of orthodoxy gave an additional twist to Alchian's (1950) original statement. In contrast to Friedman (1953), Alchian's (1950) argument does not necessarily imply that economic natural selection produces profit maximisation.

32. The use of economic 'natural selection' as survivor selection was introduced by Alchian (1950), and since Friedman (1953) it has been widely adopted (see e.g. Kay, 1995; Nelson, 1995; Schaffer, 1989).

33. The rare early exception in economics is Hamilton (1953), who used the term 'Darwinian institutionalism' to endorse a worthwhile alternative to the Newtonian mechanics associated with mainstream economics. Perhaps it should also be mentioned that Enke's (1991) and Friedman's (1953) use of the 'natural selection' metaphor is best viewed as a defence of orthodoxy, not as an endorsement of the evolutionary framework.

34. Apart from Alchian (1950) and Penrose (1959), most of these contributions have been largely forgotten. Recently, however, Hodgson (1999a), Metcalfe (1998), Nightingale (1993, 1997) and others have called attention to these works.

35. See Hodgson (1998a) for an elaboration.

36. Nelson (1994, 1995) has recognised Veblen's work as a precursor.

37. See Lester (1941), which inspired Katona's (1946) distinction between routine behaviour and genuine decisions, an ignored precursor to Nelson and Winter (1982). Also see Machlup's (1946) defence of marginalism and sharp criticism of the empirical basis for Lester's (1941) results. The debate between Lester (1941) and Machlup (1946) was a direct inspiration to Alchian (1950) and seems to have paved the way for the adoption of selection arguments as a defence of marginalism.

38. According to Sidney G. Winter in private communication, this task was left by Nelson and Winter (1982) for future development.

39. Knudsen (1998b) provides a reworking of Nelson and Winter's (1982) theory which reconciles internal and external selection processes.

40. There is much confusion on this point in evolutionary economics; however, deliberateness is not a necessary condition for Lamarckism. If routines can be changed deliberately, the explanation is certainly Lamarckian, but the reverse conclusion does not necessarily hold.

41. This point was also emphasised by Richardson (1960), who argued that some level of sluggishness in response to price changes, etc. was necessary to create a degree of stability which facilitated prediction.

42. Following a useful convention suggested in biology, adaptedness refers to the 'utility' of a trait or trait-complex in a specific environment with respect to the current circumstances. Utility refers to the expected value of the number of offspring (fitness). By contrast, adaptation denotes the process of *becoming* adapted in terms of the evolutionary history of the traits which are the centre of interest. Thus, in its present use, adaptedness is ahistorical and refers to the features of organisms; adaptation refers to the process of becoming adapted. Although the term adaptation is not settled in biology, the above uses of the term are commonly recognised as opposite poles. A third meaning of adaptation is the phenotypic adjustment to a characteristic in the environment. This use is commonly employed in economics and organisation theory but not in biology.

8. The Appearance of Lamarckism in the Evolution of Culture

John S. Wilkins[1]

> For one thing our newer style of evolution is Lamarckian in nature. The environment cannot imprint genetical information upon us, but it can and does imprint non genetical information which we can and do pass on. Acquired characters are indeed inherited. ... It is because this newer evolution is so obviously Lamarckian in nature. ... But the higher parts of the brain respond to instructive stimuli: we learn.
>
> (Medawar, 1960)

> Acquired characteristics are inherited in technology and culture. Lamarckian evolution is rapid and accumulative. It explains the cardinal difference between our past, purely biological mode of change, and our current, maddening acceleration toward something new and liberating – or toward the abyss.
>
> (Gould, 1980b, p. 84)

> Cultural (or memetic) change manifestly operates on the radically different substrate of Lamarckian inheritance, or the passage of acquired characters to subsequent generations. Whatever we invent in our lifetimes, we can pass on to our children by our writing and teaching. Evolutionists have long understood that Darwinism cannot operate effectively in systems of Lamarckian inheritance – for Lamarckian change has such a clear direction, and permits evolution to proceed so rapidly, that the much slower process of natural selection shrinks to insignificance before the Lamarckian juggernaut. ... [H]uman cultural change operates fundamentally in the Lamarckian mode, while genetic evolution remains firmly Darwinian. Lamarckian processes are so labile, so directional, and so rapid that they overwhelm Darwinian rates of change. Since Lamarckian and Darwinian systems work so differently, cultural change will receive only limited (and metaphorical) illumination from Darwinism.
>
> (Gould, 1997)

Whenever biologists and social researchers compare and contrast biological and cultural evolution, almost unanimous agreement is reached on one point – no matter what one may say about evolving culture, it is a 'Lamarckian' process, not a 'Darwinian' one. By this they do not mean that culture is a source of genetic novelty or that culture is determined by genes[2] but rather that, considered as a distinct domain of historical process, culture – including social structure, economic systems, ideological and conceptual schemes, and technological and behavioural change – behaves in ways that are analogous to how Lamarckian evolution would operate in biology rather than to how Darwinian evolution does operate. A good many authors use this disparity to argue that, in fact, 'evolution' is not the appropriate word and model for cultural change at all.[3]

As I am not very familiar with the literature, debates and issues within evolutionary economics, I wish instead to consider the biological and philosophical debates over the emergence of what I call 'cultural Darwinism'. This recent movement, which has had particular impact in archaeology and the philosophy of mind, contrasts strongly with traditional 'cultural evolutionism' in sociology and cultural anthropology, and is that which I think of as 'cultural Lamarckism'. My argument, here and elsewhere (Wilkins, 1998a, 1998b, 1999a, 1999b), is that an analogy can be made, not only approximately or metaphorically, but strictly, between biological Darwinism and cultural Darwinism; but only if a suitably broad and general notion of what constitutes Darwinian theory is adopted, and if the whole range of biology is considered, not just the evolution of sexually reproducing animals with backbones like ourselves.[4]

What Is Lamarckism, and Who Are Neo-Darwinians?

When biologists use the term 'Lamarckian' as a description of a biological hypothesis, it is usually a term of disapproval, a dismissal of the hypothesis in the way that calling it 'naïve' or 'folk biology' would be, or is a declaration of the heterodoxy of their views. I won't go far into the historical details of Lamarck's actual views but they are both more complex and less consistent than many realise.[5] The modern uses of 'Lamarckism' derive instead from the confrontation between the followers of August Weismann, called the neo-Darwinians, and the school self-described as neo-Lamarckians in the last decade of the nineteenth century and the first decade of the twentieth. As every textbook describes it, Weismann showed that acquired changes to the body of an organism during its lifetime did not affect the *gametes*, or sex cells, or the lineage of cells that led to them, called the *germ line*. This once and for all undercut the theory which Ernst Mayr (1982) has called 'soft-inheritance': that the somatic (bodily) experience of an organism was passed on to its progeny. This notion, incidentally, was accepted by no less than Charles Darwin, who called his version of it *pangenesis* (see below).

When Weismann and Alfred Russel Wallace rejected pangenesis in favour of Weismann's doctrines and stressed the universality and exclusivity of natural selection as an explanation for all biological characters, Darwin's protégé George Romanes sneeringly dubbed them 'neo-Darwinians' – more

Darwinian than Darwin – and the label stuck, later being applied to the synthesis between Mendelian genetics and Darwinian selection theory in the 1930s and 1940s, and again to the views that developed in the wake of the elucidation of molecular genetics in the 1950s and 1960s. Finally, the views that arose from the introduction of game theory into evolutionary analysis by John Maynard Smith and William D. Hamilton,[6] and the implicit gene-centrism that suggested, became the latest 'neo-Darwinism'.

In the textbook version, Weismann posited a barrier between the cells of the body (the *somatic* cells) and the sex cells. Weismann's Barrier, as it became known, found its analogue in molecular genetics in Crick and Watson's Central Dogma (Watson et al., 1987), which states that information never flows from proteins to genes, only from genes to proteins. Neo-Darwinism was triumphant and neo-Lamarckism defeated. So goes the textbook myth.

But as Kuhn (1970) reminded us, textbook histories of science are rarely correct, and this is no exception. The truth is rather more complex. Nearly all of Weismann's detailed hypotheses turned out to be wrong, although he was correct that germ-line cells had a different fate to the somatic cell lines, a process called *gamete sequestration*. The Central Dogma, for example, despite superficial similarity, is a very different notion to Weismann's Barrier – for example, it is now recognised that genomes can have genetic information inserted into them through the action of viruses, and there is a process whereby protein structure can change RNA sequences, although not DNA. The cell lineages of gametes are not as sequestered as Weismann thought (although the hypothesis is a good first approximation), and it has become clear through the pioneering work of Barbara McClintock in the late 1940s and afterwards that genes can be transferred across organismic lineages, and even between species and higher taxa, through the action of what are now known as transposable elements, mediated by pathogens and parasites (Kidwell and Lisch, 1997, 2000; Leib-Mosch and Seifarth, 1995; Syvanen, 1985, 1994).

Weismann's and Wallace's 'neo-Darwinism' was thus a very different beast to the 'neo-Darwinism' of Richard Dawkins, George C. Williams, John Maynard Smith and others today. Maynard Smith, in particular, the leading member of the so-called Oxford School of evolutionary biology, has a complex view that incorporates group selectionist accounts and the systems-theoretic work of Stuart Kauffman and shies away from simple genetic determinism and panselectionism.[7] The Oxford School is derived from the work of Ronald A. Fisher in the 1930s, who effectively started the modern synthesis. Fisher himself (1930) had shown that non-Mendelian heredity is not antithetic to Darwinian selection (Darwin himself accepted it, so how could it be?) but that with Lamarckian heredity Darwinian evolution would be much faster than with Mendelian heredity, although the dynamics of selection would be changed dramatically.[8] Consequently, to understand just what the disanalogies between culture and biology might be, we must understand the senses in which 'Lamarckian' is being used. It will become clear, I hope, that much so-called 'Lamarckism' is actually a mistake concerning the entities that evolve (a category error in philosophical parlance), and that it is not Lamarckian at all, but Darwinian evolution at a deeper or broader level.

Lamarckians make much of the origins of novelty, as do their opponents. Classic strawman Lamarckism has it that organisms (by which it is almost always meant animals, as if plants and bacteria did not evolve) assess their environmental challenges, strive to find a solution to each problem they face, and indeed generally do so. They do this through 'willing', and cultural Lamarckism involves rational planning and reflective assessment of the needs of social agents. How this is achieved is somewhat mysterious. Problem-solving is somehow thought to be clairvoyant (noted by Hull, 1988b). But the inferential process known as *induction* – generalising from past observations and experiences – is only feasible if the key terms of the induction are 'projectible' (Goodman, 1973). This means that the conditions under which the generalisation on which solutions are based are the same as the conditions in which the solution will be applied, which the philosopher David Hume famously called the Principle of Uniformity. This is exactly what is at issue under the strawman Lamarckian conception, for it is changes to the environment that cause the problems in the first place. Short of some mystical noetic faculty, it is likely that intended solutions will fail, in organisms or social agents in varying conditions.

Indeed, Lamarckians are often vague about what counts as a novelty. The 'mother' of artificial intelligence research, Margaret Boden, has clearly stated the requirements for creativity in her book *The Creative Mind: Myths and Mechanisms* (Boden, 1990), and she has distinguished between two kinds of novelty (although they shade into each other). The first kind is the shallow kind, which she calls *combinatorial novelty*. This is like being dealt different hands in games of poker, but always with the same 52 cards plus the Joker. Only the combinations are different – the 'building blocks' are potentially available at all times. The other variety is *deep novelty*. This is like adding cards to the deck, or changing the rules of the game or the value of cards, such as making one-eyed Jacks wild. At its base, all evolution ultimately depends upon deep novelty, but mostly evolution proceeds through recombination of existing alternatives in different contexts. This is why, as Darwin wrote, quoting Henri Milne Edwards, in Chapter VI of the *Origin*, 'Nature is prodigal in variety, but niggard in innovation'. Deep novelty is rare.

A nagging bit of folk psychology that often surfaces in the context of cultural evolution is the belief that, when we create something, we do so *ex nihilo*. Acts of genius are acts of *de novo* creativity, deep and founded on insight and reason. In fact, as Boden shows, acts of genius tend to rely upon a firm grounding in extant cultural traditions, and psychological sports aside, creative people either take existing alternatives and recombine them in novel ways or they generate a very large number of effectively random radical novelties and abandon or ignore all but a small few using filters derived from those traditions. In Chaim Potok's masterpiece *My Name is Asher Lev*, the Hassidic boy artist meets Jacob Kahn, an impressionist painter who is to be his teacher, and Kahn tells him, 'Only one who has mastered a tradition has a right to attempt to add to it or to rebel against it' (Potok 1973, p. 186). All genius, all creativity, depends very largely on combinatorial rather than deep novelty. When Lamarckians, particularly the mentalistic Lamarckians described in the next section, treat creativity in evolution as a kind of extreme problem-solving, this folk belief in the *sui generis* nature of novelty underlies it. But even Mozart had to do an apprenticeship of over a dozen years.

The Format and Structure of Lamarckian Processes

Before we can determine whether a process is 'Lamarckian' or not, we must first distinguish between three senses of 'Lamarckism' that occur in the biological literature. These senses are often conflated, causing all kinds of confusion. They are:

(Type 1)   Neo-Lamarckian heredity;
(Type 2)   directed variation; and
(Type 3)   the progressive evolution of complexity.

The parallel notions for an evolution of culture view would be:

(CE_1)   that culture is a process of the transmission of novel acquisitions;
(CE_2)   that cultural agents choose or predict successful variants before selection operates; and
(CE_3)   that cultural change is necessarily progressive, either in its complexity or in its approach to some ideal goal, such as truth or justice.

The philosopher David Hull (1988b, pp. 452–457) has disposed of the raw objection that culture is Lamarckian in any sociobiological sense (that genes are instructed by memes) which underlies much of the criticism mentioned above. However, there appears to be a general suspicion that culture behaves in a general way that is more formally isomorphic to Lamarckian evolution in one of these three senses than it is to neo-Darwinian (Weismannian) evolution. So, just as Hull and Dawkins (Dawkins, 1976, 1982; Hull, 1988a, 1988b) have provided a generalised, even axiomatic (Rosenberg, 1994b), characterisation of Darwinian entities in evolution, we also need to know what Lamarckian entities and processes are, in order to distinguish them from Darwinian entities and processes.

Neo-Lamarckian Inheritance and Intentional Change

It is often not realised by working biologists that Darwin was, with respect to inheritance, a Type 1 Lamarckian, in that he accepted that inheritance was modified by use and disuse (cf. Bowler, 1989b, pp. 54–64). Organs that were used were inherited in the changed state, and those that were disused withered away over generations. Neo-Lamarckian inheritance, as it was presented in the late nineteenth century following Samuel Butler's rejection of Darwinism, was the view that heredity preserved a direct record, a memory, as it were, of the experience of individual ancestors. Herbert Spencer, Ernst Haeckel and George Romanes all accepted this position. Edwin Lankester followed Weismann's neo-Darwinism (Mayr, 1982, p. 535), along with some others, but they were isolated from the mainstream of 'Darwinian' thought, which followed in the footsteps of the Master.

The other sense of Lamarckism, Type 2, largely deriving from the popularity of Samuel Butler's (see, e.g., Butler, 1911) writings, is the view that variations occur because they are selected intentionally by the 'desires' of the organisms. Fisher (1930, p. 12) puts it that

> [I]t may be supposed, as by Lamarck in the case of animals, that the mental state, and especially the desire of the organism, possess the power of producing mutations of such a kind, that these desires may be more readily gratified in the descendants. This view postulates (i) that there exists a mechanism by which the mutations are caused, and even designed, in accordance with the condition of the nervous system, and (ii) that the desires of animals in general are such that their realization will improve the aptitude of the species for life in its natural surroundings, and will also maintain or improve the aptitude of its parts to co-operate with one another, both in maintaining the vital activity of the adult animal, and in ensuring its normal embryological development.

Fisher also noted four alternatives to the idea of random variation as the basis for evolution, of which the intentional variation version above was one (A); the others were (B) use-and-disuse, (C) direct environmental control over mutation, and (D) predestined evolution through the realisation of an 'inner urge', or what would be better called an entelechy. Fisher, of course, effected the first reconciliation of Mendelian genetics and Weismannian neo-Darwinism.

Fisher is being doubly historically unjust here, for Lamarck himself thought that the 'needs' (*besoin*), not the desires, of the organism directed change (option C),[9] and neo-Lamarckians who proposed a volitional account of mutation tended to imply that this was an operation of Mind, and not of nervous systems, on the biological world, although Lamarck himself was a materialist. This is the sense of neo-Lamarckism that appears, for example, in the preface to George Bernard Shaw's *Back to Methuselah* (Shaw, 1921), and for which Arthur Koestler contends in his *Case of the Midwife Toad* (Koestler, 1971). And it remains the most common sense in which culture is regarded as Lamarckian: that culture is intentional in its variation and that this intentionality causes success in the future.

So, let us diagrammatically represent these alternative views (see Figure 8.1). Neo-Lamarckian inheritance implies that variation is 'reprogrammed' into the hereditary material on the basis of information acquired during the life of the reproducing entity. Bowler (1989b, p. 252) distinguishes Weismannian inheritance from Darwin's pangenesis view in this way:

Figure 8.1: Pangenesis and Weismannian Inheritance
Source: Modified from Bowler (1989b), p. 252.
Pangenesis

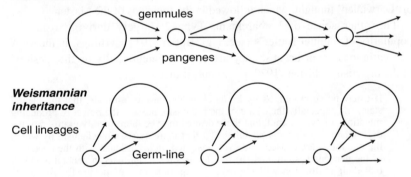

Darwin's 'gemmules' were particles that instructed the genetic material (the 'pangenes') concerning changes to the organism's body during its life to that stage. Both Lamarckian and Weismannian models of heredity and evolution recognise a distinction between heredity and the environment. The Hull-Dawkins distinction between replicators and interactors arises from the now-common recognition that Darwinian evolution is a two-step process that forms a sinusoidal wave (Lewontin, 1974; Mayr, 1982; Mayr and Provine, 1980; Sober, 1984a):

Selection (differential rates of successful completion of that stage of the cycle) takes place at the interactive stages of the wave, which means that it tends to occur during maturation (ecological selection) and reproduction

Figure 8.2: Darwinian evolution

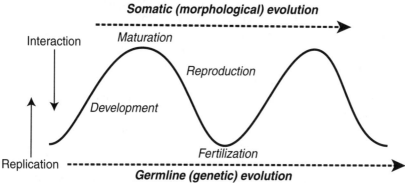

(sexual selection), although it can also occur during development (fœtal viability) and fertilisation (gamete selection). Since the processes of selection do not directly modify the hereditary information of the replicators, the soma are effects of the germ line, and the evolutionary lineage is formed by the genealogical entities, the genes.

By contrast, neo-Lamarckian inheritance involves a direct causal link from the body and its functional parts, that which we now call the *phenotype*, to the hereditary material. To avoid confusion with the Darwinian entities, let us call the Lamarckian hereditary material the *codex* (Williams, 1992), that is, that which carries the information, like a manuscript carries the written word inscribed upon it; and the end result of inheritance, the organism, the *product*, in the sense of something constructed according to the instructions of the codex. A neo-Lamarckian process is rather like a process of a chef following a recipe, and then rewriting the recipe on the basis of the qualities

Figure 8.3: Lamarckian evolution

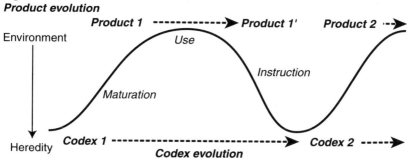

of the meal so created. This can be represented also as a sinusoidal wave (adapted from Belew and Mitchell, 1996, p. 8).

Use occurs as the products are implemented in the environment. There must be a mechanism or process by which environmental information is accrued through use and then re-encoded in the codex. The mechanism whereby changes are retranscribed depends on the variety of 'Lamarckism'. Simple neo-Lamarckian inheritance employs some process like Darwin's gemmules, a physical process that is presumably amenable to natural scientific investigation. The volitional, or intentional, version of Butler and Shaw has some mentalistic process outside the physical processes doing the re-encoding. This can involve two aspects: first, it can force the generation of promising varieties, and then it can select information that best meets the needs of the future.

The last variety of Lamarckism, Type 3, is the entelechical view, whereby all that is occurring in evolution is the progressive unfolding of innate propensities, a view largely irrelevant to the topic of this paper. Each of these, except the last, occurs at the instruction phase through some process, physical or mental.

So, the general algorithm of Type 1 Lamarckian inheritance is this:

Repeat until goal attained
1.   Construct the product from the codex (maturation)
2.   Use and modify the product as best as possible to suit the environment
3.   Instruct the codex about the changes to the product (reverse transcription)
End repeat.

In step 2, the product must have some range of states it can achieve. This is the *plasticity* of the product. In step 3, information about the end state of the product must be encoded into the codex, and this must include information about the encoding process, assuming that it also evolves. Lamarckian heredity therefore requires three transformations:

(LT_1) Expression of information
(LT_2) Implementation and modification of information
(LT_3) Encoding of revised information.

Superficially, this appears to be exemplified in cultural change, especially in learning:

(CT₁)   Cultural information is used to define a cultural agent

(CT₂)   The agent acts over time and learns, thereby modifying the cultural information

(CT₃)   The changed information is instructed to new agents.

However, transformation CT_1 is *identical* to CT_3, while LT_1 is *different* to LT_3, which is an immediate disanalogy between Type 1 Lamarckism and cultural transformation that needs explication; and further, we must ask how CT_2 occurs. In the 'Lamarckian' evolution of culture, the encoding occurs as learning takes place. If the agent learns through trial-and-error then the proper schema is shown in Figure 8.4.

Figure 8.4: Trial-and-error learning

which is just a Darwinian process occurring in the mind of an individual agent (Cziko, 1995). If, on the other hand, cultural information transforms the agent by way of instruction from the environment (that is, if experience determines mature states directly), this is some kind of cultural determinism of agents. The intuition being defended by cultural Lamarckians is that agents choose the best variants, while on this account agents would just be the products of their environment in some way.[10]

Could we introduce some *non*-environmental determinants? Lamarck's (but not Darwin's) solution was to argue that the environmental challenge 'produces in the course of time corresponding modifications in the shape and organisation of animals', for 'new needs which establish a necessity for some part really bring about the existence of that part, as a result of efforts, and that subsequently its continued use gradually strengthens, develops and finally enlarges it …' (Lamarck, 1809, chapter 7).[11] Lamarck's mechanism of instruction is habit in animals and nutrition in plants. How this could analogously work in culture is unclear. One might suppose that creativity is both encouraged and directed in times of sociocultural challenge. This would be some sort of entelechical view of culture, in which pre-existent potentialities are expressed when triggered by the environment. This is not the claim being made by cultural Lamarckians.

Directed Variation and Biased Transmission

The second sense of Lamarckism, Type 2, has to do with the denial or amelioration of the 'blindness' of variation and the 'randomness' of mutation and recombination that is claimed to be fundamental to the neo-Darwinian model (Campbell, 1960, 1965). Many writers think that what sets cultural evolution apart from biological evolution is that the variation over which selection operates in culture is not random. This is the *directed variation* objection. Now, the notion of randomness in neo-Darwinian evolution is rarely expressed clearly, but should, in the present writer's opinion, mean 'random with respect to selective gradients' (cf. Dawkins, 1982, pp. 307, 312, 1996b, pp. 70–73), a view mentioned but dismissed by Jablonka and Lamb (1995, pp. 56ff) as not what most biologists would mean. They instead propose that the common sense of 'random' is a heuristic sense: 'not possible to predict what variation will be produced next'. Nevertheless, the view propounded by Dawkins is correct, for this makes the blindness of variation a function of the biological organisms, not the biologists.

It must be recalled that artificial selection is just natural selection with a strong and directionally stable selection coefficient. Ultimately, and until we can *generate* desired genetic variation on demand, all we are doing with selective breeding is upping the ante on the fitness of genetic combinations of already extant genetic alleles. Jablonka and Lamb (1995), in an attempt to reintroduce non-nuclear inheritance into the Darwinian fold, offer the clearest recent discussion of the issues of directed variation and its relationship to guidedness of transmission and the environmental instruction of heredity. They distinguish three kinds of variation, which I name:

1. *random* variation, where any allelic variant is as likely as any other;
2. *directed* variation, where alleles that are more likely to be successful are more likely to arise; and
3. *biased* variation, where alleles of some kind are more likely to arise, without necessarily correlating with eventual success (Jablonka and Lamb, 1995, p. 58).

Some sense of 'likely' is required to make these distinctions complete; but let us take it as a propensity interpretation rather than in a Bayesian sense of likelihood relative to some theoretical understanding (Sober, 1984a) in order to avoid making these kinds of variation merely subjective or theory-dependent. Neo-Darwinian variation is either random or biased, but it cannot be directed. Indeed, it is hard to see how directed variation could arise, on pain of transgressing the problem of induction.

Progress and Perfection

The third sense of Lamarckism, Type 3, is that of directionality of the evolutionary process itself: progress towards perfection or differentiation, a view stressed repeatedly by Lamarck himself. In Herbert Spencer's philosophy (see Spencer, 1900), evolution was the inexorable movement from the simple and undifferentiated (the 'lower' or 'primitive') to the complex and differentiated ('higher' or 'modern'), a view that, when applied to culture, gave rise to the school of sociology and anthropology called Cultural Evolution (cf. Dunnell, 1978, 1988, 1992; Rindos, 1989). Most modern evolutionists are quite clear that progress of this sort is neither guaranteed by Darwinism nor is to be expected from it.[12] However, the Spencerian notion of culture as the accretion of learning is unquestioned by critics of cultural Darwinism.[13] If information once attained were indefinitely retained, this would be a telling blow against cultural Darwinism, and indeed, were it true in biology, against all Darwinism. But Weismann had it right when he noted in 1893[14] that organs needed to be maintained near their peak through selection if they were not to be slowly degraded. Entropy rules and noise causes information loss. What we have learned can be forgotten. The telling point is that when historians do attempt to survey history in the *longue duree*, they need to describe intermittent cycles of rise and fall, boom and bust, success and failure rather than a slow and steady improvement. Such exceptions as do exist tend to be in the areas of technology and science, and these appear to be of limited duration. Lost technologies are legendary if not mythical: Greek fire, gear mechanisms, Syrian steel, Chinese porcelain, folk and indigenous medicines, and so forth, have all in their history been lost and been either later rediscovered or remained lost.[15] Cultural change, including scientific progress, exhibits well the short-term local progress expected in a Darwinian account of niche expansion, but not the long-term progress of Lamarckian or Spencerian Cultural Evolution. A lot depends upon the scale used for measurement. How globally progressive western science and culture will be seen to be in another 50,000 years is unclear. Explosive niche occupation in empty adaptive landscape accounts for many progressive trends, but ecosystems eventually become close-to-carrying-capacity regimes.[16]

Each of the three senses of Lamarckism – neo-Lamarckian inheritance (Type 1), directed variation (Type 2) and progressive evolution (Type 3) – is rejected in biology, epigenetic inheritance systems notwithstanding. I consider, and will attempt to show, that they are to be rejected in culture as well. My procedure will be to consider analogues from biology to putative Lamarckism in culture in order to show how these examples are compatible with and in most cases derivable from neo-Darwinian theory.

Lamarckism and Cultural Darwinism

Panadaptationism and Fitness

If the origins of novelty in culture are effectively random, just as they are in biology, the subsequent spread and fate of those novelties can be just as Darwinian as they are in biology also. That is to say, the frequencies of instances of a practice, an idea or a technology will spread either due to natural selection or random drift. Cultural Darwinians need to be careful not to fall into the fallacies of panadaptationism or panmictic adaptation – the former is Gould's and Lewontin's term for those who think everything is the result of selection in its favour (Gould and Lewontin, 1979), while the latter refers to the fact that most selection occurs locally on subpopulations, not entire populations or species. This latter effect, sometimes called the haystack model or the Simpson's Effect,[17] shows that selection acts on an alternative relative to its nearest neighbours. If, for example, a firm adopts an egoistic Practice *A*, which in a given context out-competes an altruistic Practice *B* while it is in a local majority, it doesn't translate to the absolute equation *fitness(A)* > *fitness(B)*, because when *B* is in the majority, *A* may be very much less fit. So we often find that processes that look like Lamarckian inheritance – the classic 'for the good of the species/industry/society' claim of group selection, which requires that the parts subjugate their interests to the interest of the whole (this can only be achieved, it is claimed, through rational planning and foresight) – instead occur through individual selection in transient subpopulations of variable composition. This sort of group selection is a kind of density-dependent selection. It is one way that Darwinian evolution mimics Lamarckian evolution (Sober, 1981).

Another way is for learned behaviour to change the fitness values of random novelties. This is classically known as the Baldwin Effect (Baldwin, 1896a. 1896b; see also the chapter by Hodgson in this volume). It is the subject of a lot of confusion (principally by Piaget, 1979, who was a zoologist before he studied child psychology) so it pays us to explore it carefully. On the 'standard' misconstrual of the Baldwin Effect, behavioural changes are assimilated (in some mysterious manner) from the phenotype back into the genotype. So interpreted, it provides fruitful grounds for cultural evolutionists to reject cultural Darwinism. It transgresses the 'Weismann Barrier', or the more recent molecular version of it, the Central Dogma of molecular genetics – the idea that information from the environment cannot be transcribed from the environment into the units of heredity. Since it is everybody's intuition that exactly this happens in culture, critics claim that culture evolves in this Type 1 Lamarckian fashion.

So, what really is the Baldwin Effect? For a start, it is entirely and purely Darwinian. Suppose a population of reproducing entities is capable of a wide range of learned responses. Suppose some of them happen to learn some practice or behaviour that increases their genetic fitness – how to exploit a novel resource, enter a novel ecological niche, or employ a novel defence against predators, for example. To grant as much as possible to Lamarckians, allow that this behaviour is both the result of rational planning and that it is intentionally passed on to descendants (note that I am setting this up in a general manner that can be applied to biology or culture). Before the behaviour is learned, the fitness landscape – that is, the map of the fitness values of the combinations of traits in the population – may have been relatively smooth or the mode of the population may have been centred on a fitness peak. But the new behaviour changes all that. Although it is not initially a hereditary trait, it finds a new fitness peak, and the only way to reach it is by learning it.

However, there is a short-term and a long-term effect. The short-term one is that any entity incapable of learning the new behaviour is relatively unfit. In animals, it would be that the new behaviour is outside their phenotypic norm of reaction. These organisms (and *mutatis mutandis* firms or other cultural institutions) will tend to leave fewer progeny, or leave that population. That, in itself, is Darwinian evolution – it changes the frequencies in the population of alternatives (*alleles*). But no *new* heredity is created in this way. This is stabilising selection around the new fitness peak. Over the longer term, however, the surviving lineages will continue to generate random novelties – mutations, random with respect to the selective pressures at hand. Some of these will tend to make it easier to learn the new behaviour or put it into practice. Again, stabilising selection will favour these mutations, because it is now *cheaper* to attain the fitness peak. With enough mutations, the genetic distribution will come once again to settle on the fitness peak, and the learning requirement will be relaxed. It's all about the investment required for the return (Turney et al., 1996; Mayley, 1996; Schlichting and Pigliucci, 1998; Belew and Mitchell, 1996).

Two final points about the Baldwin Effect should be made: first, it requires both that the fitness peak attained by learning is well worth it compared to the old fitness peak and that conditions don't change over the time required to generate sufficient mutations. In a rapidly variable economy, though, it is better to be plastic than hard-wired, because then the cost/benefit ratio works against hereditary entrenchment in favour of a broader phenotypic norm of reaction. Second – and this is the crucial point – while learning may be the result of rational planning, it may also be a trial-

and-error process, which is to say, Darwinian. The overall utility of the Baldwin Effect model in the explanation of learning is insensitive to lower level intentionality, or the lack of it. In the biological case the Darwinian variation occurs not in genes but in types of behaviour as they are controlled and generated neurologically. These behaviour types are transmitted not through DNA but through what Stephen Toulmin (1972) pleonastically but neutrally called 'transmits', which are mostly but more loadedly called 'memes' these days. There is another level of Darwinian evolution – the cultural – overlaid on top of the biological. Well, one might say, that is what cultural Darwinians assume. But consider this – the way the Baldwin Effect is presented here makes no *a priori* positings about genes being involved at all. It might be the Baldwin Effect of socially-learned game-playing behaviour upon the Darwinian evolution of the IT manufacturing sector. It might, indeed, be the inverse. So long as both realms of Darwinian process occur with changes in one deforming the fitness landscape in the other, what constitutes learning with respect to the one can be a selective pressure with respect to the other. In other words, there can be Baldwin Effects *within* cultural evolution.

Dawkins's Conjecture

We can generalise this conclusion to what I call Dawkins's Conjecture – all seemingly Lamarckian processes are redescribable as Darwinian processes (Dawkins, 1982). I can't prove this conjecture, but so long as it holds up, the necessity for Lamarckian models of culture is voided. For other reasons, to do with the lack of clairvoyance in rational planning (we can only make predictions on the basis of the past, and Hume's problem of induction is now believed to be insoluble) discussed in detail by Gary Cziko (1995) and Hull (1988b), I think it is true that all learning is either trial and error or the application of prior trial and error. Learning is a Darwinian process that goes on within heads and groups of heads.

Through ordinary Darwinian processes such as the Sober and Wilson (1998) model of density-dependent selection, and the Baldwin Effect, the output of Darwinian learning gets transferred to Darwinian evolution at other scales by becoming the raw material of variation at that other scale. Moreover, the rationality and intentional nature of the behaviour of social agents also seems to be distributed over a Gaussian curve, so at the populational level it can be treated as ordinary variation (Dunnell, 1978, cf. Vromen in the present volume). What actually *is* Lamarckian at one level, if rationality actually were Lamarckian, still feeds into Darwinian processes at another.

Some social scientists seize upon seemingly Lamarckian processes in biology as proof that there is no need to be hard-nosed sociocultural Darwinians. Two such episodes are adduced – the apparent directedness of variation in bacterial antibiotic resistance, and Steele's and associates' 'somatic hypermutation feedback' hypothesis. Contrary to reportage, both are, or would be if confirmed, purely Darwinian processes.

Bacteria, like most organisms, have a fairly constant rate of mutation. It has been observed that when a colony is under stress, the rate of mutation sharply rises, as if the colony were looking for a solution to the problem posed by, say, an antibiotic medium or the lack of a food source, like lactic acid. It seems Lamarckian that favourable mutations (leading to antibiotic resistance or alternative metabolic pathways) are much more common than ordinary mutation rates would allow: this would clearly appear to be Lamarckian variation. In fact, it is not. Bacteria are generally asexual, but they have several mechanisms that allow them to share genetic material – *conjugation*, *transformation* and *transduction*. Conjugation is a physical joining of two bacteria with the subsequent mixing and then splitting of their genetic material. Like sex, conjugation allows combinatorial novelty from the deep but rare novelties of beneficial mutation which would otherwise be limited to each cell and only its daughters, along with any non-beneficial mutations. Transduction, which we will meet when we consider Steele's hypothesis below, is the insertion of some genes from one cell line into another by a class of viruses known as retroviruses (of which HIV is one). But the process going on here is transformation – the sharing of gene segments from dead bacteria within the colony (Koch, 1993; Torkelson et al., 1997; Rosenberg, 1997).

When bacteria die, their cell walls or membranes undergo disintegration, a process known as 'lysing'. Since there is no nuclear membrane in bacteria, their genes float free into the medium, and are often taken up by other bacteria, like the tools of a tradesman who has gone out of business are bought by others at auction. Mutated genes are likely to occur in non-viable combinations, which is why the bacterium died in the first instance. But one of those genes might be useful – a way of enabling a normal cell to resist the antibiotic, for instance. It gets incorporated into a viable cell, and *that* cell's lineage then rapidly takes over, through ordinary natural selection. Even if the mutation rate increased in the non-viable cell, there is nothing Lamarckian about it – systems in disequilibrium are likely to inaccurately copy genes, which is, after all, what a mutation is. It only looks Lamarckian if one regards the colony as a single entity.

Steele's somatic hypermutation feedback hypothesis is likewise a Darwinian process (Steele, 1979, 1991; Steele, Lindley, and Blanden, 1998). He posits that acquired immunological changes are inserted into the sex cells by viruses, and that this is both Type 1 Lamarckism and evolutionarily significant. First of all I should say that despite some papers in its favour, this is not widely thought to be demonstrated to occur. Immunologists – who study the immune system that keeps the body's 'self' distinct from invaders' 'non-self' – I have spoken to regard it as conjecture. There is nothing wrong with conjecture in science, so long as in the first instance the processes conjectured are possible – as Steele's are – and in the second instance that it can be shown plausibly to occur. On the second question, the jury is still out about how frequently if at all somatic hypermutation insertion into gametes actually happens. By its very nature it will be rare over ordinary timescales.[18] But all of the actual processes of transduction occur in other contexts. What I am denying is that, assuming its actuality, this process represents 'Lamarck's signature' as Steele and his collaborators subtitled a recent book (Steele, Lindley and Blanden, 1998). Instead it represents the multilevel nature of Darwin's signature.

In a kind of strawman version of neo-Darwinism, all mutations happen to genes and apart from sex all lineages of genes are distinct. The strawman version has all sex cells entirely distinct from the body – the somatic cells – so that nothing that happens to the body can affect the constitution of the sex cells. It is this strawman Darwinism that Steele contrasts with his hypothesis, and since they are clearly different, and he thinks Lamarckism is the 'only' alternative, Steele calls his view Lamarckian. But what it really is, is a Darwinism not made of straw.

The somatic hypermutation feedback hypothesis is that immune cells acquire resistance to infections in a single body, say in a defence against a parasite. Retroviruses in that body transfer these acquired immunities to the sex cells, and so fulfil the conditions of the inheritance of acquired characters – Lamarckian inheritance. But at a different scale, that of cell lines, somatic hypermutation is ordinary mutation, transduction and selection. Immune cells have a variable region in their genes that randomly mutates as they are formed. This enables them to generate vast numbers of antibodies. If one happens to bind to an infected cell it is reproduced frequently. This is the basis of immunisation – the viruses and other infectious agents in a non-viable form are introduced to the body so that immune cells that happen to bind to them will commence reproducing, so that, in turn, if the actual pathogen is encountered the body has the repertoire of antibody-producing cells already available. The process, discovered by Macfarlane Burnet and Peter Medawar, is called clonal selection, and it is a Darwinian process of variation and selection, only at the cell level, not the body level. So if somatic hypermutation feedback is confirmed, it will be another case of multilevel selection.

The point of dealing with these redescribed Darwinian processes is to stress what I have already argued elsewhere (Wilkins, 1998b): in culture, as in biology, there is no single level of evolution and no single unit of heredity. A lot of the claims about the Lamarckism of culture – both in the sense of Type 1 soft inheritance and Type 2 directed variation – depend upon a prior recognition of a privileged unit of selection and a privileged object of interaction with the environment. Generally, and understandably, Lamarckians treat the social interactor – the phenotype equivalent – as an individual human being; that is, as coterminous with the biological phenotype. This then raises the sociobiological spectre that we might reduce all social behaviour to genetic determination. But as I argued in my (1998b), what evolves in culture is not the human individual, but a *social profile*. Social profiles often are instantiated in human organisms – voter, professional, liberal, husband, wage-earner, etc. But often they are also instantiated in institutions – firm, tradition, school, party, state, etc. The easy way to see this is to ask, how do the cultural transmits or memes *constitute* a social interactor in the way genes and other biological transmits constitute an organism (Wilkins, 1999a, 1999b)? Having my memes does not constitute being a 2 metre blond endomorph bipedal mammal with a predisposition to astigmatism. Having my genes does not constitute being a philosopher who reads science fiction and fantasy novels and loves Tom Waits's version of *Somewhere*. Being me as the social agent JSW and being me as the biological progeny of two other biological organisms with a suite of adaptations and vestigial traits are two different states of affairs. Romeo by any other name.

Some Objections to Cultural Darwinism

Once we recognise the independence, at least conceptually, of the biological individual and the social profile, Lamarckian appearances dissolve. Social evolution becomes the evolution of social entities, and social transmission the transmission of cultural packets of information, from which a social profile is developed. It no more matters in principle that a meme is stored in and communicated from a biological brain or an electronic or paper medium than it matters that blue eyes are transmitted using DNA. Blue eyes might be transmitted through chromatin markings or through developmental engineering textbooks ('inhibit the X signal kinase at day 14 in order to induce blue eye phenotypes') and it would still be an evolutionary gene (if genetic engineers persisted long enough). What is a social profile depends crucially on how coherently social traits interact with their environment, and what is a social or cultural 'transmit' depends crucially on what patterns (semantic patterns) are reliably and conjointly reproduced from instantiation to instantiation ('generation to generation'). While these two distinct domains may coincide, as Boyd and Richerson (1985) and Cavalli-Sforza and Feldman (1981) assume, they need not and, I think, almost certainly will not always do so. The reason for this lies in a criticism of cultural evolutionism best expressed recently in an essay by Joseph Fracchia and Richard Lewontin (1999).

Fracchia and Lewontin attack evolutionary accounts of culture on several grounds. One is that cultural evolutionists lack a theory of inheritance, and 'do not even know whether an actor-to-actor, not to speak of a parent-to-offspring, model of the passage of culture has any general applicability' (p. 64). This, I think, is correct, and due to a failure to distinguish the social actor from the biological individual. Another problem is that cultural evolutionists, from Spencer to Marshall Sahlins and Leslie White, have treated evolution as directional and progressive, which biological evolution rarely is, and which is our Type 3 Lamarckism.[19]

Yet another of Fracchia's and Lewontin's (1999) objections to evolutionary accounts of culture is that humans can learn, reflect, imagine and plan, which is also dealt with by the distinction of a social profile.[20] But their criticism in this context concerns the fact that humans 'are always born and develop psychically in group contexts' (p. 65). By this Fracchia and Lewontin mean that enumerating facts about social agents would not give us facts about social structures. I completely agree, but I draw the opposite conclusion to them. Cultural Darwinism need not be atomistic and reductionistic, any more than biological Darwinism need be. Sometimes groups behave like individuals, and they influence the properties of their component parts. Campbell (1974b) called this 'downward causation'. If we are wedded to a privileged level of interaction through methodological individualism, and a single unit of selection, then of course Fracchia and Lewontin's critique applies, but this is no longer the received view in biology.[21]

In what is called Multilevel Selection Theory (MST), it is recognised that Hull's and Dawkins's interactor–replicator distinction is not fixed in place. It is a functional distinction that can apply whenever the conditions for replicator-hood and interactor-hood are met, and an evolutionary process (of drift plus selection) will occur at that level. Ironically, this point is due to the so-called arch genetic determinist Richard Dawkins, who noted that DNA segments ('selfish DNA') can behave as both replicators and interactors (vehicles, in his terminology), and who also relocated the replicator to culture when he coined the *meme* concept (Dawkins, 1982). If we follow this logic to its end, a replicator is whatever is instantiated with a high degree of fidelity in successive generations of interactors; and because there is no privileged substrate, memes are *types* of things – in other words, they are patterns. It is often said that genes are a bad model for a cultural replicator (Atran, 1998; Sperber, 1996; Sterelny and Griffiths, 1999) but this is only true if by 'gene' we understand a contiguous expressing stretch of DNA (cf. Griffiths and Gray, 1994). However, 'gene' is a multifaceted notion: we have DNA that is not expressed, non-DNA inheritance, and a range of operational distinctions from codons (three nucleotides) to open-reading frames (from start codons to stop codons with all exons ignored) to chromosomes to karyotypes. The *appropriate* gene-concept for analogy to culture is Williams' (1966) 'evolutionary gene', on which Dawkins based his replicators, and that is an abstract conception; Williams called it a 'cybernetic abstraction'. In effect, from an evolutionary perspective, genes are also types that govern the development of an interactive phenotype.

Interactors are also interesting. They are economic entities or characters or character suites. Their significance in the evolutionary arena is in the acquisition and disposal of economic resources relevant to reproduction. Survival of the interacting system is only relevant to an evolutionary account so long as it bears on the fitness of the replicators. Indeed, survival of the individual much past reproduction may be an economic drain on progeny, and so be selected against. It behoves us, particularly in the context of evolutionary economics, to recall that all evolution is intimately economic (Ghiselin, 1974). But since 'being an interactor' is defined by 'having hereditable traits',[22] groups having hereditable traits are interactors and are liable to evolutionary processes, just as the benchmark entities, organisms, are in (animal, sexual, vertebrate) biology.

So Fracchia's and Lewontin's problem evaporates once we abandon the notion of privileged replicators and interactors (cf. Brandon, 1988), and with it also vanish confusions about Lamarckian soft-inheritance. It isn't soft-inheritance vis à vis a firm as interactor when the firm's staff learn from experience, for selection on firms treats staff-learning as random (perhaps biased) variation relative to the population profile of all the firms in an industry (i.e., in their 'ecological niche'). Likewise, describing staff properties will not give us a description of the firm, since as a system the firm's properties are irreducible, as they depend on the interactive relationships of its parts and the interactive relationships between it and its environment (including other firms).

Fracchia and Lewontin have another criticism on which we can end this discussion. It is that the assumption that culture is progressive is not matched by Darwinian models – Lamarckian progress, or Type 3 Lamarckism. The idea that culture must evolve more or less progressively pre-dates Darwin and even Spencer. When Darwinism had been digested by the late nineteenth century, it became obvious that it would not guarantee that organisms would become more sophisticated or, except in local circumstances, adapted. In biology this led some paleontologists such as Alphaeus Packard, Edward Drinker Cope and Henry Fairfield Osborn to adopt what they termed neo-Lamarckism, predicated on the view that soft-inheritance would generate rectilinear evolution from the increasing retention of experience (see Bowler, 1983), and amongst the humanities, this view prevailed.

As Fracchia and Lewontin and others (Dunnell, 1980, 1988; Rindos, 1989) document, when cultural evolution models actually were pursued, they were progressivist. After all, it is intuitively clear that culture is accretion – we stand on the shoulders of those who came before, and all that. Technological change depends on prior technology, ideas on previous ideas, and wealth upon accrued wealth. In fact, the historical record shows as much extinction and transformation in culture as the paleontological record does in biology. One presentation of this is Jared Diamond's *Guns, Germs and Steel* (1998), which speaks of 'interrupted trajectories' of cultures through invasion, disease and the loss of habitat. The loss of political infrastructure upon the collapse of empires or of manufacturing methods with the loss of markets adds to this.

Even in science, advances can be forgotten, being rediscovered, sometimes many times, until they 'take' (and often they don't). Fracchia and Lewontin's presumption that culture is progressive where Darwinian evolution is not, is not well-founded over the longer term. Of course, neither biological nor cultural Darwinism prohibits short-term progressive trends, particularly when 'arms races' force escalation between evolutionary players (Dawkins and Krebs, 1979; Ewald, 1994; Heilman-Ternier and Harms, 1975; Nesse and Williams, [1994] (1996); Vermeij, 1987). In culture as in biology we expect to see similar patterns – a few progressive trends of varying duration and most of the time just variations on a theme. The cardinal danger in historiography is seeing only those events that lead to some final end-state, like our own, ignoring the byways and branches. It has been dubbed the Whig interpretation of history (Butterfield, 1931) and such introduced biases of linear narratives are rife in the social sciences.

Conclusion

Objections to cultural Darwinism from apparent Lamarckism in cultural change are not well-founded, since in none of the three senses of Lamarckism (above) does culture follow a Lamarckian process, at any rate not in ways that preclude a Darwinian view of cultural change. Questions of 'group selection' and 'acquired characters' in culture rest either on a category error about the populations of entities that evolve in cultural contexts, or on intuitive notions about the dynamics of culture that do not hold up under close scrutiny.

Neither the existence of the intention to solve problems rationally nor contextual definitions of groups in culture presents a major disanalogy to Darwinism. Neither does human 'creativity', since it falls on a normal distribution curve and so feeds selection. But selection is not all there is to a Darwinian account, and we have to be careful not to make the mistake made by the early neo-Darwinians that everything must be due to selection pressures for existence. There is also local density-dependent selection, and, most importantly, random sampling of subpopulations (i.e., drift) to take into account. Although selectionist models are often the reason social researchers take up a Darwinian account, the fuller and broader set of Darwinian theories needs to be assimilated.

The failure of social evolutionists to properly apply a fully Darwinian model to culture until fairly recently is in part due to the prior expectations everybody has about what cultural agents are, and partly also to popular misunderstandings about Darwinian evolution; including, it has to be said, by many biologists. It is not through lack of intelligence, but through the complexity and sometimes vagueness of presentations of Darwinism that this occurs, for 'Darwinism' is itself an evolving tradition, as all scientific theories are in the end (Hull, 1988b). This makes it hard to find the right analogies, especially if the key entities, replicators and interactors, are not at all clear in paradigm biological cases. The concept of a 'meme', like its analogy the 'evolutionary gene', has both sharpened the focus and brought into shadow relief the problems of a single unit of evolution and selection. But if we accept that in biology there are no *a priori* privileged units or levels, then neither must there be in culture. The resources of biological Darwinism – its dynamic models, life-history models, ecological models, populational dynamics, phylogenetic systematics techniques, etc. – will also become available to the social scientist. And the differences between the two domains will be as instructive as the similarities.

Notes

1.　This essay is the result of many discussions with, in particular, Hans-Cees Speel, Derek Gatherer, Jack Vromen, and Mark Mills. Thanks are especially due to Floyd Aranyosi and David Hull for discussions, comments on earlier versions of this essay, and references. Hull's (1988b) is the basis for the refutation of cultural Lamarckism presented here. Richard Lewontin kindly supplied a reprint of his and Fraccia's (1999) paper. Jeff Boyle helped me to understand the science of Steele's hypothesis. I am very grateful to the editors, John Nightingale and John Laurent, for their request for and comments on the essay.

2. Although this is often a worry expressed by opponents of cultural evolutionary models, i.e., that they are sociobiological theories in disguise.
3. A prominent example is Gould, (1996). p. 219. Others include Fracchia and Lewontin (1999), discussed below.
4. In this I am greatly influenced by, and mostly follow, Hull (1973, 1982, 1984a, 1984b, 1985, 1988a, 1988b, 1988c, 1988d), Dunnell (1978, 1979, 1988, 1992), Rindos (1984, 1989) and Plotkin (1994).
5. See, for example, Gould (1980b), Chapter 7; Packard (1901) and Mayr (1982).
6. See Maynard Smith (1975), Chapter 12, for an overview, which later became popularised and taken to its logical conclusions by Dawkins (1976).
7. Maynard Smith's views are expressed in, for example, Maynard Smith (1978, 1982, 1988) and Maynard Smith and Szathmáry (1995). Kauffman's views are found in Kauffman (1993, 1995), cf. Depew and Weber (1995) for a full review.
8. Fisher discussed blending inheritance, not the inheritance of acquired characters. The former is in contrast to Mendelian particulate inheritance, while the latter contrasts with Weismannian sequestration of reproductive cells. It is my opinion that Gould's comment in the epigram is wrong in the absolute – the coefficient of selection may have to be stronger in the case of acquired inheritance to be effective than in the case of sequestered genes, but there is no reason to think it could never be. It really depends on the rate of acquisition. For example, if Steele's hypothesis discussed below is correct, a very few events of acquisition could leave the bulk of adaptation ordinarily due to selection. Blending inheritance, on the other hand, would make selection ineffective over longer periods, and would require some Lamarckian mechanism.
9. This mistranslation of *besoin* dates back to the 1832 second volume of Lyell's *Principles of Geology* and was first noted by Packard (1901), and later argued independently by Mayr (1982, p. 357).
10. Obviously the strength of this claim is in direct proportion to the degree of constraint imposed on agents by their environment. But if we weaken the strength of environmental determinism, we also weaken the force of the Neo-Lamarckian Inheritance explanatory schema.
11. Translation of excerpts in Belew and Mitchell (1996, pp. 40–41).
12. Michael Ruse (1996) has argued that Darwin and most evolutionists of the time since have been overtly or covertly progressionists, a point that is moot in some cases but perhaps not in Darwin's writing, and certainly not in Wallace's. Nevertheless, Darwinian *theory* does not guarantee that life will become more complex or better adapted in some absolute sense, though there is room for difference of interpretation amongst the Darwinian orthodox (cf. the essays in Nitecki (1988), particularly the editor's introduction).
13. It should here be noted explicitly that Cultural Evolution, being Lamarckian (senses 1 and 2) and, as Dunnell notes, more or less 'vague and vitalistic' in its mechanisms (1988, p. 181), is quite distinct from what we are calling *cultural Darwinism*, which rests on a mechanism of natural selection.
14. Quoted in Mayr (1982), p. 116.
15. Greek fire, for example, is thought to be naphtha, but nobody is really sure and it seems no evidence is forthcoming to decide the matter.
16. The 'carrying capacity', or *r/K*, model is a somewhat simple account of the evolution of life-histories. In economies and ecologies close to their carrying capacity (K), life histories tend towards long life of organisms, slow reproduction and larger size. In less confined ecologies and economies, life histories tend towards short-lived, rapid and small reproducers *(r)*. The *r/K* model has been accepted as a useful heuristic, a rough and ready approximation, although not as a finer-grained model. The so-called 'logistic growth curve', $dx/dt = rx(1-x/K)$, where x is the population density at time t, r is the intrinsic rate of increase and K is the carrying capacity of the environment (Lloyd, 1988, p. 15), captures the dynamics. In empty ecologies, reproducers evolve in a near-hyperbolic manner,

and selection is relaxed, allowing many variants to flourish even if they are less fit. As K is approached, selection coefficients rise, and organisms need more subtle edges over their competitors. See Mueller (1997) for a case study.

17. The haystack model is Richard Lewontin's, discussed in Sober and Wilson (1998). Mice do not form a single population. At times small groups inhabit a single haystack, and the frequencies of alleles in one haystack can be a non-representative sample of the whole population. It can happen in a haystack that 'altruistic' mice meet or are in the majority, which means that more individuals from haystacks that are mainly altruistic will survive than in other haystacks where food is not shared, etc. As a result, the entire population becomes altruistic although *en masse* altruists are less fit than egoists. Sober and Wilson call this a group selection model, but I think it is a group sorting model that changes the fitness assignments of altruists, and the selection is still individualistic. It falls under the rubric of 'density-dependent selection'. Simpson's Paradox is a statistical anomaly of the same kind. Subpopulations of a sample group may have frequencies that differ from the summed frequency of the whole population. It is named after the statistician who first published it, not the evolutionary biologist G.G. Simpson.

18. The frequency of endogenous retroviral (ERV) insertion must be low, or nearly all our genes would have an ERV-origin, when between 1% to 5% of expressed mammalian genes in fact do (Hohenadl et al., 1996; Leib-Mosch and Seifarth, 1995; Patience, Wilkinson and Weiss, 1997). However a lot of the *unexpressed* genes are ERV-derived, accounting for perhaps as much as 40% of mammalian specific genomes. In other groups such as plants, ciliates and fungi, the proportion is much higher.

19. Both Dunnell (1980), and Fracchia and Lewontin explore and present this progressivist bias in cultural evolutionism. Sahlins' and White's progressivism are presented in Sahlins, 1960, and White, 1959, 1960. Dunnell and Fracchia and Lewontin document several other examples.

20. Neither social profiles nor social transmits plan, reflect, imagine or anticipate events. That psychological entities in which these things are instantiated happen to is irrelevant to the Darwinian evolution of cultural entities.

21. Cf. Brandon (1988), Goodnight and Stevens (1997), Mayr (1997), Orzack and Sober (1994), Sober and Wilson (1994,1998), Wicken (1985), Williams (1992), Wilson (1997a, 1997b). Bell (1996) provides a good overview of experimental studies on what is selected.

22. Lewontin (1974), Chapter 1, argues that Mendelian genetics and biometric models of evolution are reciprocally defined – in the former fitness is an ecological (interactive) parameter, and in the latter, the characters measured have a hereditability value.

9. The Human Agent in Evolutionary Economics

Jack J. Vromen

> As a matter of fact, for several questions related to long term development, Darwinian thought may even become a fruitful part of evolutionary economic theorising, not through metaphorical use, but through direct application. Humans, and the inherited parts of their behavioural dispositions (preferences), are a result of evolution on this planet. It may therefore be conjectured that the common genetic elements in human preferences which dictate some average tendencies in the agents' endeavours could produce some 'direction' in the path which economic evolution takes.
>
> (Witt, 1996, p. 714)

> In this [of course] we recognise one of the central issues in modern evolutionary theory, namely evolution at different levels of the economy and the interaction between them.
>
> (Metcalfe, 1998, p. 5)

Evolutionary economics has a long-standing and venerable tradition of withstanding theoretical presuppositions and doctrines underlying mainstream economic theory: rational individual behaviour and methodological individualism. Against the presupposition that individual agents behave perfectly rationally, evolutionary economists have always maintained that prevailing institutions shape individual behaviour. Notable examples are of course Veblen, with his emphasis on instincts and habits moulding individual behaviour and, more recently, Nelson and Winter, with their belief that behaviour is routinised to a large extent. And, relatedly, evolutionary economists have always resisted methodological individualism. Evolutionary economists have consistently argued that it is legitimate to invoke supra-individual entities in explaining social processes and phenomena. Here famous examples include Commons's views on collective action and, once again, Nelson and Winter's view that firms can be treated as entities in their own right (having routines, for example, that can survive replacements of employees).[1]

Those who eschew the use of biological metaphors in evolutionary economics may believe it is pointless to have a closer look at current evolutionary theory. And, indeed, there does not seem to be a compelling reason why evolutionary economists should want to check whether their presuppositions and views can be maintained in the light of new insights gained in current evolutionary theory. Evolutionary economists are free, it seems, to disregard new developments in current evolutionary theory altogether, and turn to quite different disciplines (such as social psychology, sociology and anthropology) in order to spot new insights. It is not even inconsistent, for example, to argue that firms are entangled in evolutionary processes and to deny at the same time that individual human beings are (and always have been) subject to evolutionary forces.

Yet I think there are good reasons why evolutionary economists should pay attention to new developments in evolutionary theory. The most convincing reason, I believe, is based on the principle of overall theoretical coherence. No discipline can afford to remain in a state of 'blissful ignorance' of adjacent disciplines. Indeed, one of the most serious shortcomings of mainstream economics can be said to be exactly this: it simply ignores insights and ideas developed in adjacent disciplines (see Hausman, 1992 and Wilson, 1998). Now, assuming that evolutionary economists want to avoid this shortcoming, it seems only reasonable for them to have a look at what current evolutionary theory has to say about human behaviour. This chapter discusses two relatively new theoretical developments in evolutionary theory: evolutionary psychology (EP) and multilevel selection theory.[2] But first the stage is set by discussing how the human agent is depicted in mainstream neoclassical economics and evolutionary economics.

The Human Agent in Mainstream Economic Theory: Man as a Machine?[3]

Homo oeconomicus, the creature featuring in classical economics, has been criticised right from its inception. With the advent of neoclassical economics, *Homo oeconomicus*, who is moved solely by a concern for his own material welfare, gave way to (hyper)rational economic man, who maximises some goal function subject to constraints. But this did not quieten the criticism. Quite to the contrary, criticisms only amplified. Massive criticism continued to be voiced, not only by non-economists. Economists from different persuasions have also expressed their dissatisfaction with the notion. I shall confine my attention here to the criticisms expressed by neo-institutionalists and neo-Austrians, representatives of two streams in economic thought that have demonstrably sympathised with evolutionary theorising in economics. As we shall see, based on different (and in some respects even opposite) depictions of how neoclassical economics characterises individual behaviour, neo-institutionalists and neo-Austrians advance quite different (and in some respects even opposite) criticisms of it. Yet both criticisms still shine through in attempts of present-day evolutionary economists to outline the basic features of human agents and their behaviour.

Neo-institutionalists criticise neoclassical economists for ignoring the profound influence of prevailing institutions on human behaviour.[4] It is not just that institutions shape the beliefs of individuals, they also affect their desires and preferences. Neoclassical economists are said to have a one-sided view on the relation between structure and agency. Neoclassical economists only pay attention to the consequences that the actions of individuals have for the structure. What they ignore is that changes in structure also can change the identities and basic properties of individuals.

Neo-Austrians have persistently argued that the optimising and maximising behaviour neoclassical economics describes does not involve genuine choice. Appearances notwithstanding, rational choice theory does not address rational choice at all! Genuine choice involves much more than mechanical calculation of optimal solutions to pre-fabricated problems. There are not given and well-defined choice sets in real economic life. Genuine choice starts with and essentially consists of framing the options. There is no *a priori* reason to assume that different individuals perceive problems in the same way. In particular, individuals endowed with entrepreneurial alertness display considerable ingenuity in spotting opportunities that others fail to see.

In a sense, then, while neo-institutionalists argue that individual human agents are endowed with too much autonomy in neoclassical economic theory, neo-Austrians hold that not enough autonomy is granted to them. The issue here is one of self-control and self-determination. Neo-institutionalists believe that too much self-control and self-determination is assigned to individuals in neoclassical economics. Neo-institutionalists believe that individual behaviour is to a large extent shaped by impersonal factors and forces that individual agents cannot control. By contrast, neo-Austrians emphasise the personal powers and capacities that determine how individual persons behave. By portraying man as a machine, neoclassical economics is said to underrate the imaginative and creative powers operating from within humans.

Note that the difference between neo-institutionalists and neo-Austrians is not that the second stress the purposefulness of behaviour and that this is denied or downplayed by the first. Both acknowledge the goal-directness or purposefulness of (much of) human behaviour. The difference, rather, is that neo-institutionalists stress that the terms of individual goal-directed action are to a large degree determined by prevailing social institutions, whereas neo-Austrians stress that creative and imaginative actions spring from within the individuals themselves. Neo-institutionalists believe that social institutions not only mould the beliefs and expectations of individuals, but also their wants and preferences. Neo-Austrians believe that individuals vary in their perceptions of problems and in their powers to find new unprecedented ways of handling problems.

In the eyes of neo-institutionalists, neoclassical economists rightly assume that individuals are engaged in purposeful behaviour. Where they go wrong is in their additional assumptions that the preferences and beliefs of individuals are unaffected by the social environment in which they live, and that their preferences and beliefs are invariant whatever the experiences they go through during their lifetime. In the eyes of neo-Austrians, neoclassical economists wrongly assume that individuals are engaged in mechanical, machine-like behaviour.

Who is right here? That is not easy to tell. Is behaviour portrayed as purposive or as mechanical in (expected) utility theory? At first sight, (expected) utility theory seems to present a highly idealised treatment of purposive behaviour. After all, the individual agent is assumed to pick out the option with the highest (expected) utility from the feasible set at his (or her) disposal. But appearances may be deceptive here. Right from the start there have been proponents of utility theory (such as Jevons) who likened individual agents to hedonistic machines. But there also have been spokesmen such as Robbins arguing that utility theory assumes that agents engage in deliberate conscious choice. Later on, it can be argued, exponents of (expected) utility theory in economics have tried to purge economic theory from all its psychological vestiges. Samuelson's revealed preference theory and Savage's influential (subjective) interpretation of expected utility theory testify to this. In Savage's interpretation, rational individual behaviour amounts to nothing more than consistency of behaviour over time (see, for example, Sugden, 1991). It simply does not matter whether individuals arrive at their behaviour after having gone through processes of conscious deliberation, after having mindlessly executed some rules, or whatever. As long as their behaviour displays the type consistency that expected utility demands, their behaviour can be rationalised with expected utility theory.

Thus present-day proponents of expected utility theory in economics prefer to be agnostic about the real causes (or determinants) of individual behaviour. It is true (as neo-Austrians argue) that expected utility theory ascribes decision rules (or inference rules, or algorithms, or optimisation techniques) to individual agents. And such rules are also computable on machines. They can be executed by computers, for example. But this does not imply that expected utility theory takes individual agents to *be* machines. Nor is expected utility theory committed to the belief that individual agents are conscious deliberators. Expected utility theory does not take sides here. The lesson to be learnt from this is that we should not confuse theoretical representations of individual behaviour with (underlying) beliefs about the nature and internal constitution of individuals.[5]

Theoretical Puzzles in Current Evolutionary Economics

In contemporary evolutionary economics, traces of both neo-institutionalist and neo-Austrian criticisms of rational economic man can be discerned. As we shall see in this section, the neo-institutionalist point that the behaviour of individuals and organisations is much more moulded by prevailing customs and institutions than neoclassical economics assumes shines through in contemporary evolutionary economics. And contemporary evolutionary economics also tries to come to grips with the neo-Austrians' emphasis on the imaginative and creative powers of entrepreneurs (see, for example, Loasby, 1999). As we shall also see, however, it seems that these two insights are difficult to reconcile with one another. They create a tension within the community of contemporary evolutionary economists. But before we come to this, I first want to discuss agreements among evolutionary economists.

As I see it, most evolutionary economists agree on the following:

1. Firms (or business units, see Metcalfe, 1998) are treated as individual units, and industries (or markets) as populations. In competitive markets, firms are subject to selection pressure. Evolutionary economists do not deny that the behaviour of firms is the result of the behaviour of the individuals partaking in the functioning of the firms. But they do not put much effort into showing how firm behaviour results from behaviour of individual persons and their relations. They do not seem to see much of a problem in treating firms as if they were agents *sui generis*. Thus they unhesitatingly talk about organisational learning, self-organisation and the like.
2. The assumption of perfect (or unbounded) rationality is rejected. Individual agents and firms are believed to be boundedly rational at most. Related to this is the belief that firms are unable to respond fully flexibly to unanticipated environmental changes. Firms cannot alter their operating routines overnight. Insofar as they are feasible at all, adjustments to changes take time and effort. Furthermore, the representative agent approach is rejected. It is not assumed at the outset that firms in an industry have already converged on some line of behaviour. In short, catchwords here are 'bounded rationality', '(some degree of) inertia' and 'heterogeneity of agents'.
3. Process analysis is the thing to do (see also Groenewegen and Vromen, 1999). In so far as evolutionary economics deals with static equilibrium

notions, they must be shown to be (possible) outcomes of dynamic, evolutionary processes.

Within evolutionary economics nobody seems to question that firm behaviour is rule- (or routine-) bound to some extent. Echoes of neo-institutionalism are quite clearly audible here. But at the same time all evolutionary economists seem to acknowledge that firms, or at least individuals partaking in their operations, can (and do) engage in purposeful behaviour. What is more, nobody seems to dispute that individuals (can) have imaginative and creative powers either. Individuals are able to come up with genuinely novel ideas. Here it is the neo-Austrian message that is taken to heart. But the neo-institutionalist and neo-Austrian messages do not seem to sit easily with one another. Where the one stresses external influences on behaviour, the other emphasises self-determination of autonomous agents.

There seem to be at least two theoretical puzzles here. First, how can individuals engage in purposeful, forward-looking behaviour if rules and routines, as remnants of the past, at the same time mechanically govern their behaviour?[6] Second, how can agents consciously introduce new ideas out of the blue if the agents (and their operating characteristics) are at the same time products of the past? How can internal (self-)determination and external determination be reconciled with one another?

These puzzles are reflected most clearly in the ongoing debate in evolutionary economics concerning the source of novelty. Everybody agrees that there is an incessant influx of novelty in economic systems. But how to account for this? Can a theoretical account of the source of novelty be given? Can the emergence of novelty be endogenised? On the one side, there are those who argue that the source of novelty is inexplicable (and leave it at that, see, for example, Metcalfe, 1998).[7] On the other side, some argue that this presents the major theoretical challenge for evolutionary economics (see, for example, Foster, 1999).

A first step in the direction of a resolution of these puzzles is taken by Witt (1994). Witt first makes a useful distinction between pre-revelation and post-revelation analysis. Post-revelation analysis deals with the diffusion of innovations in markets once these have emerged. This poses no problems. It is only pre-revelation analysis that poses special problems. For innovations cannot be anticipated (or foreseen) by definition. Witt argues that it is nevertheless possible to say something about the emergence of novelty.[8] We could inquire about the possible motives underlying attempts to innovate, for example. Witt argues that curiosity and the desire to improve one's own performance may prompt people to look for innovations. And we could also investigate the conditions under which innovations are likely to emerge. Are

190 *Darwinism and Evolutionary Economics*

people more likely to search for innovations if they are confronted with unsatisfactory results?

On the basis of Witt's distinctions, I propose to unpack the debate about the source of novelty even further in terms of the following subquestions:

1. What capacities do innovations presuppose?
2. What motives lie behind innovations?
3. When are innovations likely to emerge?
4. How many innovations are likely to emerge (what is the innovation rate)?
5. In which directions are innovations sought (are there positive search heuristics)?
6. What innovations do emerge?
7. What innovations are actually tried?[9]
8. What innovations eventually make it in the market?

Another theoretical puzzle occupying evolutionary economists at the moment is how to make sense of the notion of *co-evolution*. The basic idea here is simple. The behaviour of firms affects industry behaviour. But there is also a reverse arrow of causation running from (changes in) industry behaviour to firm behaviour. Firm behaviour and industry behaviour mutually affect each other. Evolution at the firm level and at the industry level go hand in hand with one another. The puzzle is not so much whether this happens. That seems obvious enough. The puzzle is, rather, how to think and theorise about it? We know that 'everything depends on everything' here. What we do not know yet is *how* everything depends on everything.

Evolutionary theory does not seem to be of much help in resolving any of these puzzles – how to theorise the source of novelty and how to theorise co-evolution. Pleas to move away from the 'biological metaphor' in evolutionary economics seem to be informed by this impression. Indeed, it even seems that evolutionary theory cannot accommodate the phenomena at stake here. Evolutionary theory cannot come to grips with the conscious creation of novelty, it seems. And it does not provide models to think of co-evolution. It may even appear that evolutionary theory, with its frequent exclusive focus on individual selection, cannot account for firm selection. In the sections to come, I argue that these impressions of evolutionary theory are misguided.

Evolutionary psychology and agency[10]

Evolutionary theory or agency?

One of the most tenacious and inhibiting misunderstandings of evolutionary theory is that it rules out (genuine) agency. Since most economists (and social scientists in general) hold that coming to grips with agency is crucial for understanding economic (and social) phenomena, many have drawn the conclusion that for the purpose of developing an economic (or social) theory, evolutionary theory is deficient. This section points out why evolutionary theory and agency are compatible with one another. What evolutionary theory rules out, first, is providence – that we can foresee all future contingencies – and second, that our capacity of volition (and its expression in action) is an uncaused cause. But providence and uncaused volition are not implied by agency. What is more, it is argued that current evolutionary theory, in the guise of evolutionary psychology (EP), sheds an interesting light on agency. Before we come to that, however, I want to discuss what features of evolutionary theory are primarily responsible for the (misguided) impression that it cannot accommodate agency.

The preliminary question to be answered, though, is, of course: what is agency? There are many different answers to this question. Dretske (1999) is a good source of further discussion. He argues that we can speak of genuine agency if someone does something because he has the desires and beliefs he has. Dretske stresses that the mere existence (and occurrence of) neurophysiological states or events underlying desires and beliefs falls short of calling the entity having them an agent. What is needed in addition are their meanings. It is the meaning of the states or events that provides the explanation. Note, however, that the agents do not need to be aware of (or be conscious of) the meaning. Dretske gives the example of a bird that learns to avoid poisonous butterflies. In learning which butterflies to avoid the bird develops an internal representation of certain types of poisonous butterflies. It is because the internal representation means that a token of a butterfly is around that the bird displays the avoidance behaviour. And because of this the bird can be called an agent (even though the bird is unlikely to be aware of this meaning).

Now, why have so many commentators believed that evolutionary theory excludes agency? One reason is to be found in the familiar characterisations of evolutionary theory. The first, probably best known, characterisation comes directly from Darwin. Darwin identified selection, variation and heredity as the three basic conditions for natural selection to bring about evolution. In the neo-Darwinian synthesis a separate mechanism is assigned to each condition. For the purpose of our present discussion the crucial thing to appreciate is that each mechanism is assumed to operate independently of the others. This means, for example, that the occurrence and direction of new variety is unrelated to prevailing selection pressure. It is typically *not* assumed that new variety makes a timely appearance under adversity (unfavourable selection pressure). This is what 'blind mutation' is all about.[11] And heredity likewise is assumed to be undirected by prevailing evolutionary pressure. Mendelian inheritance does not respond to the needs of organisms. The Mendelian laws rather specify counterfactually what would happen if differential selection were absent.

The overall picture does not seem to fit well with what happens in economies. Firms do respond to dissatisfactory results, for example. And, if possible, they anticipate future contingencies. That is, mutation does not seem to be blind here. Similarly, what operating features firms want to retain also seems to depend on their prospects of yielding satisfactory results. As a matter of fact, in economies the variety-inducing and the retention mechanisms seem to be two sides of the same coin: they both seem to stem from the desire to improve performance. This suggests that, in so far as there can be said to be three mechanisms working also in economies, goal-directed behaviour makes the functioning of the three mechanisms *inter*dependent rather than *in*dependent.

The second familiar characterisation of evolutionary theory is in a pair of concepts: 'replicators' and 'interactors' (see Hull, 1988b, and Plotkin, 1994, for example). This pair of concepts can be said to be successors and refinements of the pair Dawkins (1976) introduced: replicators and vehicles. As is well known by now, the main point Dawkins (1976) wanted to make is that, properly understood, the gene (as *the* paradigmatic example of a replicator), rather than the organism, is the unit of selection in Darwinian evolutionary theory. Especially if we look at inclusive fitness theory, Dawkins argued, it becomes clear that it is the selection of genes rather than that of individual organisms which ultimately counts in Darwinian evolutionary theory. Contrary to what Darwin thought, Darwinian evolution is driven not by selection of the individual organism, but by gene selection.

Dawkins called individual organisms the 'vehicles' of their selfish genes. In the eyes of many this fostered the impression that Dawkins portrayed individuals as lumbering robots programmed by their selfish genes. It seemed that Dawkins argued that our beloved self-image, that we ourselves decide what we do (and do not do), is deceptive. It is not we ourselves, but our selfish genes, that are in the driver's seat. Sometimes it may look as if we are truly moved by altruistic feelings. But 'deep down inside' we are governed by our selfish genes.

Now, what matters is not so much whether the above gives an accurate representation of Dawkins's ideas. As a matter of fact, I believe that it does not get Dawkins's ideas right.[12] But what matters is that many took the above to be the real message of Dawkins (1976): the genes are the real 'agents' in Darwinian evolutionary theory. This strengthened the impression that genuine agency is denied by evolutionary theory. It seemed that evolutionary theory and genetic determinism are inextricably tied with one another. Adopting the selection metaphor inevitably commits one to take genetic determinism on board as well.

The idea that evolutionary theory and agency mutually exclude each other is fostered also by the way in which agency and evolutionary theory are often depicted. Agency is often considered as a capacity (or power) residing inside the agent, whereas selection (as one of the major 'agents' in evolutionary theory) is located outside the agent. Changes in behaviour either originate from inside the agent, or are forced by outside pressures. In short, while agency is seen as an internal, personal force, selection is considered to be an external, impersonal force. Furthermore, evolution sometimes is characterised as being backward-looking in its mode of operation, whereas agency is forward-looking. Either phenomena and events are explained by referring to the expectations and anticipations of agents, or by referring to past, realised results. Once again, evolutionary theory and agency are put at opposite ends here.

A reconciliation

Despite all appearances to the contrary, it is of the utmost importance to grasp that selection does not rule out agency. Selection, which typically impinges upon individuals from the outside (see Brandon, 1990), is fully compatible with agency, stemming from somewhere inside the individual. The key to understanding this is provided by the distinction between *ultimate* and *proximate* causes. It is no exaggeration to state that current evolutionary theory cannot be understood if this distinction is disregarded (see, for example, De Waal, 1996).[13]

The distinction goes back to Mayr (1961). Mayr argues that there are several perfectly legitimate answers to the question why, for example, warblers migrate to the south when winter is about to come. What is the cause of bird migration? One legitimate answer is that migration is linked with photoperiodicity. Warblers are equipped with some internal physiological machinery that allows them to sense decreases in day length and that allows them to respond by migrating southwards. Another legitimate answer is that during the evolutionary history of the species, warblers have gained a genetic constitution making for such internal physiological machinery. Here the causes are the evolutionary forces that impinged on the ancestors of the warblers living now. Mayr calls the first class of causes 'proximate causes' and the second class 'ultimate causes'.[14]

Proximate causes refer to the decision-making machinery (or behaviour-instigating mechanisms) inside the behaving entity. They are internal to the behaving entity and they operate just before the behaviour is displayed. Ultimate causes on the other hand refer to circumstances outside ancestors of the behaving entity responsible for the behavioural profile the behaving entity has now. Thus, while proximate causes refer to causes *internal* to the behaving entity working *now*, ultimate causes refer to causes that were *external* to its ancestors *then* (that is, to causes working way back in time). The link between the two types of causes is that proximate causes are effects of ultimate causes. Ultimate causes impinging on behavioural entities in the past have produced the proximate causes that govern the behaviour of their descendants now.

One of the central (if not *the* central) ultimate causes in evolutionary theory is natural selection. But what are the paradigmatic species of proximate causes in evolutionary theory? The example of the migrating warblers given above suggests that neurophysiological processes inside organisms are prime proximate causes in evolutionary theory. If we add to this the widespread belief that neurophysiological processes are coded for in the organism's genes, then the image that emerges is one of a direct, straightforward chain running from genes over neurophysiological processes to overt behaviour. It seems we are back then at genetic determinism. Once again agency appears to have vanished from the evolutionary scene. Not we ourselves are in charge of what we do: it is our genes that, via the neurophysiological processes that they code for, determine our behaviour.

Sociobiology has often been said to endorse genetic determinism. And evolutionary psychology is often said to be sociobiology in disguise (or sociobiology garbed in a new dress).[15] But EP differs from sociobiology in that much more attention is paid to an intermediate link between neurophysiological processes and brain architecture on the one hand, and behaviour on the other. Indeed, EP has been introduced by its pioneers as an attempt to provide *the* missing link in evolutionary theory (Cosmides and Tooby, 1987). EP situates this link at the level of the human mind. To be more precise, EP postulates the existence of a multitude of psychological mechanisms (or modules) working at the level of the human mind (Buss, 1999). In this sense, EP identifies psychological mechanisms as *the* proximate causes of human behaviour.

What exactly are psychological mechanisms, and with what psychological mechanisms are we equipped according to EP? EP is often circumscribed as 'cognitive science meets evolutionary theory'. From cognitive science (see particularly Fodor, 1983), EP takes over the idea that the human mind consists of modules. Typically, when confronted with some task, not all of the human mind is mobilised. Only one module – as a part of the mind – is activated. What part is activated depends on the domain to which the task belongs. Now, what domains are there and, relatedly, what modules does our mind consist of? Here evolutionary theory comes in. EP holds that in order to tell what modules we have and in what domains they are triggered, we have to look at the evolutionary (sub)problems our ancestors had to cope with. The idea here is that, although it is clear that individual differential reproductive success was decisive in the evolution of the human species, our ancestors were never directly faced with the problem of how to maximise their individual reproduction rate. What they were directly faced with instead was some component of this. In order to achieve a favourable reproduction rate, several evolutionary subproblems had to be solved. Obviously, finding a suitable individual of the opposite sex to mate with was such an evolutionary subproblem. And so are successes in withstanding climatological changes, in staying away from predators and in solving co-operation problems in groups. A central hypothesis in EP is that domains correspond to such evolutionary (sub)problems and that our modules evolved to solve these problems.

Perhaps the best worked out example of a module is the cheater-detection algorithm discussed by Cosmides and Tooby (1992).[16] Cosmides and Tooby argue that in order to have 'tit for tat' sustain a social contract, the people in question must be good at spotting cheaters. If people were not good at this, they would be unable to punish cheaters. And the latter of course is crucial to 'tit for tat'. In Cosmides and Tooby's opinion, the existence of a specialised cheater-detection algorithm is confirmed by the findings in the Wason Selection Task. Peter Wason devised his Selection Task to find out whether people perform well in applying *modus tollens*, the logical rule underlying Popper's falsificationism. To his surprise, people tended to perform quite poorly. The only exception to this tendency was when a specific type of propositional content was given to the problem. When the problem was framed in terms of a social contract problem, the performance rate increased dramatically from less than 25% to 75%. Apparently, then, Cosmides and Tooby conclude, people avail of a content-specific algorithm, an algorithm that is activated only if the problem has the right propositional content.

EP advances a 'Swiss army knife' model of mind in which the human mind consists of a multitude of such special-problem devices. Each of these devices evolved to solve a specific evolutionary (sub)problem in times long gone, EP argues. But they can still be triggered if people are provided with the right informational input. In this sense, our skulls still house a stone-aged mind. EP revitalises the view that people all around the world share the same basic repertoire of modules. Human nature is said to be the same everywhere. But it is important to recognise that human nature, as EP sees it, is not of a piece. What module is activated, to repeat, depends on the informational input provided. This explains why the same people who behave altruistically in some settings (as in following 'tit for tat' in social contract settings) behave much more self-regardingly in other contexts.

Some have likened modules to preferences. Others compare them with instincts. Who is right? The answer to this question may seem to have some bearing on economics. For it seems that EP voices a view on human behaviour that is either compatible with mainstream neoclassical economics or underwrites 'old' Veblen-type institutionalism. This impression is misleading. In EP's loose use of the terms,[17] 'preference' and 'instinct' refer to pretty much the same thing: to predispositions (or inclinations) to learn and behave in certain ways. They are more like preferences in that they do not fully specify exactly what to do in particular situations. But they are more like instincts in that they usually prestructure our perceptions and our experiences, but also our behavioural responses, in an unconscious way. We cannot choose our own modules. They are already there before we make our choices and decisions.

Do our modules prompt us to behave rationally? Among other things this depends on how well adapted modules were to ancestral circumstances, and to what extent our present-day circumstances resemble these ancestral circumstances. Behaviour that was optimal then may well be far from optimal now. Cosmides and Tooby (1994) suggest that behaviour prompted by our modules may make for better than rational behaviour. What they mean by this is that having a rich repertoire of special problem-solving devices (as EP claims) may be more efficient than having just one general problem-solving device. Modules as special problem-solving devices function as shortcuts, facilitating 'fast-track' learning. Hence they save on time and energy. The other side of this, however, is that our stone-aged skull may be poorly adapted to solve today's problems. Our modules may prevent us from quickly learning certain useful things. Thus modules enable and facilitate, but they also inevitably constrain and confine what can be learned or done.

But where does all this leave agency? We started our discussion of EP by noting that, compared to sociobiology, EP inserts an extra layer between neurophysiological processes and brain architecture on the one hand, and behaviour on the other. But, if it is still the case that genes are believed to determine neurophysiological processes, that these processes in turn determine our mind's modules, and that these modules finally determine our behaviour, is not EP committed to genetic determinism after all? As far as I can see,[18] there are at least two reasons for believing that EP has left genetic determinism behind. The first is that EP believes the route between genes and behaviour to be more complex than genetic determinism suggests. Environmental influences enter the picture at least at two moments. They affect the ontogenetic development of brain structure;[19] and they intervene in the translation of the mind's modules into behaviour. The mind's modules typically are conditional. The same module thus may lead to different behavioural responses to different circumstances. In this way EP tries to account for cultural diversity. EP's notion of 'evoked culture' is meant to convey the idea that people across all kinds of culture have the same underlying (conditional) modules in common with one another: the fact that they are faced with different circumstances evokes different cultural responses.

But sensitivity to environmental influences still does not bring us agency. Behaviour prompted by 'modules as predispositions' seems to be more similar to mechanical rule-governed behaviour than to conscious purposeful action. But 'modules as predispositions' need not and often do not fully specify behaviour. They leave room for deliberate choice. Rather than fully specified programmes for action, they provide positive heuristics for learning. By delimiting and structuring the set of options that are taken into consideration, they guide and facilitate choice. But they almost never uniquely single out one course of action. As Symons (1992) (following William James) argues, the mind's modules may establish fixed ends. But they do allow for flexibility in the choice of means.

Thus reason may serve as the slave of our predispositions, to paraphrase Hume. Reason may not only greatly facilitate prudential behaviour (or, in general, help in satisfying self-regarding 'passions'). Reason may also help in turning 'social instincts' into co-operative behaviour that is satisfactory to all involved, as Darwin (n.d.) already noted: the love of praise and the fear of blame are among the most prominent of the social instincts, Darwin argued. If reason allows man to anticipate the judgements of his fellows, as Darwin thinks it does, then he knows pretty well how to obtain praise and avoid blame from his fellows. In general, Darwin suggested that what sets *Homo sapiens* apart from less developed species is not its possession of special instincts but its endowment with the power of reasoning: 'Although man ... has no special instincts to tell him how to aid his fellow-men, he still has the impulse, and with his improved intellectual faculties would naturally be much guided in this respect by reason and experience' (Darwin, n.d., p. 481).[20]

Reason may also sometimes overrule our predispositions. We are not the prisoners of our modules. It may be that we inherited a taste for fatty food from our ancestors, for example. But our worry about getting overweight may be sufficiently strong that we choose to stick to a less tasty diet. It may seem that some kind of free-floating reason here gets the last word after all. This impression is wrong, however. To see this, let us unpack the impression into two parts. First, in acknowledging that reason can overturn predispositions, is reason given the role of final arbiter here? Second, does reason enter the scene here as a *deus ex machina*? Let us deal with both parts in turn.

Reasoned action is no longer the rule or norm here. Our lust for fatty food is no longer an aberration of this. It is rather the other way around. Our primary reward system, driven by predispositions, provides the basis for behaviour. Conscious deliberation can break in to change the odds. Furthermore, the fact (if it is one) that we can use our capacity to think and reason to go against our natural appetites does not imply that we often exploit this capacity. It may well be the case that more often we go along with our natural appetites. And when we do so, we follow our appetites unconsciously. This also gives some determinacy and predictability to our actions. Thus, for purposes of a positive social theory with predictive aspirations, reliance on dispositions may make perfectly good sense.

Reason does not enter the story as a *deus ex machina*. Although much may still be wanting, the capacity (uniquely human or not) to overrule is itself explained in evolutionary terms. Evolutionary theory demands that reason itself is a product of evolution. Introducing uncaused causes goes against the grain of evolutionary theory. As Dennett (1995) puts it, evolutionary theory does not allow for 'skyhooks', devices that fall as manna from heaven. But it does allow for 'cranes': devices that can change or speed up evolutionary processes, and that are themselves shown to be products of antecedent evolutionary processes. Cranes enable scaffolding. Evolutionary processes can build upon the results obtained in earlier evolutionary processes.

In a sense, then, the main message of evolutionary theory can be said to be that the past continues to cast its shadow over the present and future. What happened in the past still determines what can happen now and in the future. Everything is history-dependent. But, as we have seen, this does not imply that 'future-oriented and anticipating' elements can find no place in evolutionary theory. Evolutionary theory does not rule out the possibility of forward-looking action. What is ruled out is the existence of providentially forward-looking actors. Evolutionary theory is idle in a world inhabited by creatures equipped with perfect foresight.

Implications for (evolutionary) economics?

So far, the conclusion to be drawn from our discussion of EP seems to be primarily a negative one: acknowledging genuine agency does not demand that we leave evolutionary theory. But EP also seems to have a few positive messages for economic theory in the offing. Consider opportunism.

Economic theories of organisation (such as transactions cost economics, see Williamson, 1985) typically assume that individuals tend to behave opportunistically. This tendency is assumed to be independent of the organisational context in which individuals function. Hierarchical control within organisations is often presented as the most efficient way to curtail this tendency. By contrast, EP suggests that the disposition to behave opportunistically may depend on organisational context (see, for example, Nicholson, 1997). The disposition may be triggered in the one context, and not in the other. Organisational contexts that give employees the impression that a precious social contract is to be upheld, for example, may foster a much more trusting and co-operative attitude among employees. In other words, hierarchical control may be the problem rather than the cure.

This example also vividly illustrates the point that far from portraying us human beings as passive victims of prevailing circumstances, EP portrays us as beings that can actively change circumstances in order to activate the modules in us that we want to activate. This also has repercussions for how to approach the theoretical puzzle of the sources of novelty introduced above. Recall that I unpacked this puzzle into eight subquestions. This section's discussion has shown, I think, that evolutionary theory in general and EP in particular can shed some light on the first five subquestions. First, evolutionary theory is able to explain the capacity of innovators to engage in deliberate search as the outcome of preceding evolutionary processes. Second, let us assume that Witt (1994) is right in saying that curiosity and the desire to improve one's own performance are the main motives underlying innovations. The challenge for EP would be to show that these motives had survival value in certain problem contexts in the past. Third, the conditions to be met for innovations to emerge need not pertain only to experiences of adversity. They may also pertain to contexts in which the disposition to search is activated. Here we see again that one of the main lessons to draw from EP may be that we actively change the circumstances in which we operate in such a way that the right predispositions are triggered. Fourth, the same argument can be invoked to point out that innovation rates are context-dependent. And again, creating the right circumstances may also help increase the innovation rate. EP may be of much help, especially in answering the fifth subquestion. For in a sense positive search heuristics is what EP is all about. Identifying our mind's modules means finding out what learning procedures people follow in different contexts.

This leaves us with subquestions 6 and 7. Even if we had perfectly determinate answers to the first five subquestions, we would still be unable to answer the sixth one. In a sense, genuinely new ideas come out of the blue. This merely paraphrases that they are not predictable. It is true that evolutionary theory cannot predict this process. But neither can any other theory! So evolutionary theory cannot be discarded on the ground that it cannot account for the innovative process. If evolutionary theory is to be condemned for this, then every other theory has to await the same fate.

Multilevel Selection Theory

As we have seen, most evolutionary economists take firms (or business units) as the elementary units of analysis. No attempts are made to explain how firm behaviour results from the relevant properties of the individuals involved in the functioning of the firm (their interests, beliefs, etc.) and the ways in which they are related to one another in the firm organisation. This does not fit in nicely with methodological individualism. Nelson and Winter (1982) acknowledge this. They concede that it may be more realistic to analyse firm behaviour as the outcome of the firm members and the contractual relations that obtain between them. But they argue that, for their own purposes (that are close to those of orthodox economics, as they themselves note),[21] they need not look into the interior of the 'black box'. If we want to give an evolutionary explanation of industry behaviour, Nelson and Winter argue, then we can treat firms as elementary units of analysis because in competitive markets there is evolutionary pressure exerted on firms *as units*.

Witt (1987) is one of the few evolutionary economists who explicitly discusses evolutionary economics in relation to methodological individualism. Witt wants to adhere to methodological individualism, if only for the reason that novelty (which Witt puts centre stage in evolutionary economics) is created, applied and disseminated by individuals and not by firms as some sort of collective agents (Witt, 1987, p. 14). Witt characteristically is not too much concerned with how the activities of all the individuals in the firm (novelty-creating or not) intermingle so as to produce the behaviour of the firm. In fact, in line with the venerable Austrian tradition, Witt simply seems to equate firm behaviour with the behaviour of the entrepreneur.

The problem with this is, of course, that we cannot take it for granted that entrepreneurs (or stockholders or managers, for that matter) succeed in acquiring unconditional support from their employees. The plans of entrepreneurs can meet resistance within the organisation. For we cannot take it for granted that the interests of all who affect the functioning of the organisation are perfectly aligned with one another. As a consequence, the behaviour of the organisation taken as a whole need not be perfectly in line with the wishes and goals of entrepreneurs.

If we want to understand why firms behave the way they do, it seems we have to look both at what happens between firms at the level of industries (at interfirm interaction, as Nelson and Winter, 1982, emphasise), and at what happens within firms at the level of individual contractants (at intrafirm interaction, as contractual theories of organisation stress). We can generalise this point by saying that we have a hierarchy of evolutionary processes concurrently going on. At each level of organisation in this hierarchy, the behaviour of units is affected not only by what happens 'outside', at higher levels of organisation, but also by what happens 'inside' the units, at lower levels of organisation. This, I venture to suggest, is an interesting rendering of what co-evolution in economics could be all about.[22] Co-evolution does not merely recognise that the consequences of the interaction of units at a higher level feed back to (and possibly alter) the relevant properties of the units themselves. Firms can change themselves, for example, as a consequence of the changes that their interactions produce at the industry level. But that is not all. There is more to co-evolution than 'reconstitutive downward causation', as Hodgson (1999b) calls it. What more there is, is that at each level of the hierarchy the relevant properties of the units in question (and, hence, their behaviour) depend also on what happens at lower levels of organisation. In a sense, then, there is reconstitutive upward as well as downward causation. It is here that Sober and Wilson's multilevel selection theory comes in. Sober and Wilson's multilevel selection theory (henceforth: MST) holds out the promise to shed light on exactly this broader notion of co-evolution.

Group selection[23]

In order to understand MST, let us first have a look at the notion of group selection.[24] Group selection became a discredited notion for many soon after Wynne-Edwards (1962) invoked the notion as an explanation of ultrasocial behaviour in nature. There seem to have been two major reasons for this. The first reason is empirical. Starting with Williams (1966), many biologists (and evolutionary theorists in general) have not so much doubted that 'group selection' denotes a genuine possibility in nature, as that the conditions for the force of group selection to be stronger than that of individual selection are so severe that they are not likely to be met in reality. The second reason is conceptual. Biologists increasingly felt that, on the basis of Hamilton's (1964) inclusive fitness theory (based on kin selection), and of Trivers's (1971) theory of reciprocal altruism, they could explain all kinds of ultrasocial behaviour in what was regarded as orthodox Darwinian terms of individual, or even gene, selection (Dawkins, 1976). Hence there was believed to be no need for the notion of group selection.

Sober and Wilson (1998; see also Wilson and Sober, 1994) want to rehabilitate the notion of group selection. What Sober and Wilson want to show is both that a clear and coherent notion of group selection can be developed and that group selection is going on more often than ardent opponents of group selection are willing to accept. While I do not think Sober and Wilson (1998) were entirely successful, they do have many valuable insights to offer. The problem is that they want to argue two things that do not fit nicely with one another. The first thing they argue for is that in discussing group selection the theoretical perspective adopted should be clearly distinguished from the causal processes analysed. The relevant issue here is whether there are processes in which groups (rather than individual organisms) are selected and not whether a theoretical perspective can be upheld which maintains, for example, that it ultimately is 'selfish genes' that count. The second thing Sober and Wilson argue is that altruism requires group selection to evolve. It is argued that altruism cannot evolve if there is only individual selection going on. In establishing their second argument, Sober and Wilson develop a comprehensive theoretical perspective that, as we shall see, sometimes spots two different causal processes, whereas in reality there seems to be one process going on only. Thus, Sober and Wilson themselves do not seem to distinguish clearly between theoretical perspective and actual causal processes.

Sober and Wilson warn against confusing the theoretical perspective adopted with the causal processes analysed. Following Dawkins (1976), 'selfish gene' adepts have insisted that genes are *the* units of selection in biological evolution. Sober and Wilson argue that they are right to the extent that what ultimately counts in biological evolution is how gene frequencies change in a population's gene pool. But this is merely a matter of *ex post* bookkeeping. It is the way to keep track of the effects of evolutionary processes. However, it does not tell us anything about the causes of changes in gene frequencies. And even if we confine our attention to natural selection (as one of the possible causes of evolution), it is by no means self-evident that changes in gene frequencies can only result from natural selection impinging on individual organisms.[25] For individual organisms need not be the only possible vehicles in biological evolution. Groups may be vehicles as well. And since 'group selection is a question about vehicles, not replicators' (Sober and Wilson, 1998, p. 92), the 'selfish gene' perspective does not rule out the possibility of group selection. Indeed, Sober and Wilson go on to argue, groups sometimes are vehicles, and, hence, there is group selection going on. In insisting that there nevertheless is no such thing as group selection, 'selfish gene' adepts commit the *averaging fallacy*: in taking the average fitness over groups these adepts argue as if there were no population structure (the way in which the population is divided into groups). 'Selfish gene' adepts argue that there is only one causal process going on, to wit, one of individual selection, whereas in fact there are two causal processes going on, both individual and group selection.

But what exactly is group selection? The answer suggested by the above discussion is that there is group selection if natural selection impinges on groups rather than on individuals. Groups apparently, then, must exhibit some sort of wholeness or unity comparable to that of individual organisms. This indeed seems to be the guiding idea of Sober and Wilson (1998). Groups are said to have (differential) fitness in much the same way as individual organisms have (p. 37).[26] And it is argued that groups are internally integrated (p. 145), co-ordinated, and display some internal harmony (p. 87). This can be called their 'common fate' idea. In groups, individuals are bound together by their common fate. Its constituent members all suffer, for example, if a group perishes. This does not imply that there cannot be any conflict of interest between the individual members at all. Their interests may conflict to some extent. But, as Sober and Wilson are eager to note, a complete lack of conflicting interests need not hold for individual organisms either. The unity of individual organisms neither is a pre-ordained 'state of nature'. Individual organisms also must withstand 'mutiny from within' (see, for example, Ridley, 1996). If 'selfish gene' adepts are willing to accept individual organisms as vehicles, and if groups display the same sort of unity as individual organisms, Sober and Wilson ask rhetorically, then why don't they also accept groups as vehicles?

The second thing Sober and Wilson (1998) argue for, as we saw, is that it takes group selection for altruism to evolve. More precisely, for altruism to evolve the strength of group selection must outweigh that of individual selection. According to Sober and Wilson, individual selection is always omnipresent, irrespective of whether there is also group selection going on. And they argue that individual selection always favours egoism. 'Egoistic' behaviour is defined by Sober and Wilson as behaviour that promotes one's own fitness at the expense of the fitness of others. Sober and Wilson are well aware of the fact that they go against the stream here. Many take kin selection ('inclusive fitness') theory and game-theoretic accounts of the evolution of reciprocal altruism to be evidence for the thesis that altruism can evolve also if there is only individual selection going on. Sober and Wilson go at great length in arguing that this is based on a misunderstanding. They argue that kin selection theory and game theory tacitly invoke group selection. I concentrate on their account of game theory. For it is here, I submit, that the conflict with their own plea to distinguish clearly between perspective and process is most poignantly brought out.

In their account of game theory, Sober and Wilson proceed as follows. They argue that there is both individual and group selection. Groups are identified here as the possible pairwise encounters between two individuals.

If games are represented in normal form, each box in the matrix is assumed to signify a group. The effects of group selection depend on how the sum totals of the different possible pairs of individuals compare to each other. The effects of individual selection depend on how the individual fitnesses of the constituent 'members' within the group compare to each other. The end result depends on the relative strengths of the two selection processes.

The notion of a group at stake here is a very minimal one. The number of individual members need not be larger than two. And the individuals need to meet only once. More importantly, the individuals can be different in all respects except one. The only thing they need to have in common with each other is that there is a non-negligible probability that they meet each other. The internal harmony and coordination of groups that Sober and Wilson stress so much in their first argument is not required here. Groups here do not need to operate as units.[27]

In fact it seems to be quite contrived to speak of natural selection acting on groups (as units) here. There is much in the standard interpretation in terms of individual selection, I submit, that recommends itself here. The distinction Sober and Wilson make between individual and group selection seems to be rather artificial. There seems to be one process, and one process only, going on. What Sober and Wilson do here seems to be opposite to the averaging fallacy they accuse 'selfish gene' adepts of: spotting two causal processes whereas there is only one going on.[28] But underlying this, it can be argued, the same mistake is made: attributing causal significance to how processes are carved up in some theoretical framework.

I suggest that dropping the second argument best relieves the tension between Sober and Wilson's arguments. Altruism does not require group selection to evolve. Processes of individual selection can take place under a variety of conditions, and under some of them (if there is assortative mating, for example) altruism may evolve. Dropping the second argument also obviates any compelling reasons to accept the minimal notions of group and group selection. The more substantive notions of group and group selection that are implied in the first argument are to be retained. A set of individuals only makes for a group if the individuals share some fate with one another. This allows us to speak of the set of individuals acting as a unit. And it is upon units like this that selection can impinge.

Multilevel selection processes in market economies

Turning back to economics now, it seems that examples of groups and of group selection (in the substantive sense outlined above) are readily discernible. As many economists have observed, there is something like competitive (or market) selection going on between firms in market economies. Firms normally seem to exhibit the type of unity required for treating them as groups. Thus what economists call competitive selection pretty much resembles what Sober and Wilson call group selection. Viewed in isolation (*ceteris paribus*, as economists would have it), competitive selection favours firms with co-operatively behaving individuals. Furthermore, within firms there seems to be the problem of 'free riding' (or shirking) individuals that Sober and Wilson associate with individual selection. *Ceteris paribus*, free-riding individuals are by definition better off than the individuals the efforts of whom they free ride upon. 'Individual selection' within firms thus seems to favour egoistic free riding. All aspects of Sober and Wilson's multiselection theory therefore do seem to have counterparts in actual selection processes in market economies. Competitive selection and free riding pull the behaviour of individuals in opposite directions in much the same way that group selection and individual selection do in Sober and Wilson's MST theory.

The implications for the study of firm behaviour are that both processes of 'group selection' and of 'individual selection' have to be taken into account. Firms have to withstand both internal (intrafirm) and external (interfirm) pressure. There is no *a priori* reason to believe that the two pressures call for the same optimal solution. The optimal solution to the problem of how to align the different interests of individuals within firms (cf. Nelson and Winter, 1982, pp. 107–2: 'routine as a truce') is likely to differ from the optimal solution of how to outperform competing firms. Therefore firms presumably strike a balance between the two. What balance they strike depends on the relative strengths of the two pressures. The picture gets more complex (but also more plausible, I think) by inserting extra layers between individuals and firms, for example, groups or divisions of employees (see Campbell, 1994) and between firms and industries, such as business groups (see Granovetter, 1998). But the overall idea remains the same: what happens at each level of organisation is a function of the net effect of different pressures working at adjacent levels.

MST thus explains how the functioning of firms partly depends on what is going on, one level of organisation below, between individuals within firms. Conversely, it also sheds light on Hodgson's (1999b) reconstitutive downward causation: relevant properties of agents depend also in part on the firms in which they function. As Sober (1980) points out, individuals who otherwise differ from each other may nevertheless behave similarly when placed in the same organisational setting. This explains why a firm's routines may survive replacements of employees. *Vice versa*, the same individual may behave differently in different organisational settings. As particularly Simon (1990, 1991, 1993) has pointed out, individuals-*qua*-'member'-of-some-firm may behave differently from individuals-*qua*-

'member'-of some-other-firm (or than individuals in other roles, as individuals-*qua*-citizens, for example).

In other words, Sober and Wilson's MST seems to provide a promising starting point for analysing co-evolutionary processes in market economies. What it convincingly shows, I think, is that neither the operating characteristics of firms, nor the relevant properties of individual agents, can be treated as given data. They concurrently evolve in interlocked ways. It may well turn out that Sober and Wilson's theory has to be adapted, refined, completed or repaired. But at least it does not rest content with vague allusions to the effect that everything-depends-on-everything. It provides us with a clear, coherent and comprehensible model to start thinking about co-evolution in market economies.

Concluding Remarks

Contrary to popular understanding, evolutionary theory does not rule out agency. In particular, evolutionary theory can accommodate the deliberate creation of novelty. The biological metaphor should not be eschewed in evolutionary economics on the ground that it cannot make sense of the incessant endogenous emergence of novelty in market economies. Evolutionary psychology holds out the hope that we will enhance our understanding of the sources of novelty. Furthermore, evolutionary theory is no longer dogmatically committed to the view that there can only be individual (or gene) selection. Understandably, this dogmatic commitment also stood in the way of accepting the biological metaphor in evolutionary economics. For it seems obvious that in economies several interrelated evolutionary processes unfold simultaneously at different levels of organisation. Even though Sober and Wilson's MST has its limitations, it provides a clear, coherent and comprehensive model of such interdependent multilevel evolutionary processes.

This is not to say, however, that evolutionary theory is able to provide all the conceptual and theoretical resources needed to understand these complex issues. Additional resources may be drawn from other *social* sciences such as social psychology. In general, it can be argued that evolutionary psychology gives unwarrantedly short shrift to cultural factors. Little attention is paid to transmitted culture (as opposed to evoked culture), the diffusion of ideas via imitation and social learning. And MST seems to underrate the impact group membership can have on the ways in which individuals behave. Theories about cultural (memetic) evolution and about group dynamics (see, for example, Tajfel, 1981, and Brown, 1988) in social psychology could be of help here.

Notes

1. I am aware that I assume much more continuity here between the views of the old institutionalists, Veblen and Commons, and those of Nelson and Winter, than many commentators would deem defensible. I do not deny that there are huge differences between these views. But I think I can defend my claim that their views on the issues discussed here resemble one another to a considerable degree.
2. It is frankly admitted that to some extent this is an arbitrary selection. Recently there have appeared also interesting new treatments of cultural evolution (such as Sperber, 1996 and Blackmore, 1999), for example.
3. Unless specified otherwise, I will take 'agent' to mean individual human being in this paper.
4. Neo-institutionalism is not to be confused with New Institutional Economics (NIE). See Groenewegen and Vromen (1999) for a discussion of the distinction between the two.
5. This also holds for evolutionary economics. It is sometimes argued that self-organisation theory does more justice to genuine agency than traditional Darwinian evolutionary theory. I believe this view is mistaken. All of these theories are applicable to mechanical (thermodynamic) systems – as a matter of fact they all originated from thermodynamics. They may also be invoked to study non-mechanical systems. But none of them imply (belief in) the existence of genuine agency.
6. See also Vromen (1995) and (1997) for a discussion of this.
7. Some also argue that the inexplicability of the origin of novelty poses no problem for evolutionary theory. Robert C. Dunnell, for example, argues: 'The first consequence of assuming an evolutionary point of view is that the specific origin or invention of new elements becomes a trivial inquiry. What is important is why a new element becomes fixed or accepted ... . [A]nd thus visible in the archaeological record. ... Invention is analogous to mutation in biological systems. On a global scale, it is probably a useful heuristic position to assume that invention is a random phenomenon, and thus, that the total number of people is the major constraint on the raw material of culture change'. (Dunnell, 1996, p. 118; I owe this reference to John Wilkins)
8. Concerning pre-revelation analysis, see also Nightingale's (1993) interesting discussion of Jack Downie's Innovation Mechanism.
9. The difference between (sub)questions 6 and 7 is that not all of the ideas entertained in the thoughts of innovators (as in some sort of 'vicarious selection', see Campbell, 1960 and Cziko, 1995) need be put into practice.
10. For a more detailed and elaborate discussion, see Vromen (1999a).
11. Some would argue that this is exactly what makes economic (and cultural) evolution Lamarckian. But see Speel, Wilkins and Vromen (forthcoming) for a critique of this view.
12. Dawkins never denied the existence of genuine altruism. More importantly, Dawkins argued that understanding cultural, memetic evolution may be more important for understanding human behaviour. He even suggested that we can escape the tyranny of both our genes and memes.
13. But sometimes even theorists advocating an evolutionary approach fail to grasp this distinction. See, e.g., Binmore (1994), who seems to believe that adopting an evolutionary approach implies the belief that we are machines driven by our genes and memes.
14. Actually, Mayr discusses two more classes of causes. They too can be classified in terms of proximate and ultimate causes. But for the purpose of this paper discussion of the two classes of causes mentioned suffices.

15. It has to be noted that EP is far from uncontroversial. There also seem to be different views within EP. Indeed, central notions do not seem to be unambiguously defined. For more on this, see Vromen (1999a).
16. The most controversial example of a module no doubt concerns mate preference.
17. The loose and often ambiguous way in which concepts are used in EP of course complicates efforts to present a clear discussion of it. But, as for example Sugden (1999) argues, economists also use 'preference' in a loose way. According to Sugden, in economics 'preferences' also refer to dispositions to behave in certain ways.
18. I cannot claim to have a complete overview of EP. Problems are compounded because it seems there are a lot of ambiguities (and perhaps even disagreements) in EP.
19. It should perhaps be added here that no sociobiologist ever held that genes fully determine brain structure, regardless of the environmental conditions prevailing during ontogenetic development.
20. It was John Laurent who alerted me to this passage.
21. It has been noted that, allegations to the contrary notwithstanding, textbook neoclassical economics (with its assumptions of firms and households as units) for quite some time also did not live up to the standards of methodological individualism either. It can even be doubted that it did so with its 'microfoundations' program (see Janssen, 1993).
22. Co-evolution in economics can mean many different things, it seems. It could mean, for example, that firms not only have to adapt 'passively' to prevailing circumstances, but can also actively change their environment. Or it could mean that two things at the same level of organisation (such as a firm's organisational form and its technology) in an interrelated way evolve simultaneously. The interpretation given here is especially interesting for the ongoing debate in the social sciences on whether it is 'structure' or 'agency' that should be given explanatory primacy.
23. There has been a debate going on as to whether Hayek invoked group selection in his ideas about cultural selection (and, if so, whether it was legitimate to do so). See Vanberg (1986) and Hodgson (1991). See also Vromen (1995).
24. For a more detailed analysis and discussion of Sober and Wilson's notion of group selection, see Vromen (1999b).
25. Even the staunchest defenders of the 'selfish gene' perspective acknowledge that natural selection normally does not act directly on genes as the paradigmatic examples of *replicators*, but indirectly, *via* individual organisms (as the paradigmatic examples of *vehicles*, or *interactors*).
26. Unless specified otherwise, page numbers refer to Sober and Wilson (1998).
27. As Trivers (1999) notes, this is a far cry from what immediately comes to mind when talking about group selection: tribes, gangs, or gangs combatting each other as units (as in genocidal warfare, for example). See also Darwin (n.d.), who writes about herds, packs, flocks and 'bodies'.
28. This could be called the *decomposing fallacy*.

References

Alchian, A.A. (1950), 'Uncertainty, evolution, and economic theory', *Journal of Political Economy*, **58**, 211–21.

Allen, G. (1979), *Life Science in the Twentieth Century*, Cambridge: Cambridge University Press.

Anderson, R.W. (1995), 'On the maternal transmission of immunity: a molecular attention hypothesis', *Biosystems*, **34**, 87–105.

Arndt, H.W. (1981), 'Economic development: a semantic history', *Economic Development and Cultural Change*, **29**, 457–66.

Atran, S. (1998), 'Folk biology and the anthropology of science: cognitive universals and their cultural particulars', *Behavioral and Brain Sciences*, **21** (4), 547–609.

Bagehot, W. (1879), *Physics and Politics* (5th ed.), London: C. Kegan Paul & Co.

Baldwin, J.M. (1896a), 'A new factor in evolution', *American Naturalist*, **30**, 441–51, 536–53.

Baldwin, J.M. (1896b), 'Heredity and instinct (I and II)', *Science*, 20 March and 10 April, 438–41, 558–61.

Baldwin, J.M. (1909), *Darwin and the Humanities*, Baltimore: Review Publishing.

Baltimore, D. (1970), 'RNA–dependent DNA polymerase in virions of RNA tumor viruses', *Nature*, **226**, 1209–11.

Becker, G.S. (1976), *The Economic Approach to Human Behavior*, Chicago: University of Chicago Press.

Belew, R.K. and M. Mitchell (eds) (1996), *Adaptive Individuals in Evolving Populations: Models and Algorithms,* New York: Perseus Press.

Bell, G. (1996), *Selection: The Mechanism of Evolution*, New York: Chapman and Hall.

Bergin, J. and B.L. Lipman (1996), 'Evolution with state–dependent mutations', *Econometrica*, **64**, 943–56.

Bernstein, R.E. (1984), 'Darwin's alter ego: co–originator Alfred Wallace', *Perspectives in Biology*, **27** (2), 234–7.

Besant, A. (1887), *Is Socialism Sound?* London: Progressive Publishing Co.

Bickerton, D. (1990), *Species and Language*, Chicago: Chicago University Press.

Binmore, K. (1994), *Game Theory and the Social Contract, Vol. I: Playing Fair,* Cambridge, MA: MIT Press.

Black, M. (1962), *Models and Metaphors: Studies in Language and Philosophy*, Ithaca: Cornell University Press.

Blake, R.R., W.E. Avis and J.S. Mouton (1966), *Corporate Darwinism*, Houston, TX: Gulf Publishing Company.

Blackmore, S.J. (1999), *The Meme Machine*, Oxford: Oxford University Press.

Blume, L. and D. Easley (1992), 'Evolution and market behavior', *Journal of Economic Theory*, **58**, 9–40.

Boden, M.A. (1990), *The Creative Mind: Myths and Mechanisms*, London: Weidenfeld and Nicolson.

Boesiger, E. (1974), 'Evolutionary theories after Lamarck and Darwin', in F.J. Ayala' and T. Dobzhansky (eds), *Studies in the Philosophy of Biology*, London, Berkeley and Los Angeles: Macmillan and University of California Press, 21–44.

Bortis, H. (1998), *Institutions, Behaviour and Economic Theory: A Contribution to Classical–Keynesian Political Economy*, Cambridge, UK: Cambridge University Press.

Boulding, K.E. (1950), *A Reconstruction of Economics*, New York: Wiley.

Boulding, K.E. (1981), *Evolutionary Economics*, Beverly Hills: Sage.

Boulding, K.E. (1992), 'Punctuationism in societal evolution', in A. Somit and S.A. Peterson (eds), *The Dynamics of Evolution: The Punctuated Equilibrium Debate in the Natural and Social Sciences*, Ithaca, NY and London: Cornell University Press, 171–86.

Boulding, K.E. (1993), 'The basic evolutionary model', in U. Witt (ed.), (1993), pp. 523-48.

Bowler, P.J. (1983), *The Eclipse of Darwinism: Anti-Darwinian Evolution Theories in the Decades around 1900*, Baltimore, VA: Johns Hopkins University Press.

Bowler, P.J. (1989a), *The Mendelian Revolution: The Emergence of Hereditarian Concepts in Modern Science and Society*, Baltimore, VA: Johns Hopkins University Press.

Bowler, P.J. (1989b), *Evolution: the History of an Idea*, Berkeley, CA: University of California Press.

Boyd, R. and P.J. Richerson (1985), *Culture and the Evolutionary Process*, Chicago: University of Chicago Press.

Boyd, R. and P.J. Richerson (1992), 'Cultural inheritance and evolutionary ecology', in E. A. Smith and B. Winterhalder, (eds), *Evolutionary Ecology and Human Behavior*, New York: De Gruyter, 61–92.

Brandon, R.N. (1988), 'The levels of selection: a hierarchy of interactors', in H. Plotkin (ed.), *The Role of Behavior in Evolution*, Cambridge, MA: MIT Press, 51–71.

Brandon, R. (1990), *Organism and Environment*, Princeton: Princeton University Press.

Brodie, R. (1996), *Virus of the Mind: The New Science of the Meme*, Seattle, WA: Integral Press.

Brown, R. (1988), *Group Processes: Dynamics within and between Groups*, Oxford: Basil Blackwell.

Bryant, K. and A. Wells (1998), *A New Economic Paradigm? Innovation-Based Evolutionary Systems*, Canberra: Department of Industry, Science and Resources.

Bücher, K. [1893] (1922), *Die Entstehung der Volkswirtschaft (I)*, Tübingen: Lau

Burkhardt, R.W. Jr. (1977), *The Spirit of System: Lamarck and Evolutionary Biology*, Cambridge, MA: Harvard University Press.

Burkhardt, R.W. Jr (1984), 'The zoological philosophy of J.B. Lamarck', in Lamarck (1984), xv–xxxix.

Burkhardt, R.W. Jr. (1995), *The Spirit of the System*, *Lamarck and Evolutionary Biology*, Cambridge, MA: Harvard University Press.

Buss, D.M. (1999), *Evolutionary Psychology: The New Science of the Mind*, Needham Heights, MA: Allyn & Bacon.

Butler, J., Ll. D. (1824), *The Analogy of Religion, Natural and Revealed, to the Consititution and Course of Nature* (new edition, corrected), London: C. and J. Rivington.

Butler, S. (1911) *Evolution, Old & New*, 3rd ed., London: Jonathon Cape.

Butterfield, H. (1931), *The Whig Interpretation of History*, London: Bell.

Byles, J.B. (1894), *Sophisms of Free-Trade and Popular Political Economy Examined*, London: Bodley Head.

Callebaut, W. (1993), *Taking the Naturalistic Turn, or, How Real Philosophy of Science is Done*, Chicago: University of Chicago Press.

Camic, C. (1986), 'The matter of habit', *American Journal of Sociology*, **91**, 1039–87.

Campbell, D.T. [1960] (1987), 'Blind variation and selective retention in creative thought as in other knowledge processes', in G. Radnitzky and W.W. Bartley III (eds), *Evolutionary Epistemology, Rationality, and the Sociology of Knowledge*, New York NY: Open Court, 91–114. Originally published in *The Psychological Review*, **67**, 380–400.

Campbell, D.T. (1965), 'Variation, selection and retention in sociocultural evolution', in H.R. Barringer, G.I. Blanksten and R.W. Mack (eds), *Social Change in Developing Areas: A Reinterpretation of Evolutionary Theory*, Cambridge, MA: Schenkman, 19–49. Reprinted in *General Systems*, **14** (1969), 69–85 and in Hodgson (1998c), 354–370.

Campbell, D.T. (1974a), 'Evolutionary epistemology', in P.A. Schilpp (ed.), *The Philosophy of Karl Popper*, **14**, I & II, *The Library of Living Philosophers*, La Salle, IL: Open Court, 413–63.

Campbell, D.T. (1974b), '"Downward causation" in hierarchically organized biological systems', in F.J. Ayala and T. Dobzhansky (eds), *Studies in the Philosophy of Biology*, London: Macmillan, 179–86.

Campbell, D.T. (1975), 'On the conflicts between biological and social evolution and between psychology and moral tradition', *American Psychologist*, **30** (12), December, 1103–26.

Campbell, D.T. (1994), 'How individual and face-to-face group selection undermine firm selection in organizational evolution', in J.A. Baum, and J.V. Singh, (eds), *Evolutionary Dynamics of Organizations*, Oxford, Oxford University Press, 23–8

Campbell, J.H. (1987), 'The new gene and its evolution' in K. Campbell and M.F. Day (eds) (1987), *Rates of Evolution,* London: Allen and Unwin, 283–309.

Campbell, M. (1984), *A Century since Mendel*, Wollongong: Illert Publications.

Campbell, M. and J. Laurent (1987), *The Eye of Reason: Charles Darwin in Australasia*, Wollongong, NSW: University of Wollongong Press.

Carey, J. (1992), *The Intellectuals and the Masses: Pride and Prejudice Among the Literary Intelligentsia, 1880–1939*, London: Faber.

Carroll, J. (1994), 'Marx and Darwin–humanist wreckers of western culture', *Quadrant*, **36**, 8–15.

Castoriadis, C. (1987), *The Imaginary Institution of Society*, Cambridge: Polity Press.

Cavalli-Sforza, L.L. and M.W. Feldman (1981), *Cultural Transmission and Evolution: A Quantitative Approach*, Princeton, NJ: Princeton University Press.

Chilvers, H.A. (1929), *The Seven Wonders of Southern Africa*, Johannesburg: Administration of the South African Railways and Harbours.

Chomsky, N. (1986), *Knowledge of Language: Its Nature, Origin, and Use*, New York: Praeger.

Clark, R.W. (1984), *The Survival of Charles Darwin: A Biography of a Man and an Idea*, New York: Random House.

Clements, H. (1983), *Alfred Russel Wallace: Biologist and Social Reformer*, Hutchinson: London.

Coffin, J.M., S.H. Hughes and H.E. Varmus (1997), *Retroviruses: Homage to Howard Temin*, Plainview, NY: Cold Spring Harbor Laboratory Press.

Cohen, J. and I. Stewart (1994), *The Collapse of Chaos: Discovering Simplicity in a Complex World*, London and New York: Viking.

Commons, J.R. (1934), *Institutional Economics – Its Place in Political Economy*, New York: Macmillan, reprinted with a new introduction by M. Rutherford (1990), New Brunswick, NJ: Transaction.

Cosmides, L. and J. Tooby (1987), 'From evolution to behavior: evolutionary psychology as the missing link', in J. Dupré (ed.), *The Latest or the Best*, Cambridge: MIT Press, 277–306.

Cosmides, L. and J. Tooby (1992), 'Cognitive adaptations for social exchange', in J.H. Barkow, L. Cosmides and J. Tooby (eds), *The Adapted Mind*, Oxford: Oxford University Press, 163–228.

Cosmides, L. and J. Tooby (1994), 'Better than rational: evolutionary psychology and the invisible hand', *American Economic Review*, **84**, 327–32.

Cottrell, A. and M.S. Lawlor (1991), '"Natural Rate" Mutations: Keynes, Leijonhufvud and the Wicksell Connection', *History of Political Economy*, **23** (4), 625–43.

Cowles, T. (1936), 'Malthus, Darwin and Bagehot: a study in the transference of a concept' *Isis*, **26**, 341–8.

Cox, J. (1995), *A Catalogue of the Papers of John Maynard Keynes in King's College Library*, Cambridge: Chadwyck-Healey Ltd.

Cronin, H. (1991), *The Ant and the Peacock*, Cambridge: Cambridge University Press.

Crozier, J.B. (1906), *The Wheel of Wealth: Being a Reconstruction of the Science and Art of Political Economy on the Lines of Modern Evolution*, London: Longman, Green & Co.

Cyert, R.M. and J.G. March (1963), *A Behavioral Theory of the Firm*, Englewood Cliffs: Prentice–Hall.

Cziko, G. (1995), *Without Miracles: Universal Selection Theory and the Second Darwinian Revolution*, Cambridge, MA: MIT Press.

Darwin, C. (1868), *The Variation of Animals and Plants under Domestication* (2 vols), London: John Murray.

Darwin, C. [1872 and 1874] (n.d.), *On the Origin of Species* (6th ed), and *The Descent of Man and Selection in Relation to Sex* (2nd ed), New York: The Modern Library.

Darwin, C. (1890), *Journal of Researches into the Natural History and Geology of the Countries Visited during the Voyage of H.M.S. 'Beagle' Round the World*, London: Ward, Lock & Co, Ltd.

Darwin, C. (G. de Beer, ed.) (1974), *Autobiographies / Charles Darwin, Thomas Henry Huxley*, with an introduction, Oxford: Oxford University Press.

Darwin, F. (ed.) (1887), *The Life and Letters of Charles Darwin, Including an Autobiographical Chapter* (3 vols), London: John Murray.

Darwin, G. (1909), 'Preface', in Rev. J.O. Bevan, *Egypt and the Egyptians: Their History, Antiquities, Language, Religion, and Influence over Palestine and Neighbouring Countries*, London: George Allen & Sons.

Darwin, L. (1897), *Bimetallism: A Summary of the Arguments for and against a Bimetallic System of Currency*, London: John Murray.

Darwin, L. (1903), *Municipal Trade*, London: John Murray.

Darwin, L. (1921), *Organic Evolution*, Cambridge, UK: Cambridge University Press.

Darwin, L. (1928), *What is Eugenics?* London: Watts & Co.

Davidson, K. (1987), 'How the Right gets its arithmetic wrong', in K. Coghill (ed.), *The New Right's Australian Fantasy*, Ringwood, Vic: Penguin, 67–73.

Davis, J.B. (1994), *Keynes's Philosophical Development*, Cambridge, UK: Cambridge University Press.

Dawkins, R. (1976), *The Selfish Gene*, Oxford: Oxford University Press.

Dawkins, R. (1982), *The Extended Phenotype: The Gene as the Unit of Selection*, Oxford: Oxford University Press.

Dawkins, R. (1983), 'Universal Darwinism', in D.S. Bendall (ed.), *Evolution from Molecules to Man*, Cambridge: Cambridge University Press, 403–25.

Dawkins, R (1986), *The Blind Watchmaker*, Harlow: Longman.

Dawkins, R. (1989), *The Selfish Gene* (new edition), Oxford: Oxford University Press.

Dawkins, R. (1996a), *The Blind Watchmaker*, New York: W.W. Norton and Company, Inc.

Dawkins, R. (1996b), *Climbing Mount Improbable*, New York: Norton.

Dawkins, R. and J.R. Krebs (1979), 'Arms races between and within species', *Proceedings of the Royal Society of London*, Series B, **205**, 489–511.

De Bresson, C. (1987), 'The evolutionary paradigm and the economics of technological change', *Journal of Economic Issues*, **21** (2), June, 751–61.

Degler, C.N. (1991), *In Search of Human Nature: The Decline and Revival of Darwinism in American Social Thought*, Oxford and New York: Oxford University Press.

Dennett, D.C. (1995), *Darwin's Dangerous Idea: Evolution and the Meaning of Life*, London: Allen Lane.

Depew, D.J. and B.H. Weber (1995), *Darwinism Evolving: Systems Dynamics and the Genealogy of Natural Selection*, Cambridge, MA: MIT Press.

Desmond, A. and J. Moore (1991), *Darwin*, London: Michael Joseph.

De Waal, F. (1996), *Good Natured: The Origins of Right and Wrong in Humans and Other Animals*, Cambridge, MA: Harvard University Press.

Diamond, J.M. (1998), *Guns, Germs and Steel: A Short History of Everybody for the Last 13,000 Years*, London: Vintage.

Downie, J. (1958), *The Competitive Process*, London: Duckworth.

Dretske, F.I. (1999), 'Machines, plants and animals: the origins of agency', *Erkenntnis*, **51**, 10–31.

Dunnell, R.C. (1978), 'Style and function: a fundamental dichotomy', *American Antiquity*, **43**, 192–202. Reprinted in M.J. O'Brien (ed.) (1996),

Evolutionary Archaeology, Salt Lake City: University of Utah Press, 112–22.

Dunnell, R.C. (1980), 'Evolutionary theory and archeology', in M.B. Schiffer (ed.), *Advances in Archælogical Method and Theory, Vol. 3*, New York: Academic Press, 35–99.

Dunnell, R.C. (1988), 'The concept of progress in cultural evolution', in M.H. Nitecki (ed.), *Evolutionary Progress*, Chicago: University of Chicago Press, 169–94.

Dunnell, R.C. (1992), 'Archaeology and evolutionary science', in L. Wandsnider (ed.), *Quandaries and Quests: Visions of Archaeology's Future*, Center for Archaeological Investigations, Occasional Paper No. 20, 30–67. Reprinted in M.J. O'Brien (ed.) (1996), *Evolutionary Archaeology*, Salt Lake City: University of Utah Press, 98–106.

Dunnell, R.C. and R.J. Wenke (1979). 'An evolutionary model of the development of complex society', Unpublished paper presented at the 1979 Annual Meeting of the American Association for the Advancement of Science, San Francisco, in the symposium *New Approaches to Explaining Cultural Complexity*.

Durant, J.R. (1979), 'Scientific naturalism and social reform in the thought of Alfred Russel Wallace', *British Journal for the History of Science*, **12**, 31–58.

Durham, W.H. (1991), *Coevolution: Genes, Culture, and Human Diversity*, Stanford: Stanford University Press.

Edelman, G.M. (1987), *Neural Darwinism: The Theory of Neuronal Group Selection*, New York: Basic Books.

Eldredge, N. (1986) Progress in Evolution?, *New Scientist*, 5 June, 54–7.

Endler, J.A. (1992), 'Natural selection: current usages', in: E. Fox Keller, and E.A. Lloyd (eds), *Keywords in Evolutionary Biology*, Cambridge, MA: Harvard University Press, 220–24.

Engels, F. [1884] (1977), *The Origin of the Family, Private Property and the State, in the Light of the Researches of L.H. Morgan*, Moscow: Progress Publishers.

Enke, S. (1951), 'On maximizing profits: a distinction between Chamberlin and Robinson', *American Economic Review*, **61**, 566–78.

Evans, C. et al. (1993a), 'On the meaning of alarm calls: functional reference in an avian vocal system', *Animal Behaviour*, **46**, 23–8.

Evans, C. et al. (1993b), 'Variation among mammalian alarm call systems and the problem of meaning in animal signals', *Ethology*, **93**, 177–97.

Ewald, P.W. (1994), *Evolution of Infectious Diseases*, New York: Oxford University Press.

Figuier, L. (1872), *The Ocean World*, London: Cassell, Petter, Galpin & Co.

Fishburn, G. (1995), 'Henry Fawcett: his role in the Darwinian revolution', *History of Economics Review*, **24**, 79–86.

Fisher, R.A. [1930] (1958), *The Genetical Theory of Natural Selection*, Revised edition, New York: Dover.

Fitzgibbons, A. (1988), *Keynes's Vision: A New Political Economy*, Oxford: Clarendon Press.

Fitzgibbons, A. (1995), *Adam Smith's System of Liberty, Wealth and Virtue: The Moral and Political Foundations of 'The Wealth of Nations'*, Oxford: Clarendon Press.

Fodor, J. (1983), *The Modularity of Mind*, Cambridge: MIT Press.

Foster, J. (1997), 'Economics and the diffusion of communication and information technology: Schumpeter and the self–organisation approach', *Prometheus*, **15** (1), 57–71.

Foster, J. (1999), 'The interaction of economic self–organisation and competitive processes', Paper presented at workshop *Progress in the Study of Economic Evolution*, Ancona, 20–22 May.

Fracchia, J. and R.C. Lewontin (1999), 'Does culture evolve?' *History and Theory*, **38** (4), 52–78.

Francis, M. (1986), 'Herbert Spencer and the mid–Victorian scientists', *Metascience*, **4**, 2–21.

Freeden, M. (1978), *The New Liberalism: An Ideology of Social Reform*, Oxford: Clarendon Press.

Freeden, M. (1986), *Liberalism Divided: A Study in British Political Thought, 1914–39*, Oxford: Clarendon Press.

Freeman, C. (1992), *The Economics of Hope: Essays on Technical Change, Economic Growth and the Environment*, London and New York: Pinter.

Friedman, M. (1953), *Essays in Positive Economics*, Chicago: Chicago University Press.

Futuyama, D.J. (1998), *Evolutionary Biology* (3rd ed), Sunderland, MA: Sinauer Associates, Inc.

Gaffney, M. (1997), 'Alfred Wallace's campaign to nationalise land: how Darwin's peer learned from John Stuart Mill and became Henry George's ally', *American Journal of Economics and Sociology*, **56**, 609–15.

Galton, F. [1853] (1889), *Travels in South Africa*, London: Ward, Lock & Co.

Ghiselin, M.T. (1974), *The Economy of Nature and the Evolution of Sex*, Berkeley: University of California Press.

Goodman, N. (1973), *Fact, Fiction, and Forecast* (3rd ed.), Indianapolis: Bobbs–Merrill.

Goodnight, C.J. and L. Stevens (1997), 'Experimental studies of group selection: what do they tell us about group selection in nature?', *American Naturalist*, **150**, Supplement, July: 'Multilevel selection: a symposium organized by David Sloan Wilson', S59–S79.

Gordon, S. (1989), 'Darwin and political economy: the connection reconsidered', *Journal of the History of Biology*, **22**, 437–59.

Gould, P.C. (1988), *Early Green Politics: Back to Nature, Back to the Land, Socialism in Britain 1880–1900*, Sussex: Harvester's Press.

Gould, S.J. (1980a), 'Darwin's deceptive memories', *New Scientist*, **21**, 577–9.

Gould, S.J. (1980b), *The Panda's Thumb: More Reflections in Natural History*, New York: Norton.

Gould, S.J. (1983), 'Our Natural Place?', in S.J. Gould, *Hen's Teeth and Horse's Toes*, London and New York: W.W. Norton & Company, 241–50.

Gould, S.J. (1996), *Life's Grandeur*, London: Cape.

Gould, S.J. (1997), 'Darwinian fundamentalism', *New York Review*, 12 June, 34–7.

Gould, S.J. and R.C. Lewontin (1979), 'The spandrels of San Marco and the Panglossian paradigm: a critique of the adaptationist programme', *Proceedings of the Royal Society of London, Series B*, **205**, 581–98.

Granovetter, M. (1998), 'Coase revisited: business groups in the modern economy', in G. Dosi, D.J. Teece and J. Chytry (eds), *'Technology, Organization and Competitiveness'*, Oxford: Oxford University Press, 67–103.

Gray, J. (1984), *Hayek on Liberty*, Oxford: Basil Blackwell.

Griffiths, P.E. and R.D Gray (1994), 'Developmental systems and evolutionary explanation', *Journal of Philosophy* **91** (6), 277–304.

Groenewegen, J. and J. Vromen (1999), 'Implications of evolutionary economics: theory, method and policies', in J. Groenewegen and J.Vromen (eds), *Institutions and the Evolution of Capitalism: Implications of Evolutionary Economics*, Cheltenham, UK and Northhampton, MA, US: Edward Elgar, 1–16.

Groenewegen, P. (1988), 'Alfred Marshall and Australian economics', *HETSA Bulletin No. 9*, Winter, 1–15.

Groenewegen, P. (1995), *A Soaring Eagle: Alfred Marshall 1843–1924*, Aldershot, UK and Brookfield, US: Edward Elgar.

Gross, P. and N. Levitt (1994), *Higher Superstition: The Academic Left and Its Quarrels with Science*, Baltimore: John Hopkins University Press.

Gruber, H. (1974), *Darwin on Man*, New York: E.P. Dutton & Co. Inc.

Haldane, J.B.S. (1932), *The Inequality of Man and Other Essays*, London: Chatto & Windus.

Hamilton, D. (1953), *Newtonian Classicism and Darwinian Institutionalism*, New Mexico: University of New Mexico Press.

Hamilton, D. [1970] (1999), *Evolutionary Economics. A Study in Economic Thought*, with a new introduction by the author, New Brunswick: Transaction Publishers.

Hamilton, W.D. (1964), 'The genetical theory of social behavior', *Journal of Theoretical Biology*, **7**, 1–32.

Hannan, M.T. and J. Freeman (1989), *Organizational Ecology*, Cambridge, MA: Harvard University Press.

Hardy, A.C. (1965), *The Living Stream: A Restatement of Evolution Theory and Its Relation to the Spirit of Man*, London: Collins.

Harrod, R. (1939), 'An essay in dynamic theory', *Economic Journal*, **49**, 14–33.

Harrod. R.F. (1951), *The Life of John Maynard Keynes*, London: Macmillan.

Hartman, H. (1990), 'The evolution of natural selection: Darwin versus Wallace', *Perspectives in Biology and Medicine*, **34**, 78–88.

Hausman, D. (1992), *The Separate and Inexact Science of Economics*, Cambridge: Cambridge University Press.

Haycroft, J.B. (1895), *Darwinism and Race Progress*, London: C. Kegan Paul.

Hayek, F.A. (1988), *The Fatal Conceit: The Errors of Socialism. The Collected Works of Friedrich August Hayek*, Vol. I, London: Routledge.

Hayek, F.A. (1990), *New Studies in Philosophy, Politics, Economics and the History of Ideas*, London: Routledge.

Hearn, W.E. (1856), *A Lecture on the Proposed Formation of Adult Educational Classes, Delivered before the Members of the Melbourne Mechanics' Institution, Wednesday, June, 18th, 1856*, Melbourne: Wilson, Mackinnon and Fairfax.

Hearn, W.E. (1863), *Plutology, or the Theory of the Efforts to Satisfy Human Wants*, Melbourne: George Robertson.

Heilbroner, R. and W. Milberg (1996), *The Crisis of Vision in Modern Economic Thought*, Cambridge: Cambridge University Press.

Heilman-Ternier, J. and V.L. Harms (1975), 'Plant ecology–taxonomy, Final report – Churchill River Study 5', Saskatoon: Dept of Plant Ecology, University of Saskatchewan.

Henry, J.F. (1995), 'Professor Stigler's report on Alfred Marshall's *Lectures on Progress and Poverty*, an addendum', *Marshall Studies Bulletin*, **5**, 39–40.

Hesse, M.B. (1966), *Models and Analogies in Science*, Notre Dame: University of Notre Dame Press.

Hirshleifer, J. (1977), 'Economics from a biological viewpoint', *Journal of Law and Economics*, **20** (1), 1–52. Reprinted in Hodgson (1995), 87–138.

Hirshleifer, J. (1982), 'Evolutionary models in economics and law: cooperation versus conflict strategies', in R.O. Zerbe Jr and P.H. Rubin (eds), *Research in Law and Economics*, **4**, 1–60.

Hirst, P.Q. and P. Woolley (1982), *Social Relations and Human Attributes*, London: Tavistock.

Ho, M-W. and P.T. Saunders (eds) (1984), *Beyond Neo-Darwinism: An Introduction to the New Evolutionary Paradigm*, London: Academic Press.

Hobhouse, L.T. (1896), *The Theory of Knowledge: A Contribution to Some Problems of Logic and Metaphysics*, London: Methuen & Co.

Hobhouse, L.T. [1906] (1925), *Morals in Evolution*, London: Chapman & Hall.

Hobhouse, L.T. (1911), *Liberalism*, London: Oxford University Press.

Hobson, J.A. (1895), *The Evolution of Modern Capitalism*, London: W. Scott.

Hobson, J.A. (1922), *The Economics of Unemployment*, London: George Allen & Unwin Ltd.

Hobson, J.A. (1929), *Wealth and Life: A Study in Values*, London: Macmillan.

Hobson, J.A. (1936), *Veblen*, London: Chapman and Hall.

Hobson, J.A. and A.F. Mummery [1888] (1956), *The Physiology of Industry*, New York: Kelley & Millman.

Hocket, C.F. (1960), 'The origin of speech', *Scientific American*, **203**, 88–96.

Hodgskin, T. (1966), *Popular Political Economy*, New York: Kelley.

Hodgson, G.M. (1988), *Economics and Institutions*, Cambridge, UK: Polity Press.

Hodgson, G.M. (1991), 'Hayek's theory of cultural evolution', *Economics and Philosophy*, **7**, 67–82.

Hodgson, G.M. (1993), *Economics and Evolution: Bringing Life Back into Economics*, Cambridge: Polity Press and Ann Arbor, MI: University of Michigan Press.

Hodgson, G.M. (1994), 'Theories of Economic Evolution', in G.M. Hodgson, W.J. Samuels and M.R. Tool (eds), *The Elgar Companion to Institutional and Evolutionary Economics*, Aldershot, UK and Brookfield, US: Edward Elgar, 218–24.

Hodgson, G.M. (ed.) (1995), *Economics and Biology*, Aldershot, UK and Brookfield, US: Edward Elgar.

Hodgson, G.M. (1997a), 'The ubiquity of habits and rules', *Cambridge Journal of Economics*, **21** (6), 663–84.

Hodgson, G.M. (1997b), 'The evolutionary and non–Darwinian economics of Joseph Schumpeter', *Journal of Evolutionary Economics*, **7**, 130–35.

Hodgson, G.M. (1998a), 'The approach of institutional economics', *Journal of Economic Literature*, **36** (1), 166–92.

Hodgson, G.M. (1998b), 'On the evolution of Thorstein Veblen's evolutionary economics', *Cambridge Journal of Economics*, **22** (4), July, 415–31.

Hodgson, G.M. (ed.) (1998c), *The Foundations of Evolutionary Economics, 1890–1973* (2 vols), Cheltenham, UK and Northhampton, MA, US: Edward Elgar.

Hodgson, G.M. (1998d), 'Emergence', in J.B. Davis, D.W. Hands, and U. Mäki (eds), *Handbook of Economic Methodology*, 156–60.

Hodgson, G.M. (1999a), *Evolution and Institutions: On Evolutionary Economics and the Evolution of Economics*, Cheltenham, UK and Northampton, MA, US: Edward Elgar.

Hodgson, G.M. (1999b), *Structures and Institutions: Reflections on Institutionalism, Structuration Theory and Critical Realism*, presented at the 'Realism and Economics' workshop, King's College, Cambridge, and at EIPE, Rotterdam.

Hodgson, G.M. (1999c), 'Darwin, Veblen and the problem of causality in economics', University of Hertfordshire (unpublished), mimeo.

Hofer, R. and W. Polt (1998), 'Evolutionary innovation theory and innovation policy: an overview', in K. Bryant and A. Wells (eds), *A New Economic Paradigm? Innovation-based Evolutionary Systems*, Canberra: Department of Industry, Science and Resources.

Hofstadter, D.R. (1979), *Gödel, Escher, Bach: An Eternal Golden Braid*, New York: Basic Books.

Hofstadter, R. (1955), *Social Darwinism in American Thought*, Boston: Beacon Press.

Hohenadl, C., C. Leib-Mosch, et al. (1996), 'Biological significance of human endogenous retroviral sequences', *Journal of Acquired Immune Deficiency Syndromes and Human Retrovirology*, **13**(1), S268–73.

Hull, D.L. (1973), *Darwin and His Critics: The Reception of Darwin's Theory of Evolution by the Scientific Community*, Cambridge: Harvard University Press.

Hull, D.L. (1980), 'Individuality and selection', *Annual Review of Ecology and Systematics*, **11**, 311–32.

Hull, D.L. (1981), 'Units of evolution: a metaphysical essay', in U.L. Jensen and R. Harré (1981), *The Philosophy of Evolution*, Brighton: Harvester Press, 23–44. Reprinted in R.N. Brandon and R.M. Burian (eds) (1984), *Genes, Organisms, Populations: Controversies over the Units of Selection*, Cambridge, MA: MIT Press.

Hull, D.L. (1982), 'The naked meme', in H.C. Plotkin (ed.), *Learning, Development and Culture: Essays in Evolutionary Epistemology*, New York: Wiley, 273–327.

Hull, D.L. (1984a), 'Historical entities and historical narratives', in C. Hookway (ed.), *Minds, Machines, and Evolution*. Cambridge, Cambridge University Press, 17–42.

Hull, D.L. (1984b), 'Lamarck among the anglos', in Lamarck (1984), xl–lxvi.

Hull, D.L. (1985), 'Darwinism as a historical entity: a historiographic proposal', in D. Kohn (ed.), *The Darwinian Heritage*, Princeton: Princeton University Press, 773–812.

Hull, D.L. (1988a), 'Interactors versus vehicles', in H.C. Plotkin (ed.), *The Role of Behavior in Evolution*, Cambridge, MA: MIT Press, 19–50.

Hull, D.L. (1988b), *Science as a Process: An Evolutionary Account of the Social and Conceptual Development of Science*, Chicago: University of Chicago Press.

Hull, D.L. (1988c), 'A mechanism and its metaphysics: an evolutionary account of the social and conceptual development of science'. *Biology and Philosophy*, **3**, 123–55.

Hull, D.L. (1988d), 'A period of development: a response', *Biology and Philosophy*, **3**, 241–61.

Hume, D. (1739), *A Treatise of Human Nature* (2 vols.), London: printed for John Noon.

Hume, D. (Kemp Smith, ed.) (1935), *Hume's Dialogue's Concerning Natural Religion*, Oxford: Oxford University Press.

Huxley, J. (1933), *What Dare I Think? The Challenge of Modern Science to Human Action and Belief*, London: Chatto & Windus.

Huxley, T.H. (1888), 'The struggle for existence: a programme', *Nineteenth Century*, **132**, 161–80.

Irvine, R.F. (1913), *Report of the Commission of Inquiry into the question of the Housing of Workmen in Europe and America*, Sydney: W.A. Gullick, Government Printer.

Irvine, R.F. (1914), *The Place of the Social Sciences in a Modern University*, Sydney: Angus & Robertson.

Irvine, R.F. (1933), *The Midas Delusion*, Adelaide: Hassell Press.

Irvine, R.F. and O.T.J. Alpers (1902), *The Progress of New Zealand in the Century*, Toronto and Philadelphia: Linscott Publishing Company.

Jablonka, E. and M.J. Lamb (1995), *Epigenetic Inheritance and Evolution: The Lamarckian Dimension*, Oxford, New York: Oxford University Press.

Jablonka, E., M. Lachmann and M.J. Lamb (1992), 'Evidence, mechanisms and models for the inheritance of acquired characters', *Journal of Theoretical Biology*, **158**, 245–68.

Jacob, F. (1985), *Mulighedernes Spil – Om Det Levendes Mangfoldighed (Le Jeu des Possible)*, Copenhagen: Hekla.

James, W. (1890), *The Principles of Psychology*, New York: Holt.

James, W. (1897), *The Will to Believe and Other Essays in Popular Philosophy*, New York and London: Longmans Green.

James, W. [1923] (1977), 'Psychological foundations', Excerpt from W. James, *Psychology: Briefer Course*, New York: Henry Holt and Co, in J.J. McDermottt (ed.), *The Writings of William James: A Comprehensive Edition*, Chicago and London: The University of Chicago Press, 134–50.

Janssen, M. (1993), *Microfoundations: A Critical Inquiry*, London: Routledge.

Jordanova, L.J. (1984), *Lamarck*, Oxford: Oxford University Press.

Katona, G. (1946), 'Psychological analysis of business decisions and expectations', *American Economic Review*, **36**, 44–62.

Kauffman, S.A. (1993), *The Origins of Order: Self-organisation and Selection in Evolution*, Oxford and New York: Oxford University Press.

Kauffman, S.A. (1995), *At Home in the Universe: the Search for Laws of Self-Organization and Complexity*, New York: Oxford University Press.

Kay, N.M. (1995), 'Alchian and "the Alchian Thesis"', *Journal of Economic Methodology*, **2**, 281–86.

Kelm, M. (1997), 'Schumpeter's theory of economic evolution: a Darwinian interpretation', *Journal of Evolutionary Economics*, **7**, 97–130.

Kevles, D. (1985), *In the Name of Eugenics: Genetics and the Uses of Human Heredity*, New York: Knopf.

Keynes, J.M. (1908), *Principles of Probability* (2 vols), Fellowship dissertation, submitted Dec. 1908 (KCKP, MM/6).

Keynes, J.M. (1913), *Indian Currency and Finance*, London: Macmillan.

Keynes, J.M. (1919), *The Economic Consequences of the Peace*, London: Macmillan.

Keynes, J.M. (1921), *A Treatise on Probability*, London: Macmillan.

Keynes, J.M. (1922), *A Revision of the Treaty*, London: Macmillan.

Keynes, J.M. (1923), *A Tract on Monetary Reform*, London: Macmillan.

Keynes, J.M. (1924), *Alfred Marshall 1842–1924: A Memoir* (reprinted from *Economic Journal,* September 1924).

Keynes, J.M. (1926), *The End of Laissez-Faire*, London: Leonard and Virginia Woolf at the Hogarth Press.

Keynes, J.M. (1930a), *A Treatise on Money* (2 vols.), London: Macmillan.

Keynes, J.M. (1930b), 'Economic possibilities for our grandchildren', *The Nation and Anthenaeum*, 11 October, 36–7 and 18 October, 96–8.

Keynes, J.M. (1933), *The Means to Prosperity*, London: Macmillan.

Keynes, J.M. (1936), *The General Theory of Employment, Interest and Money*, London: Macmillan.

Keynes, J.M. (1938a), 'Art and the state', in C. Williams-Ellis (ed.), *Britain and the Beast*, London: Reader's Union, 1–7.

Keynes, J.M. (1938b), 'My early beliefs', Paper read at Tilton, 11 September, in *Collected Works*, **X**, London: Macmillan, for the Royal Economic Society, 433–50.

Khalil, E.L. (1993), 'Neo–classical economics and neo–Darwinism: clearing the way for historical thinking', in Hodgson (1995), 548–98.

Kidd, B. (1898), *Social Evolution*, London: Macmillan.

Kidwell, M.G. and D.R. Lisch (1997), 'Transposable elements as sources of variation in animals and plants', *Proceedings of the National Academy of Sciences USA*, **94**, 7704–11.

Kidwell, M.G. and D.R. Lisch (2000), 'Transposable elements and host genome evolution,' *Trends in Ecology and Evolution*, **15** (3), 95–9.

Klamer, A. and T.C. Leonard (1994), 'So what's an economic metaphor?', in Mirowski (1994), 20–51.

Knudsen, T. (1998a), 'Local emulative selection', Stanford, CA: Scancore, Stanford University (mimeo).

Knudsen, T. (1998b), 'Wither economic natural selection?', Scancor Seminar *Samples of the Future*, Stanford, CA: Scancore, Stanford University, September.

Koch, A.L. (1993), 'Genetic response of microbes to extreme challenges', *Journal of Theoretical Biology*, **160** (1), 1–21.

Koestler, A. (1971), *The Case of the Midwife Toad*, London: Hutchinson.

Kottler, M.J. (1985), 'Charles Darwin and Alfred Russel Wallace: two decades of debate over natural selection', in D. Kohn (ed.), *The Darwinian Heritage*, Princeton, NJ: Princeton University Press.

Krabbe, J.J. (1996), *Historicism and Organicism in Economics: The Evolution of Thought*, Dordrecht: Kluwer Academic Publishers.

Krugman, P. (1996), 'What economists can learn from evolutionary theorists', Talk given to the European Association for Evolutionary Political Economy, Antwerp, November.

Kuhn, T.S. (1970), *The Structure of Scientific Revolutions*, Chicago: University of Chicago Press.

Lamarck, J.B. de (1779), *Flore François*, Paris (not in print).

Lamarck, J.B. de (1809), *Philosophie Zoologique, ou, Exposition des Considérations Relative à l'Histoire Naturelle des Animaux*, Paris: Chez Dentu [et] L'Auteur.

Lamarck, J.B. de [1809] (1984), *Zoological Philosophy: An Exposition with Regard to the Natural History of Animals*, translated by Hugh Elliot from the 1st French edition of 1809 with introductory essays by D.L. Hull and R.W. Burkhardt, Chicago: University of Chicago Press.

Lamarck, J.B. de (1815–22), *Histoire Naturelle des Animaux sans Vertebres* [Natural History of Invertebrates], 7 vols, Paris.

Laming, A. (1959), *Lascaux*, Harmondsworth, Middlesex: Penguin.

La Nauze, J.A. (1949), *Political Economy in Australia*, Melbourne: Melbourne University Press.

La Nauze, J.A. (1972), 'Hearn, William Edward (1826–1888)', *Australian Dictionary of Biography*, Vol. 4, 1851–1890 (D–J), Melbourne: Melbourne University Press, 370–2.

Laurent, J. (1988), *Tom Mann's Social and Economic Writings*, Nottingham: Spokesman and Sydney: AMWU.

Laurent, J. (1991), 'Evolution and organic analogy in R.F. Irvine's economics', *History of Economics Review*, **16**, 1–9.

Laurent, J. (1994), 'Varieties of social Darwinism in Australia, Japan and Hawaii, 1883–1921', in R. MacLeod and P. Rehbock (eds), *Darwin's Laboratory: Evolutionary Theory and Natural History in the Pacific*, Honolulu: University of Hawaii Press, 474–510.

Laurent, J. (in press), 'Alfred Marshall's annotations on Herbert Spencer', *Marshall Studies Bulletin*.

Lawson, T. (1997), *Economics and Reality*, London: Routledge.

Leakey, L. [1934] (1953), *Adam's Ancestors: An Up-to-date Outline of the Old Stone Age (Palaeolithic), and What is Known about Man's Origin and Evolution*, London: Methuen & Co.

Leakey, R. (1995), *The Origin of Humankind*, London: Methuen & Co.

Leib-Mosch, C. and W. Seifarth (1995), 'Evolution and biological significance of human retroelements', *Virus Genes*, **11** (2–3), 133–45.

Leijonhufvud, A. (1968), *On Keynesian Economics and the Economics of Keynes: A Study in Monetary Theory*, London: Oxford University Press.

Leonard, T.C. (1999), 'Private Vices, Scientific Virtues: A Substantive Case for Economics in the Theory of Science', Princeton: Princeton University, manuscript.

Lester, R.A. (1941), *Economics of Labor*, New York: Macmillan.

Lewin, R. (1992), *Complexity: Life at the Edge of Chaos*, New York: Macmillan.

Lewin, R. (1998), *The Origin of Modern Humans* (2nd ed.), New York: Scientific American Library.

Lewis, P.A. (1996), 'Metaphor and Critical Realism', *Review of Social Economy*, **54** (4), Winter, 487–506.

Lewontin, R.C. (1974), *The Genetic Basis of Evolutionary Change*, Columbia Biological Series, no. 25., New York: Columbia University Press.

Li, W.H. (1997), *Molecular Evolution*, Sunderland, MA: Sinauer Associates.

Lieberman, P. (1991), *Uniquely Human*, Cambridge, MA: Harvard University Press.

Limoges, C. and C. Menard (1994), 'Organization and the division of labor: biological metaphors at work in Alfred Marshall's Principles of Economics', in Mirowski (ed.) (1994), 336–59.

Lloyd, E.A. (1988), *The Structure and Confirmation of Evolutionary Theory*, New York: Greenwood Press.

Loasby, B. (1991), *Equilibrium and Evolution: An Exploration of Connecting Principles in Economics*, Manchester: Manchester University Press.

Loasby, B. (1998), 'The organisation of capabilities', *Journal of Economic Behavior and Organization*, **35**, 139–60.

Loasby, B.J. (1999), *Knowledge, Institutions and Evolution in Economics*, London: Routledge.

Lotka, A.J. (1956), *Elements of Mathematical Biology*, New York: Dover.

Luo, G.Y. (1995), 'Evolution and market competition', *Journal of Economic Theory*, **67**, 223–50.

Lynch, A. (1996), *Thought Contagion: How Beliefs Spread Through Society*, New York: Basic Books.

Maasen, S. (1995), 'Who is afraid of metaphors?', in S. Maasen, E. Mendelsohn and P. Weingart (eds), 'Biology as Society, Society as Biology: Metaphors', *Sociology of the Sciences Yearbook*, **18** (1994), Boston: Kluwer, 11–35.

Machlup, F. (1946), 'Marginal analysis and empirical research', *American Economic Review*, **36**, 519–54.

Maeterlinck, M. (1914), contribution to H. Caine (ed.), *King Albert's Book*, London: The Daily Telegraph, 188.

Magnusson, L. and J. Ottosson (1997), *Evolutionary Economics and Path Dependence*, Aldershot, Hants: Edward Elgar.

March, J.G. (1999), 'The evolution of evolution', in J.G. March (ed.), *The Pursuit of Organizational Intelligence*, Malden, MA: Blackwell Publishers.

March, J.G. and H.A. Simon (1958), *Organizations*, New York: John Wiley.

Margolis, H. (1994), *Paradigms and Barriers: How Habits of Mind Govern Scientific Beliefs*, Chicago: University of Chicago Press.

Marshall, A. [1867] (1990), 'The Law of Parcimony', in T. Raffaelli (ed.), *The Early Philosophical Writings of Alfred Marshall*, Firenze Marshallian Studies no. 6, Florence: Università Degli Studi di Firenze, 47–56.

Marshall, A. [1869] (1990), 'Ye Machine', in T. Raffaelli (ed.), *The Early Philosophical Writings of Alfred Marshall*, Firenze Marshallian Studies no. 6, Florence: Università Degli Studi di Firenze, 72–93.

Marshall, A. (1889), *Presidential Address to the Twenty-first Annual Co-operative Congress*, Manchester: Co–operative Union Ltd.

Marshall, A. (1890), *Principles of Economics* (1st ed.), London: Macmillan.

Marshall, A. (1898), 'Distribution and exchange', *Economic Journal*, **8** (1), 37–59.

Marshall, A. (1919, 1920), *Industry and Trade* (3rd ed.), London: Macmillan.

Marshall, A. (1923), *Money, Credit and Commerce*, London: Macmillan.

Marshall, A. (1961), *Principles of Economics*, Variorum edition edited by C.W. Guillebaud, London: Macmillan, for the Royal Economic Society.

Marshall, A. (P. Groenewegen, ed.) (1997), *Collected Essays, 1872–1916*, Tokyo: Kyokuto Shoten Limited and Bristol: Overstone Press.

Marshall, A. and M.P. Marshall (1879), *Economics of Industry*, London: Macmillan.

Marshall Library of Economics (1927), *Catalogue*, Cambridge: Cambridge University Press for Faculty of Economics.

Marx, K. (1906), *Capital: A Critique of Political Economy*, Vol.1, Chicago: Charles H. Kerr & Company.

Marx, K. (1941), *Selected Correspondence 1846–1895, [between] Karl Marx and Frederick Engels, with commentary and notes*, London: Lawrence and Wishart.

Marx, K. [1859] (1977), *A Contribution to the Critique of Political Economy*, Moscow: Progress Press.

Mayley, G. (1996), 'Landscapes, learning costs and genetic assimilation', *Evolutionary Computation*, **4** (3), 213–34.

Maynard Smith, J. (1975), *The Theory of Evolution* (3rd ed.), Harmondsworth: Penguin.

Maynard Smith, J. (1978). *The Evolution of Sex*, Cambridge: Cambridge University Press.

Maynard Smith, J. (1982), *Evolution and the Theory of Games*, Cambridge: Cambridge University Press.

Maynard Smith, J. (1988), *Did Darwin Get It Right? Essays on Games, Sex and Evolution*, New York: Chapman and Hall.

Maynard Smith, J. (1989), *Evolutionary Genetics*, Oxford: Oxford University Press.

Maynard Smith, J. (1998), *Shaping Life: Genes, Embryos and Evolution*, London: Weidenfeld and Nicholson.

Maynard Smith, J. and E. Szathmáry (1999), *The Origins of Life: From the Birth of Life to the Origin of Language*, Oxford: Oxford University Press.

Mayr, E. (1961), 'Cause and effect in biology', *Science*, **134**, 1501–6.

Mayr, E. (1982), *The Growth of Biological Thought: Diversity, Evolution, and Inheritance*, Cambridge, MA: Belknap Press.

Mayr, E. (1997), 'The objects of selection', *Proceedings of the National Academy of Sciences of the United States of America*, **6**, 2091–4.

Mayr, E. and W.B. Provine (eds) (1980), *The Evolutionary Synthesis: Perspectives on the Unification of Biology*, Cambridge, MA: Harvard University Press.

McFarlane, B. (1966), *Professor Irvine's Economics in Australian Labour History*, Canberra: Australian Society for the Study of Labour History.

McKelvey, W. (1982), *Organizational Systematics: Taxonomy, Evolution, Classification*, Berkeley, CA: University of California Press.

McKenna, E.J. and D. Zannoni (1997–8), 'Post Keynesian economics and the philosophy of individualism', *Journal of Post Keynesian Economics*, **20** (2), 235–49.

McKie, R. (1967), *The Company of Animals*, Melbourne: Angus & Robertson.

Medawar, P. (1990) (D. Pyke, ed.), *The Threat and the Glory: Reflections on Science and Scientists*, Oxford: Oxford University Press.

Metcalfe, J.S. (1993), 'Some Lamarckian themes in the theory of growth and economic selection: a provisional analysis', *Revue Internationale de Systemique*, **7**, 487–504.

Metcalfe, J.S. (1998), *Evolutionary Economics and Creative Destruction*, London and New York: Routledge.

Mill, J.S. (J.M. Robson ed.) [1848] (1974), *Principles of Political Economy*, Toronto: University of Toronto Press.

Minkler, A.P. (1993), 'The problem with dispersed knowledge: firms in theory and practice', *Kyklos*, **46**, 569–87.

Mirowski, P. (1989), *More Heat than Light: Economics as Social Physics, Physics as Nature's Economics*, Cambridge: Cambridge University Press.

Mirowski, P. (ed.) (1994), *Natural Images in Economic Thought: Markets Read in Tooth and Claw*, Cambridge: Cambridge University Press.

Moggridge, D. (1992), *Maynard Keynes: An Economist's Biography*, London: Routledge.

Mogie, M. (1996), 'Malthus and Darwin: world views apart', *Evolution*, **50**, 2086–8.

Mokyr, J. (1990), *Twenty-five Centuries of Technological Change: An Historical Survey*, Chur, Switzerland: Harwood Academic Publishers.

Monod, J. (1971), *Tilfældigheden og Nødvendigheden (Le Hazard et la Nécessité)*, Copenhagen: Fremad.

Monod, J.L. (1997), 'On the molecular theory of evolution', in M. Ridley (ed.), *Evolution*, Oxford: Oxford University Press, 389–95.

Moore, G.E. (1903), *Principia Ethica*, Cambridge, UK: Cambridge University Press.

Moore, J. (1997), 'Wallace's Malthusian moment: the common context revisited', in B. Lightman (ed.), *Victorian Science in Context*, Chicago: University of Chicago Press, 290–331.

Morgan, C.L. (1896), *Habit and Instinct*, London and New York: Edward Arnold.

Morin, E. (1974), *Det Glemte Mønster: Den Menneskelige Natur (Le Paradigme Perdu: La Nature Humaine)*, Copenhagen: Gykdendal.

Morin, E. (1990), *Metoden: Kendskabet til Kundskaben – En Erkendelsens Antropologi (La Connaisance de la Connaissance)*, Aarhus: Ask.

Morin, E. (1992), *Method: Towards a Study of Humankind. Vol. 1: The Nature of the Nature*, New York: Peter Lang.

Muggeridge, M. (1988), *Conversion: A Spiritual Journey*, London: Collins.

Mueller, L.D. (1997), 'Theoretical and empirical examination of density-dependent selection', *Annual Review of Ecology and Systematics* **28**, 269–288.

Muller, H.J. (1939), 'The dominance of economics over eugenics', *Fact*, March, 53–73.

Murphy, J.B. (1994), 'The kinds of order in society', in P. Mirowski (ed.) (1994), 536–82.

Nelson, R.R. (1962), 'The link between science and invention: the case of the transistor', in National Bureau of Economic Research Conference, Vol. 13, *The Rate and Direction of Inventive Activity*, Princeton: Princeton University Press for the National Bureau of Economic Research, 549–83.

Nelson, R.R. (1994), 'Routines', in G.M. Hodgson, W. Samuels and M.R. Tool (eds), *The Elgar Companion to Institutional and Evolutionary Economics*, Aldershot, UK and Brookfield, USA: Edward Elgar, 249–53.

Nelson, R.R. (1995), 'Recent Evolutionary Theorizing About Economic Change', *Journal of Economic Literature*, **33**, 48–90.

Nelson, R.R. and S.G. Winter (1982), *An Evolutionary Theory of Economic Change*, Cambridge, MA: Harvard University Press.

Nesse, R.M. and G.C. Williams [1994] (1996), *Why We Get Sick: The New Science of Darwinian Medicine*, New York: Vintage Books.

Nicholson, N. (1997), 'Evolutionary psychology: toward a new view on human nature and organizational society', *Human Relations*, **50**, 1053–78.

Nightingale, J. (1993), 'Solving Marshall's problem with the biological analogy: Jack Downie's *Competitive Process*', *History of Economics Review*, **20**, 74–95. Reprinted in Hodgson (1995), 299–318.

Nightingale, J. (1997), 'Anticipating Nelson and Winter: Jack Downie's theory of evolutionary economic change', *Journal of Evolutionary Economics,* **7**, 147–68.

Nightingale, J. (2000), 'Universal Darwinism and social research: the case of economics', in W. Barnett, C. Chiarella, S. Keen, R. Marks and H. Schnabl (eds*), Commerce, Complexity and Evolution*, Cambridge: Cambridge University Press, 22–38.

Nitecki, M.H. (ed.) (1988), *Evolutionary Progress*. Chicago, IL: University of Chicago Press.

O'Brien, D. (1994), *Introduction to Marshall, Alfred and M.P. (1879)*, London: Thoemmes Press.

O'Donnell, R.M. (1989), *Keynes: Philosophy, Economics and Politics: The Philisophical Foundations of Keynes's Thought and Their Influence on His Economics and Politics*, New York: St. Martin's Press.

Ogilvie, D. (1990), *The Truth Seeker*, Brisbane: University of Queensland, School of External Studies and Continuing Education.

Orzack, S.H. and E. Sober (1994), 'Optimality models and the test of adaptationism', *American Naturalist,* **143** (3), 361–80.

Packard, A. (1901). *Lamarck, the Founder of Evolution: His Life and Work*, New York: Longmans, Green and Co.

Patience, C., D.A. Wilkinson, et al. (1997), 'Our retroviral heritage', *Trends in Genetics*, **13**(3), 116–20.

Peirce, C.S. [1878] (1958), 'How to make our ideas clear', *Popular Science Monthly*, **12**, January, 286–302. Reprinted in C.S. Peirce, *Selected Writings (Values in a Universe of Chance)*, edited with an introduction by P.P.Wiener, New York: Doubleday.

Peirce, C.S. (1992), *Reasoning and the Logic of Things: The Cambridge Conferences Lectures of 1898*, introduced by K.L. Ketner and H. Putnam, Cambridge, MA: Harvard University Press.

Penrose, E.T. (1952), 'Biological analogies in the theory of the firm', *American Economic Review*, **42**, 804–19. Reprinted in Hodgson (1998c), 264–79.

Penrose, E.T. [1959] (1995), *Theory of the Growth of the Firm*, Oxford: Basil Blackwell.

Piaget, J. (1979), *Behaviour and Evolution*, translated from the French edition of 1976 by D. Nicholson-Smith, London: Routledge and Kegan Paul.

Pinker, S. (1994), *The Language Instinct*, New York: William Morrow.

Plotkin, H.C. (1988), 'Behavior and evolution', in H.C. Plotkin (ed.), *The Role of Behavior in Evolution*, Cambridge, MA: MIT Press, 1–18.

Plotkin, H.C. (1994), *Darwin Machines and the Nature of Knowledge: Concerning Adaptations, Instinct and the Evolution of Intelligence*, London: Allen Lane, The Penguin Press.

Polanyi, M (1967), *The Tacit Dimension,* London: Routledge and Kegan Paul.

Popper, K.R. (1972), *Objective Knowledge: An Evolutionary Approach,* Oxford: Oxford University Press.

Popper, K.R. (1974), 'Scientific reduction and the essential incompleteness of all science', in F.J. Ayala and T. Dobzhansky (eds), *Studies in the Philosophy of Biology,* London, Berkeley and Los Angeles: Macmillan and University of California Press, 259–84.

Potok, C. (1973), *My Name is Asher Lev*, Harmondsworth, UK: Penguin.

Prigogine, I. and I. Stengers (1984), *Order Out of Chaos: Man's New Dialogue With Nature*, London: Heinemann.

Pusey, M. (1991), *Economic Rationalism in Canberra*, Cambridge: Cambridge University Press.

Ramsey, F.P. (1932), *The Foundations of Mathematics and other Logical Essays*, London: Macmillan.

Ramstad, Y. (1994), 'On the nature of economic evolution: John R. Commons and the metaphor of artificial selection', in L. Magnusson (ed.), *Evolutionary and Neo-Schumpeterian Approaches to Economics*, Boston: Kluwer, 65–121.

Reber, A.S. (1993), *Implicit Learning and Tacit Knowledge: An Essay on the Cognitive Unconscious*, Oxford: Oxford University Press.

Reijnders, J. (ed.) (1997), *Economics and Evolution*, Cheltenham, UK and Lyme, US: Edward Elgar.

Ricardo, D. [1821] (1973), *Principles of Political Economy and Taxation*, London : Dent.

Richards, R.J. (1987), *Darwin and the Emergence of Evolutionary Theories of Mind and Behavior*, Chicago: University of Chicago Press.

Richards, R.J. (1992), 'Evolution', in E. Fox Keller and E.A. Lloyd (eds), *Keywords in Evolutionary Biology*, Cambridge, MA: Harvard University Press, 95–105.

Richardson, G.B. (1960), *Information and Investment*, Oxford: Clarendon Press.

Ridley, M. (1996), *The Origins of Virtue*, London: Penguin Group.

Rindos, D. (1984), *The Origins of Agriculture: an Evolutionary Perspective*. Orlando, FL: Academic Press.

Rindos, D. (1989), 'Undirected variation and the Darwinian explanation of cultural change', in M.B. Schiffer (ed.), *Archaeological Method and Theory*, Vol. I, Tucson: University of Arizona Press, 1–45.

Robinson, J. (1953), *On Re-reading Marx*, Cambridge: Students Bookshops Ltd.

Rose, N. (1998), 'Controversies in meme theory', *Journal of Memetics*, **2** (1), June, 66–76.

Rose-Ackerman, S. (1996), 'Altruism, nonprofits, and economic theory', *Journal of Economic Literature*, **34**, 701–28.

Rosenberg, A. (1994a), 'Does evolutionary theory give comfort or inspiration to economics?', in Mirowski (1994), 384–407.

Rosenberg, A. (1994b), *Instrumental Biology, or, The Disunity of Science*, Chicago: University of Chicago Press.

Rosenberg, S.M. (1997), 'Mutation for survival', *Current Opinion in Genetics & Development,* **7** (6), 829–34.

Rousseau, G. (1969), 'Lamarck et Darwin', *Bulletin du Muséum National d'Histoire Naturelle.*, **41**, 1029–41.

Ruse, M. (1996), *Monad to Man: the Concept of Progress in Evolutionary Biology*, Cambridge, MA: Harvard University Press.

Sahlins, M. (1960), 'Evolution: specific and general', in M. Sahlins and E. Service (eds), *Evolution and Culture*, Ann Arbor, MI: University of Michigan Press.

Salter, W.E.G. (1960), *Productivity and Technical Change*, Cambridge: Cambridge University Press.

Samuelson, P.A. (1947), *Foundations of Economic Analysis*, Cambridge: Harvard University Press.

Schabas, M. (1994), 'The greyhound and the mastiff: Darwinian themes in Mill and Marshall', in Mirowski (1994), 322–35.

Schaffer, M.E. (1989), 'Are profit maximizers the best survivors?', *Journal of Economic Behavior and Organization*, **12**, 29–45.

Schlichting, C.D. and M. Pigliucci (1998), *Phenotypic Evolution: A Reaction Norm Perspective*, Sunderland, MA: Sinauer Associates.

Schmoller, G. (1900), *Grundriss der Allgemeinen Volkwirtschaftslehre*, vols I and II, Leipzig: Duncker and Humblot.

Schumpeter, J.A. (1954), *History of Economic Analysis*, New York: Oxford University Press.

Schweber, S. (1980), 'Darwin and the political economists: divergence of character', *Journal of the History of Biology*, **13** (2), 195–289.

Setterfield, M. (1997), 'Should economists dispense with the notion of equilibrium?' *Journal of Post Keynesian Economics*, **20** (1), 47–76.

Shackle, G.L.S. (1967), *The Years of High Theory: Invention and Tradition in Economic Thought 1926–1939*, Cambridge: Cambridge University Press.

Shaw, G.B. [1921] (1945), *Back to Methuselah: A Metabiological Pentateuch*, Oxford: Oxford University Press.

Simon, H.A. (1976), *Administrative Behavior*, New York: Free Press.

Simon, H.A. (1981), *The Sciences of the Artificial* (2nd ed.), Cambridge, MA: MIT Press.

Simon, H.A. (1990), 'A mechanism for social selection and successful altruism', *Science*, **250**, 1665–8.

Simon, H.A. (1991), 'Organizations and markets', *Journal of Economic Perspectives*, **5**, 25–44.

Simon, H.A. (1993), 'Altruism and economics', *American Economic Review*, **83**, 156–61.

Skidelsky, R. (1983), *John Maynard Keynes, Vol. 1 – Hopes Betrayed, 1883–1920*, London: Macmillan.

Skidelsky, R. (1992), *John Maynard Keynes, Vol. 2 – The Economist as Saviour, 1920–1937*, London: Macmillan.

Skidelsky, R. (1997), 'Keynes and Cambridge Arts Theatre', in R. Christianson (ed.), *Cambridge Arts Theatre: Celebrating Sixty Years*, Cambridge: Granta Editions, 1–23.

Smith, A. [1759] (1853), *The Theory of Moral Sentiments*, London: Henry G. Bohn.

Smith, A. [1776] (1904–50), *The Wealth of Nations*, London: Methuen.

Smolin, L. (1997), *The Life of the Cosmos*, London: Weidenfeld and Nicholson.

Smuts, J.C. (1926), *Holism and Evolution*, London: Macmillan.

Snell, H. (1906), 'Socialism and co–operation', *Co-operative Wholesale Society Annual*, 149–74.

Snell, H. (1936), *Men, Movements, and Myself*, London: J.M. Dent & Sons.

Sober, E. (1980), 'Evolution, population thinking, and essentialism.' *Philosophy of Science*, **47**, 350–83.

Sober, E. (1981), 'Holism, individualism, and the units of selection', in P.D. Asquith and R.N. Giere (eds), *Philosophy of Science Association 1980*, **2**, East Lansing, MI: Philosophy of Science Association, 93–121.

Sober, E. (1984a), *The Nature of Selection: Evolutionary Theory in Philosophical Focus*, Cambridge, MA: MIT Press.

Sober, E. (ed.) (1984b), *Conceptual Issues in Evolutionary Biology: An Anthology*, Cambridge, MA: MIT Press.

Sober, E. and D.S. Wilson (1994), 'A critical review of philosophical work on the units of selection problem', *Philosophy of Science*, **61**, 534–55.

Sober, E. and D.S. Wilson (1998), *Unto Others: The Evolution and Psychology of Unselfish Behavior*, Cambridge, MA: Harvard University Press.

Speel, H.C., J. Wilkins and J. Vromen (1999), 'Why memetic evolution is not Lamarckian' (mimeo).

Spencer, H. (1851), *Social Statics: Or the Conditions Essential to Human Happiness Specified, and the First of Them Developed*, London: John Chapman.

Spencer, H. (1881), *The Study of Sociology* (10th ed.), London: Kegan Paul.

Spencer, H. (1900), *First Principles* (6th ed.), London: Williams and Norgate.

Sperber, D. (1996), *Explaining Culture: A Naturalistic Approach*, Oxford, UK and Cambridge, MA: Blackwell.

Steele, E.J. (1979), *Somatic Selection and Adaptive Evolution: On the Inheritance of Acquired Characteristics*, Toronto: Williams-Wallace International.

Steele, E.J. (1991), *Somatic Hypermutation in V-regions*, Boca Raton: CRC Press.

Steele, E.J. and J.W. Pollard (1987), 'Hypothesis: somatic hypermutation by gene conversion via the error prone DNA—>RNA—>DNA information loop', *Molecular Immunology*, **24**, 667–73.

Steele, E.J., H.S. Rothenfluh, G.L. Ada and R.V. Blanden (1993), 'Affinity maturation of lymphocyte receptors and positive selection of T Cells in the thymus', *Immunological Reviews*, **135**, 5–49.

Steele, E.J., H.S. Rothenfluh and R.V. Blanden (1997), 'Mechanism of antigen-driven somatic hypermutation of rearranged immunoglobulin V(D)J genes in the mouse', *Immunology and Cell Biology*, **75**, 82–95.

Steele, E.J., R.A. Lindley and R.V. Blanden (1998), *Lamarck's Signature: How Retrogenes are Changing Darwin's Natural Selection Paradigm*, Sydney: Allen & Unwin and New York: Perseus Press.

Steindl, J. (1952), *Maturity and Stagnation in American Capitalism*, Oxford: Blackwell.

Sterelny, K. and P.E. Griffiths (1999), *Sex and Death: An Introduction to Philosophy of Biology: Science and its Conceptual Foundations*, Chicago: University of Chicago Press.

Stigler, G.J. (1941), *Production and Distribution Theories. The Formative Period*, New York: Macmillan.

Sugden, R. (1991), 'Rational choice: a survey of contributions from economics and philosophy', *Economic Journal,* **101**, 751–85.

Sugden, R. (1999), 'Team preferences', paper presented at *Seminar on Rationality and Intentions*, Amsterdam, 15 October.

Sutherland, A. (1898), *The Origin and Growth of the Moral Instinct*, London: Longmans, Green & Co.

Symons, D. (1992), 'On the use and misuse of Darwinism in the study of human behavior', in J.H. Barkow, L. Cosmides and J. Tooby (eds), *The Adapted Mind*, Oxford: Oxford University Press, 137–59.

Syvanen, M. (1985), 'Cross–species gene transfer; implications for a new theory of evolution', *Journal of Theoretical Biology* **112** (2), 333–43.

Syvanen, M. (1994), 'Horizontal gene transfer: evidence and possible consequences', *Annual Review of Genetics*, **28**, 237–61.

Tajfel, H. (1981), *Human Groups & Social Categories*, Cambridge: Cambridge University Press.

Taylor, A. (1989), 'The significance of Darwinian theory for Marx and Engels', *Philosophy of the Social Sciences*, **19**, 409–23.

Temin, H.M. (1964), 'Nature of the provirus of rous sarcoma', *National Cancer Institute Monograph*, **17**, 557–70.

Temin, H.M. and S. Mizutani (1970), 'RNA-directed DNA polymerase in virions of rous sarcoma virus', *Nature*, **226**, 1211–13.

Thomas, B. (1991), 'Alfred Marshall on economic biology', *Review of Political Economy*, **3** (1), 1–14. Reprinted in Hodgson (1995), 259–72.

Torkelson, J.R., S. Harris, M.J. Lombardo, J. Nagendran, C. Thulin and S.M. Rosenberg (1997), 'Genome-wide hypermutation in a subpopulation of stationary-phase cells underlies recombination-dependent adaptive mutation', *EMBO Journal*, **16** (11), 3303–11.

Toulmin, S. (1972), *Human Understanding*, Cambridge: Cambridge University Press.

Toye, J. (1997), 'Keynes on population and economic growth', *Cambridge Journal of Economics*, **21**, 1–26.

Treloar, A. and J. Pullen (1998), 'Hearn's "Plutology" or Hearn's "Olbology"?' *History of Economics Review*, **27**, 16–20.

Trent-Band, H. (1991), 'Why Engels linked Marx and Darwin at Marx's graveside', *Michigan Academician*, **23**, 285–94.

Trivers, R. (1971), 'The evolution of reciprocal altruism', *Quarterly Review of Biology*, **46**, 35–57.

Trivers, R. (1999), 'As they would do to you (review of "Unto Others")', *Skeptic*, **6** (4) 81–3.

Tullock, G. (1979), 'Sociobiology and economics', *Atlantic Economic Journal of Economics*, **21**, 1–26.

Turner, F.M (1974), *Between Science and Religion: The Reaction to Scientific Naturalism in Late Victorian England*, New Haven, CO: Yale University Press,.

Turney, P. D. Whitley and R. Anderson (1996), 'Evolution, learning, and instinct: 100 years of the Baldwin Effect', *Evolutionary Computation*, **4**, (3) 213-329. Also at http://ai.iit.nrc.ca/baldwin/toc.html.

Udéhn, L. (1992), 'The limits of economic imperialism', in U. Himmelstrand (ed.), *Interfaces in Economic and Social Analysis*, London: Routledge, 239–80.

Urina, E.M. (1977), 'Marx and Darwin', *History of Political Economy*, **9**, 548–59.

Vanberg, V. (1986), 'Spontaneous market order and social rules: a critical examination of F.A. Hayek's theory of cultural evolution', *Economics and Philosophy*, **2**, 75–100.

Veblen, T.B. (1898), 'Why is economics not an evolutionary science?', *Quarterly Journal of Economics*, **12**, 373–97. Reprinted in Veblen [1919] (1994), 56–81.

Veblen, T.B. [1899] (1961), *The Theory of the Leisure Class: An Economic Study in the Evolution of Institutions,* New York: Macmillan. Republished New York: Random House.

Veblen, T.B. [1904] (1975), *The Theory of Business Enterprise*, New York: Charles Scribners. Reprinted by Augustus Kelley.

Veblen, T.B. [1914] (1990), *The Instinct of Workmanship, and the State of the Industrial Arts*, New York: Macmillan. Reprinted with a new introduction by Murray G. Murphey and a 1964 introductory note by J. Dorfman, New Brunswick, NJ: Transaction Publishers.

Veblen, T.B. [1919] (1990), *The Place of Science in Modern Civilisation and Other Essays,* New York: Huebsch. Reprinted with a new introduction by W. J. Samuels, New Brunswick, NJ: Transaction Publishers.

Veblen, T.B. (1934) (Leon Ardzrooni, ed.), *Essays on Our Changing Order*, New York: Viking Press.

Vermeij, G.J. (1987), *Evolution and Escalation: An Ecological History of Life*, Princeton, NJ: Princeton University Press.

Vromen, J. (1995), *Economic Evolution*, London: Routledge.

Vromen, J. (1997), 'Evolutionary economics: precursors, paradigmatic propositions, puzzles and prospects', in J. Reijnders (ed.) *Economics and Evolution*, Cheltenham, UK and Lyme, NH, US: Edward Elgar, 41–68.

Vromen, J. (1999a), 'Evolutionary psychology and economic theory', paper presented at *1999 ISNIE–Conference*, Washington, 17–19 September.

Vromen, J. (1999b), 'Group selection rehabilitated?' Erasmus Institute for Philosophy and Economics, Erasmus University of Rotterdam, mimeo.

Waddington, C.H. (1969), 'The theory of evolution today', in A. Koestler and J.R. Smythies (eds), *Beyond Reductionism: New Perspectives in the Life Sciences,* London: Hutchinson, 357–74.

Waddington, C.H. (1975), *The Evolution of an Evolutionist*, Edinburgh and Ithaca: Edinburgh University Press and Cornell University Press.

Wallace, A.R. (1870), *Contributions to the Theory of Natural Selection*, London: Swan Sonnenschein.

Wallace, A.R. (1878), *Tropical Nature and Other Essays*, London: Macmillan.

Wallace, A.R. (1879), *Australasia*, London: Edward Stanford.

Wallace, A.R. (1890), *Darwinism: An Exposition of the Theory of Natural Selection, with Some of Its Applications*, London: Macmillan.

Wallace, A.R. (1892), *Land Nationalisation: Its Necessity and its Aims*, London: Swan Sonnenschein.

Wallace, A.R. (1895), 'The social economy of the future', in A. Reid (ed.), *The New Party*, Melbourne : E.W. Cole.

Wallace, A.R. (1898), *The Wonderful Century*, London: Swan Sonnenschein

Wallace, A.R. (1900), *Studies Scientific and Social* (2 vols), London: Macmillan.

Wallace, A.R. (1905), *My Life* (2 vols), London: Chapman and Hall.

Wallace, A.R. (1913a), *The Revolt of Democracy*, London: Cassell.

Wallace, A.R. (1913b), *Social Environment and Moral Progress*, London: Cassell.

Wallace, A.R. (1916), *Alfred Russel Wallace. Letters and Reminiscences*, J. Marchant (ed.), London: Cassell & Co.

Wallace, A.R. (1991) (C.H. Smith ed.), *An Anthology of his Shorter Writings*, Oxford: Oxford University Press.

Watkins, J.P. (1998), 'Towards a reconsideration of social evolution: symbiosis and its implications for economics', *Journal of Economic Issues*, **32** (1), 87–105.

Watson, J.D., N.H. Hopkins, J.W. Roberts, J.A. Steitz and A.M. Weiner (1987), *Molecular Biology of the Gene*, Vol. 1. (4th ed.), Menlo Park, CA: Benjamin/Cummings.

Webb, S. (1896), *The Difficulties of Individualism*, London: Fabian Society.

Webb, S. (1916), *Towards Social Democracy? A Study of Social Evolution during the Past Three-quarters of a Century*, London: Fabian Society.

Weikart, R. (1995), 'A recently discovered Darwin letter on social Darwinism', *Isis*, **86**, 609–11.

Weingart, P., S.D. Mitchell, P.J. Richerson and S. Maasen (eds) (1997), *Human by Nature: Between Biology and the Social Sciences*, Mahwah, NJ: Lawrence Erlbaum Associates.

Weismann, A. (1893), *The Germ-plasm: A Theory of Heredity*, translated by W.N. Parker and H.R. Ronnfeldt, London: Walter Scott.

Wells, H.G. (1917), *The Soul of a Bishop*, London: Cassell & Co.

Wells, H.G. (1926), *The World of William Clissold* (3 vols), London: Macmillan.

Wells, H.G. (1932), *The Work, Wealth and Happiness of Mankind*, London: William Heinemann Ltd.

Wesson, R. (1993), *Beyond Natural Selection*, Cambridge, MA: MIT Press.

Whitaker, J.K. (1975), *Early Writings of Alfred Marshall*, London: Macmillan.

Whitaker, J.K. (1996), *The Correspondence of Alfred Marshall*, London: Macmillan, for the Royal Economic Society.

White, L. (1959), *The Evolution of Culture: The Development of Civilization to the Fall of Rome*, New York: McGraw–Hill.

White, L. (1960), 'Preface', in M. Sahlins and E Service (eds), *Evolution and Culture*, Ann Arbor, MI: University of Michigan Press.

Wicken, J.S. (1985), 'An organismic critique of molecular Darwinism', *Journal of Theoretical Biology,* **117** (4), 545–61.

Wilkins, J.S. (1998a), 'The evolutionary structure of scientific theories', *Biology and Philosophy,* **13** (4), 479–504.

Wilkins, J.S. (1998b), 'What's in a Meme? Reflections from the perspective of the history and philosophy of evolutionary biology', *Journal of Memetics*, **2**, 2–33. <http://www.cpm.mmu.ac.uk/jom-emit/1998/vol2/wilkins_js.html>.

Wilkins, J.S. (1999a), 'Memes ain't (just), in the head', *Journal of Memetics*, **3**, 48–55. <http://www.cpm.mmu.ac.uk/jom-emit/1999/vol3/wilkins_j.html>.

Wilkins, J.S. (1999b), 'On choosing to evolve: strategies without a strategist', *Journal of Memetics,* **3**, 81–3. <http://www.cpm.mmu.ac.uk/jom-emit/1999/vol3/wilkins_j2.html>.

Williams, G.C. (1966), *Adaptation and Natural Selection: A Critique of Some Current Evolutionary Thought*, Princeton, NJ: Princeton University Press.

Williams, G.C. (1986), 'A defence of reductionism in evolutionary biology', *Oxford Surveys in Evolutionary Biology*, **2**, 1–27.

Williams, G.C. (1992), *Natural Selection: Domains, Levels, and Challenges*, New York: Oxford University Press.

Williamson, O.E. (1985), *The Economic Institutions of Capitalism*, New York: Free Press.

Wills, C. (1989), *The Wisdom of the Genes: New Pathways in Evolution*, New York: Basic Books.

Wilson, D.S. (1997a), 'Introduction: multilevel selection theory comes of age', *American Naturalist*, **150**. Supplement, July: 'Multilevel selection: a symposium organized by David Sloan Wilson', S1–S4.

Wilson, D.S. (1997b), 'Altruism and organism: disentangling the themes of multilevel selection theory', *American Naturalist*, **150**. Supplement, July: 'Multilevel selection: A Symposium Organized by David Sloan Wilson', S122–S134.

Wilson, D.S. and E. Sober (1994), 'Reintroducing group selection to the human behavioral sciences', *Behavioral and Brain Sciences*, **17**, 585–654.

Wilson, E.O. (1975), *Sociobiology: The New Synthesis*, Cambridge, MA: Harvard University Press.

Wilson, E.O. (1998), *Consilience: The Unity of Knowledge*, London: Little, Brown and Company.

Wimsatt, W.C. (1980), 'Reductionist research strategies and their biases in the units of selection controversy', in T. Nickles (ed.), *Scientific Discovery, Volume II, Historical and Scientific Case Studies*, Dordrecht, Holland: Reidel. Reprinted in Sober (1984b), 213–59.

Winter, S.G. (1964), 'Economic "natural selection" and the theory of the firm', *Yale Economic Essays*, **4**, 225–72.

Witt, U. (1987), *Individualistische Grundlagen der Evolutorischen Ökonomik*, Tübingen: J.C.B. Mohr (Paul Siebeck).

Witt, U. (ed.) (1992), *Explaining Process and Change: Approaches to Evolutionary Economics*, Ann Arbor, MI: University of Michigan Press.

Witt, U. (ed.) (1993), *Evolutionary Economics*, Aldershot, UK and Brookfield, US: Edward Elgar.

Witt, U. (1994), 'Endogenous change – causes and contingencies', *Advances in Austrian Economics*, **1**, 105–17.

Witt, U. (1996), 'A "Darwinian revolution" in economics?', *Journal for Institutional and Theoretical Economics*, **152**, 707–15.

Witt, U. (1997), 'Self-organisation and economics – what is new?', *Structural Change and Economic Dynamics*, **8**, 489–507.

Worster, D. (1994), *Nature's Ecology: A History of Ecological Ideas* (2nd ed.), Cambridge: Cambridge University Press.

Wynne–Edwards, V.C. (1962), *Animal Dispersion*, Edinburgh: Oliver & Boyd.

Young, R.M. (1985), *Darwin's Metaphor: Nature's Place in Victorian Culture*, Cambridge: Cambridge University Press.

Author Index

Subject Index

agent, agency (human) , 8–10, 35, 80, 106, 109, 116, 118–20, 124, 163–4, 169, 174, 176–9, 181, 184–9, 191, 193–4, 196–8, 200, 205–8,
  representative 188
altruism 7, 34, 47, 72, 84, 139, 172, 183, 185, 192, 196, 201–4, 207
analogy 17, 30, 89
  biological 1, 16, 17, 21–3, 29, 33, 63, 88, 122, 124, 146, 148–9, 151, 153, 160–1, 166, 184, 207
  organic 64, 80
  of nature 32
anthropology 161, 171, 185
Apostles, Cambridge University 73
artificial intelligence 122

Baldwin effect 4–6, 10–12, 99–100, 103, 119, 172–4
baseline problem 122, 142, 148–51, 153–54
Bayesian 170
behaviour 16, 173–4
  adaptive 111
  collective 18, 34
  co–operative 18–9, 28, 34
  competitive 28
  institutions and 177
  learned 4–6, 172
  purposive v mechanical 182, 192
  realistic portrayal of 55
  routine 159
  rules of thumb 149
  evolution in 55
besoin 128, 166
biological sciences 58, 88, 99, 161

Capital, Marx's 22, 23, 34
causal explanation, processes 94–5, 97–9, 102, 105–6, 109, 116–8, 202–4
  ultimate v proximate 193–4, 207
  reconstitutive downward (upward) 201, 205
central dogma 121, 127, 133–4, 136–7, 141–2, 155, 162, 172

change, social or economic 20, 76, 88, 143, 150,, 160–1, 164, 168–9, 171–2, 180, 201, 207–8
cheater detection algorithm 195
choice 9–10, 114, 116, 119, 130, 153, 196–7
  theories of 186–7
climax theory 131
Communist Manifesto, Marx and Engels's 41
competition 4, 70, 72, 79, 80
  competitive, markets 6, 46, 65, 75,
  struggle for subsistence 64–6, 69, 72, 79
complexity 4, 8, 10, 53, 90–2, 94–5, 97, 102, 116–7, 119, 122–3, 125, 127, 130, 134, 138–9, 141–2, 148, 150, 152, 154, 156–7, 164, 171
co–operation 70, 80
cranes and skyhooks 198
creative -ity 10, 55, 145, 163–4, 169, 181, 186, 188–9
cultural diversity 197
culture as ideas 108, 110–1
cumulative change, causation 133, 143–4, 149–50, 158

Darwinian theory 15, 21, 25–6, 28–9, 30–3, 35, 64, 76–7, 83, 87–120, 121–159, 160–183, 184, 192–3, 201, 207
  concepts 16, 65
  beliefs 37
  Neo–Darwinian -Darwinist 5, 16, 93–6, 101, 121, 127, 132, 137, 139, 161–4, 165, 181, 191
Darwinism 1–2, 5, 7, 15, 31, 36, 46, 48, 63, 75, 88, 93–100, 103, 105, 110–1, 114, 116–8, 120, 160–183
  cultural 161, 171–2, 177–80
  social 19, 54, 68, 79, 147
Dawkins's conjecture 174–7
Descent of Man, Darwin's 3, 17,18, 23, 24, 25, 30, 33, 66, 70, 73
descent with modification 131, 152
division of labour 33, 51
double helix 135–6

economic
  biology 49
  organism 63
economics
  (neo) Austrian 151, 185–9, 200
  neo–institutionalists 185–7, (v New
    Institutionalists) 207
  classical 145
  Darwinian 15–6, 18, 21, 25–6, 31, 33,
    139, 148, 151
  evolutionary 1–10, 15, 17, 20, 21, 31–2,
    49, 64, 80, 116, 139, 143–4, 146, 155,
    159, 184–6, 188–90, 200, 206–7
  Marxist 142
  neoclassical (mainstream) 103, 142–4,
    147, 185–8, 196, 208
  Post–Keynesian 142
  transactions costs 199
emergent, emergence 89, 91–2, 102, 105,
  118–9, 144, 149, 156
  pointillism as 102
environment 3, 8–9, 11
  degradation 38
equilibrium 30, 43, 131, 133, 142–3, 188–9
eugenics 54, 66–9, 72, 80–1
Malthusian League 67
evolution 2, 15–6, 20, 27–8, 30, 33–5, 37, 44,
  50, 57–60
  biological 76, 83, 88, 90, 92, 98, 103–7,
    110, 116, 127–142, 147, 162
  co-evolution 147, 190, 201, 206, 208
  collectivist 72
  cultural 3–4, 6–7, 83, 87–120, 127, 161,
    171, 182–3, 206–7
  economic 9, 10, 30, 58, 87–120
  genetic 89, 93–4, 96–7, 100, 102, 104,
    111, 119, 160
  horizontal/vertical 131–2
  human 16, 67, 70
  individual 16, 19, 23–4, 29
  of complex systems 104–5, 116
  of purposive action 76
  Panglossian view of 116, 147
  Path (history) -dependent 198
  progress of 127, 130, 147, 150–1
  social 3–4, 8, 9, 20, 24, 29, 70–1, 80,
    87–120, 122–3, 125, 132, 141, 145,
    147–8, 151, 153–6

evolutionary
  ethics 74
  epistemology 1, 77, 104
  explanation,
    developmental 123, 125–6, 156,
    phylogenetic 7, 123, 125–6, 156, 158
  hierarchically structured theory 104
  psychology 119, 185, 191–200, 206, 208
  relationships 51
  thought, doctrine 49–52, 85
  writers 51–2

Fabian Socialist 31
Fabian Society 71–2
falsificationism 195
far–from–equilibrium thermodynamics 7
firm 30, 54–5, 125, 146, 148–50, 152, 154,
  164, 172–3, 177, 179, 184–5, 188–90, 192,
  200–1, 204–6, 208
  as units of selection 179, 188–90, 204–6
First Principles, Spencer's 50–1, 62
fitness 46, 84, 95, 132–3, 145–6, 159, 170,
  172–4, 179, 183, 192, 201–4
free trade 38–9, 46, 69
free traders 47, 75
full employment 64

General Theory, Keynes's 63–5, 72,
  74–5, 77–8
genes 11, 84, 92, 95–7, 100, 103, 107–8,
  111–2, 114–117, 122, 124, 134–6, 138,
  140, 142, 146, 148–51, 154, 158, 162, 164,
  167, 174–6, 177, 179, 182–3, 194, 196,
  201, 206
  selfish 192, 202–4, 208
  agents as 193, 196
genetic(s) 7, 8, 83–4, 193
  assimilation 102, 122
  code 97, 121, 123–5, 134–5, 138, 142,
    155–6
  determinism 148, 167, 194, 196–7, 208
  and economics 148–9, 154
  epigenetic inheritance 132, 148, 171
  explanation 123–5, 156
  language as 153
  recipe 124, 138, 148
  transmission 6
genotype 94–7, 99, 101, 108, 115, 118,
  132–3, 149, 172
gold standard 46